The GarageBand Book

The GarageBand Book

Tony Bove

WILEY

Wiley Publishing, Inc.

The GarageBand Book

Published by
Wiley Publishing, Inc.
111 River Street
Hoboken, NJ 07030
www.wiley.com

Copyright © 2005 by Wiley Publishing, Inc..

Published by Wiley Publishing, Inc., Indianapolis, Indiana
Published simultaneously in Canada

ISBN: 0-7645-7322-5

Manufactured in the United States of America

10 9 8 7 6 5 4 3 2 1

1V/QU/RQ/QU/IN

For general information on our other products and services or to obtain technical support, please contact our Customer Care Department within the U.S. at (800) 762-2974, outside the U.S. at (317) 572-3993 or fax (317) 572-4002.

Wiley also publishes its books in a variety of electronic formats. Some content that appears in print may be available in electronic books.

Library of Congress Control Number: 2004112338

This book is dedicated to John Lennon, who showed us all how to sing and play harmonica (at the same time even), and Jimi Hendrix, who didn't need a wah-wah but used one anyway, and to my sons John Paul and Jimi Eric.

Credits

Acquisitions Editor
Michael Roney

Project Editor
Timothy J. Borek

Technical Editor
Small Green Alien Productions, LLC

Copy Editors
Kim Heusel
Scott Tullis

Editorial Manager
Robyn Siesky

Vice President & Executive Group Publisher
Richard Swadley

Vice President and Publisher
Barry Pruett

Project Coordinator
Maridee Ennis

Layout and Graphics
Amanda Carter
Carrie A. Foster
Jennifer Heleine
Lynsey Osborn

Quality Control Technicians
Susan Moritz
Brian H. Walls

Proofreader
Christine Pingleton

Indexer
Rebecca R. Plunkett

Special Help
Adrienne Porter
Maureen Spears

Foreword

By and large, life really isn't fair. If you were to take the time and bother to find the pot of gold at the end of the rainbow, you'd find that it contains not untold wealth and riches but a discount coupon book for area restaurants. And even so, a homicidal demi-elf is willing to kill you and all the members of your immediate family in highly creative and dramatic ways to get it back.

You're reminded of this on a regular basis here on planet Earth, but it's never underscored more dramatically than when you and your schoolmates take up musical instruments. Some people have it and some people don't. You have all the passion for music and Lord knows you worked twice as hard as any other kid in the class, but the fact remains that through the first two weeks of school you were progressively downgraded from violin to recorder to the two sticks that you're supposed to bang together and finally the kid who turns the pages for the xylophone player.

Trust me, I know. I've been a keyboard player all my life, and my commitment and love of the piano is demonstrated by the fact that after all this time I'm still pretty awful at it. I made steady progress up the point where I had to learn how to make my left hand do something that's slightly out of phase with what my right hand is up to. If you're challenging me to play something by Randy Newman — where every tune sounds like a toilet-paper jingle and you're never supposed to use both hands at the same time — I'm good. But when I visit a friend of mine who's a *real* keyboard player and he sits down at the Steinway in his living room, I'm like a squirrel witnessing the opening shots of the Battle of Gettysburg. I have enough wit and insight to understand that something rather big is going on, but I can't understand it beyond the idea that I should climb up into a tree and keep out of the way.

So many Salieris, so few Mozarts. It's little wonder that the state of music education has declined to its current sorry state.

I was there when Steve Jobs formally announced GarageBand. He did it in typical, understated fashion, telling a packed keynote hall that Apple was adding a whole new component to the iLife suite and spending five minutes building up to it. Since its introduction, iLife had only grown more and more impressive. Create and manage a music library from your CDs. Edit and share your home videos with the style and panache of a professional. Create full-featured DVDs without buying any special hardware. It was hard to figure out what the topper for all of that was going to be. The boy was CEO of Pixar. Was it too big a stretch to guess that maybe it'd be the slickest and most proletarian animation tool the industry had ever seen?

Foreword

I wouldn't have guessed "music composition and editing tool." There are those with talent who play their accordions at family functions or sing in the community choir or started touring with The Who after John Entwistle decided to quit the group and reunite with Keith Moon. And then there are those who never picked up an instrument since the last day of school in Grade 6, when they realized that they would never be forced to learn "Twinkle, Twinkle Little Star" ever again under any circumstances.

But music is more than mastering intricate technique. It's actually a language skill and as such, it's something that anyone can plug into and express in some fashion if given the tools and the opportunity. I used to scorn "sampling," a style of music that involves mixing and matching sound bites from other songs. "Big deal," I used to say. "So you took the elements of a hit record and turned them into...*another* hit record." Then a kid explained the concept to me. He didn't know enough musicians to form a band of his own, and he certainly couldn't afford to buy instruments or rent time in a studio. But he could easily afford two tape decks, and with a library of music passages taped off of the radio, he had the power of a god. He could grab three seconds of a 40-piece orchestra, nine seconds of the most talented guitarist on the planet, and build a loop from a drum machine that was way too complicated for him to ever learn how to program.

Result: Sampling allowed him to express his passion for creating music even though he was just a lone 16-year-old with a part-time job at Wendy's. He didn't have to learn how to do it or prove to anyone that he *could* do it: all he needed was the desire and the determination to take matters into his own hands.

This is at the very root of GarageBand's unique mojo. It takes the complex act of making music and turns it into something you can *play* with...and that's every bit as revolutionary as iMovie or iDVD. If you've never played music before, you can discover the almost hypnotically entertaining process of assembling increasingly complex music from pre-established clips. If you're an amateur, you've never had a better friend for the process of learning and honing a song than GarageBand's ability to take your live performance and embroider it with virtual instruments. Even if you're a professional, the app will allow you to rehearse with your whole band even though they're scattered to all corners of the Earth. And when you compose your next hit single on your front porch, you won't have to spend hours in the studio later on playing a clumsy demo tape and patiently explaining to your bandmates that the *phhhrt-phhhhhhht* sounds you made with your mouth are where the horns are supposed to come in.

GarageBand really is that powerful and accessible. It's so appealing to nonmusicians and is so engaging that it actually take a once-complex creative process and reduces it to just another activity you can do from 9:10 A.M. to 9:55 in lieu of actual work. In this vein, Apple has turned music composition into a more sophisticated form of Solitaire...and nothing could be better for the future of music education.

Andy Ihnatko
Series Author

Preface

How did the garage become a metaphor for recording a band? The Beatles started in a backyard and then moved to an urban cavern. The Rolling Stones started out in jazz clubs. The Who, the Kinks... well, you get the idea. In fact, all these bands were part of the British Invasion of the early 1960s. In America, young musicians reacted to this invasion by starting their own bands. As garages are more commonplace in America than in Britain, many of these startup American bands formed in garages. (I joined one, and we practiced every night in a garage near Wayne, Pennsylvania.)

Many of the bands of that period sounded like they played in garages, emphasizing their amateurishness, playing the same three chords, bashing their guitars, and growling their vocals. While hundreds of these bands popped up around America, only a handful of them — such as Shadows of Knight, The Count 5, The Seeds, The Standells — had hits. The Kingsmen rocketed straight into rock music history with a cover of "Louie Louie" (a song by Richard Berry that hadn't charted), and is perhaps the best example of the garage rock of the time: the group literally practiced in each other's garages in Portland, Oregon.

In the 1980s, there was a garage rock revival that fed into the alternative rock movement and future grunge music explosion, which was partially inspired by garage rock from Seattle (such as the Sonics). Another revival has started again in the 2000s with bands like the White Stripes, the Hives, and the Strokes. But the dungy garage has long been abandoned for the cushy comforts of the studio outfitted with the latest in Mac audio gear, such as Digidesign Pro Tools, and sound engineers well versed in multitrack recording techniques.

GarageBand represents the next generation of audio tools — ones designed for ordinary folks like us. It brings some of the basic functions of a Pro Tools setup down to the level of the rank amateur rocking out for the fun of it, or the professional eager to make a demo of a new composition without having to go into a recording studio. In short, GarageBand is for those of us who prefer working in garages, at least in spirit.

Everything you compose in GarageBand can be copied directly into iTunes and used in your iPod. You can even compose on the fly with nothing more than a laptop, or add a keyboard or even record parts you play yourself on real guitars and instruments, or vocals (or in my case, harmonica). My own experience may be typical: I became addicted to GarageBand as soon as I sat down and played a MIDI keyboard (the software version, MidiKeys, works in a pinch very well) with it.

Preface

Since then I've written songs, added vocal parts to professionally-recorded tracks, accompanied myself on eight different instruments, and played through my Mac (using GarageBand as my pre-amplifier) on stage in live performances. In this book I provide not only tips I picked up from others and my own experiences, but also the perspectives of professional musicians, studio engineers and technicians, and producers. This GarageBand stuff is outtasight.

What You Need to Know

I expect you to know how to use the Mac to do simple things like copying files and dragging and dropping songs into iTunes. You should have used Copy and Paste at least once in your life.

I get to introduce a lot of music stuff in this book, but I'm gentle about it, delegating the details you don't need into sidebars. Even if you have talent, you have to learn how to work the controls.

You don't have to know how to read music. The entire point of GarageBand is that you can do it yourself, without any special training. "If I was trained," Mick Jagger of the Rolling Stones once said, "I would write really good things that I can't write. I could write a symphony." Yes, and how far would you have gotten in the world of classical music, Mick? He started the world's greatest garage band and laughed all the way to the bank, so no sympathy from me.

On the other hand, his partner Keith Richards often said that you only needed to know three chords to play rock guitar. I don't know which three chords he meant, but I show in this book how to use GarageBand to do everything from writings songs to creating CD-quality music and recording performances with real instruments.

Elements Used in this Book

So, how get you started? First, let's introduce you to the unique structure of the book that you hold in your hands. There are a couple of book elements that you need to know about.

Sidebars

You'll notice these sidebars scattered here and there throughout the pages of the book. Sidebars are where I take the opportunity to digress. I share information that might enhance your understanding of the topic at hand, that add new perspective, or that I just plain find interesting.

Ideally, the effect of these footnotes will be like the "commentary track" you'd find on a good DVD of a great movie. Possibly it's like having some idiot in the audience yelling at the screen while you're trying to enjoy *Vertigo*. Hard to tell. My hopes are high, and frankly you might as well just grin and bear it because there really isn't much you can do about it at this point.

A BOOK YOU SHOULD BUY AFTER BUYING THIS ONE

Actually, I got the idea from Martin Gardner's *The Annotated Alice*, in which the complete text of Lewis Carroll's classic is accompanied by sidebars that explain just exactly what the guy was talking about. You know, on the off-chance that you're *not* aware that mercurous nitrate was a key chemical used in the manufacture of felt, and hatmakers often suffered from mercury poisoning and exhibited psychotic behavior.

The book's still in print and led to a whole line of "annotated" classics. Definitely worth a look.

Though I suppose you *could* just put this book back on the shelf and spend the dough on Roger Ebert's *Movie Yearbook* instead. Hmm. That honestly never occurred to me. Well, okay, the man has a Pulitzer and everything, but did he ever teach you how to network two computers via Firewire? Just don't do anything rash; that's all I ask.

Notes

And then there are those comments that I inserted because I'm undisciplined and uncontrollable — and I need to comment on the discussion at hand. Right now. With Sidebars, there's sort of an implied warranty. If you read the sidebar, you'll probably learn something useful but not essential. But Notes are mostly here because I have a hard time controlling my impulses. All I can promise is that each note certainly seemed like a good idea at the time, and my heart was in the right place, absolutely.

 NOTE

See, as a writer, the most difficult part of the job is figuring out just how much Coke you need to drink before sitting down at the keyboard and how often to redose over the course of the day. Some people need the assistance of university medical facilities and complex nuclear imaging devices to monitor the seratonin levels of their brains. All *I* have to do is read back the stuff I've written over the past hour or so. I'm on an HMO, so it's a real time and money-saver.

Book Organization

The book's divided into five sections:

Part I: Kick Out the Jams

Okay, here we go: start a music project, add loops, make tracks, mix the tracks, and export the song into iTunes — all in five easy pieces. You learn about GarageBand by *using* it. At the end of this section you already know how to create a song in GarageBand and play it in iTunes.

Part II: Careful with That Axe, Eugene

You want to play screaming electric guitar and pound the beat with bongo fury. Or you want to groove on the sounds of exotic software-generated instruments you could never afford and don't even know how to play. This section is all about using Real Instruments, using Software Instruments, and recording performances with them. You even learn the best way to use microphones for vocal recording.

Part III: In Search of the Lost Chord

Music production is all about editing, effects, and mixing. This section offers everything you need to know about editing the notes of a Software Instrument performance, editing the sound of a Real Instrument recording, using audio effects and simulated amplifiers to improve the sound, and using GarageBand's track-mixing functions to produce a high-quality stereo song.

Part IV: Sympathy for the Demo

If you're looking for a record deal or a gig, you need a demonstration CD. This section describes how to use iTunes to store your song with all your other tunes, burn CDs, and synchronize your iPod with your music so that you can play it anywhere, for anybody.

Part V: When the Music's Over

Turn out the lights... and put on the slide show or video. This section shows you what you can do with your GarageBand tunes. Build slide shows with your photos and music. Edit video clips with a groovy soundtrack. Assemble rockumentaries you can publish on the Web and burn onto DVD. You can even learn how to get the best performance out of GarageBand and how to join a like-minded community of GarageBand composers who share their music.

Acknowledgments

I owe a considerable debt of gratitude to my family, and especially my sons John Paul and Jimi Eric, founders of my favorite garage band, and Cheryl Rhodes for all her patience and support.

I want to thank my Wiley project editor, Timothy Borek, and Editorial Manager, Robyn Siesky, for ongoing assistance that made my job so much easier. I also thank Maureen Spears, Kim Heusel, Scott Tullis, and Debbie Gates for editing and improving this book immensely. A book this timely places a considerable burden on a publisher's production team, and I thank the production crew at Wiley for diligence beyond the call of reason.

I owe thanks and a happy hour or three to Carole McLendon, my agent at Waterside. And I have acquisitions editor Mike Roney at Wiley to thank for coming up with the idea for this book.

A special thanks and my eternal gratitude goes out to the folks who contributed original material for this book, including track wizard Stacy Parrish, studio samurai L. Henry Sarmiento II, the master of time Jimmy Sanchez, the master of the mambo Bill Payne, and the man in the black hat — the legendary Pete Sears.

Finally, my heartfelt thanks to members of my band, the Flying Other Brothers (Pete Sears, Barry Sless, Jimmy Sanchez, Bill Bennett, Bert Keely, TBone, and Roger and Ann McNamee) for the music that inspired me while writing this book, and for appearing in photos.

About the Author

Tony Bove has played harmonica since he was nine, in various bands you never heard of (such as the Graceful Duck, the Mystic Valley Ramblers, and the Great Next Whatever). But as a founding member of the Flying Other Brothers (`www.flyingotherbros.com`), Tony has recently performed with Hall-of-Fame rockers and now uses GarageBand to compose songs.

Tony has kicked around the computer industry for decades, editing the influential *Inside Report on New Media* newsletter and writing for weekly and monthly magazines, including *Computer Currents, Nextworld, The Chicago Tribune* Sunday Technology Section, and *NewMedia*. He also co-founded and edited *Desktop Publishing/Publish* magazine. Computer trade shows and conferences were known for their informal music gatherings, and Tony was a founding member of Random Axes and other nerd-musician configurations at these events.

When not playing music or doing all those other things, Tony found time to write 20 books on computing, desktop publishing, and multimedia, including *The iLife '04 Book* with Andy Ihnatko, *iLife All-in-One Desk Reference For Dummies,* and *iPod and iTunes For Dummies* with Cheryl Rhodes, and a series of books about Macromedia Director, Adobe Illustrator, and PageMaker. Tony has also worked as a director of enterprise marketing for a large software company and as a communications director and technical publications manager. (Got work? Look him up at his site, `www.rockument.com/bove.html`.)

Tracing the personal computer revolution back to the Sixties counterculture, Tony went out on a limb and produced a CD-ROM documentary in 1996, *Haight-Ashbury in the Sixties* (featuring music from the Grateful Dead, Janis Joplin, and the Jefferson Airplane). Tony also developed the Rockument music site (`www.rockument.com`), with commentary and radio programs focused on rock music history.

Contents

Contents

Contents

Contents

PART I

Kick Out the Jams

Songs in the Key of iLife

In This Chapter

Overview of GarageBand and the iLife package • Connecting a MIDI keyboard
Opening and playing songs • Starting a new song project, and
setting its tempo, time signature, and key

Nothing moves you quite like a song. People have always gravitated around the source of music since the dawn of time. Making music is a tradition in every culture on the planet, and serves as a global language that everyone recognizes and understands. Blind Lemon Jefferson wrote songs over a century ago, traveled around the dusty countryside singing and playing the blues, and died penniless, but one of his songs is included in a probe that is heading out of our solar system. The man's music will live on forever. Your music could, too.

Making music has been part of the Mac culture since day one, when Steve Jobs introduced the original Mac to an audience and used it to play music (simple tones, but it was the first personal computer with built-in sound). Jazz great Herbie Hancock jumped on the Mac bandwagon early, using it to control synthesizers and compose music, as did electronic music godfather Vladimir Ussachevsky and pop/rock icon Todd Rundgren.

The first true program to make music on the Mac was MusicWorks from Hayden Software, written by Jay Fenton (who went on to create VideoWorks, the basis for Macromedia Director). Today, the Mac is the dominant platform in professional music and audio recording, and Mac software has won awards in the music industry; Digidesign's Pro Tools even won an Oscar. GarageBand brings the lofty capabilities inherited from a legacy of innovative music software down to the level of the rest of us who just want to make music.

PETE SEARS: EXPERIMENTING WITH GARAGEBAND

"Composing music is experimental by its nature. If you can experiment with sounds, chord progressions, and rhythm tracks whenever the moment strikes you — a professional musician could be incredibly more productive just in getting sounds and melodies together, and composing bits and pieces, then playing them back. GarageBand is a very powerful tool for pulling ideas together."

In his 34 years as a musician, Pete Sears has played keyboards and bass guitar with a large variety of artists, including Rod Stewart on the classic albums *Gasoline Alley, Every Picture Tells a Story, Never a Dull Moment,* and *Smiler.* He was with Jefferson Starship from 1974 to 1987, and has performed with Phil Lesh and Steve Kimock, John Lee Hooker, Warren Haynes, Ron Wood, Jerry Garcia, Peter Rowan, Los Lobos, Taj Mahal, Mickey Hart, Bob Weir, Leftover Salmon, Mike Bloomfield, Roy Harper, Ike and Tina Turner, Shana Morrison, and many others, playing sessions on more than a hundred albums. Sears also plays in the Jorma Kaukonen Trio and Hot Tuna, and joined the Flying Other Brothers in the summer of 2000.

Like the name implies, you can kick out the jams and record studio-quality music in your garage, or home, or wherever you use your Mac — even at your favorite coffeehouse. GarageBand turns your Mac into a portable recording studio with built-in instruments, special effects, thousands of prerecorded loops, and the wisdom of at least one or two recording engineers. You can use royalty-free loops in your songs, play the synthesized instruments supplied with GarageBand (and add more from extra instrument packs), and even plug in a real guitar and use GarageBand's built-in amplifier simulators.

You may not think you are capable of reaching the top of the pop charts anytime soon, but GarageBand has other important uses, such as making original music for your slideshows. You can then post the slideshows on the Web or distribute them with legal music *you own*. Professionals and small businesses sometimes need jingles and music for advertising spots and videos. Maverick directors need music for their independent underfunded movie projects. Why pay exorbitant licensing fees? The music you make is yours to distribute and copy as you wish.

WHAT YOU HAVE... AND WHAT YOU NEED

GarageBand is part of the iLife set of applications that comes with every Mac: iTunes, iPhoto, iMovie, and iDVD. (Some say GarageBand should have been called iMakeMusic). If you don't already have it, you can get the entire suite from Apple on DVD (the fastest and easiest way) for under $50 (as of this writing).

The iLife suite helps you organize the media in your life. You can use iTunes to download songs from the Internet, rip CDs, or export songs you create in GarageBand to your iTunes library. You can then bring the songs into iPhoto, iMovie, and iDVD, burn them onto CD, or import them into your iPod. You can import photos from digital cameras into iPhoto — where you can enhance and arrange them into slideshows along with your songs — and then send them out into the world on Web pages, in email attachments, and on DVDs. By transferring video from a digital camcorder into iMovie, you can organize and edit video clips into movies, complete with special effects and your songs for a soundtrack. You can then burn these music videos onto DVD.

GarageBand lets you combine separately recorded *tracks* (see Figure 1-4). Your instrumental performances and prerecorded loops are stored in each track in a way that makes isolating and changing the sounds without affecting other tracks easy. GarageBand offers two types of tracks:

- **Real Instrument tracks:** These are used for vocals, and for performances and loops recorded with actual musical instruments (such as your favorite electric guitar) through a microphone (such as the built-in microphone in your Mac) or a line-in connection. Real Instrument tracks are represented as *waveforms* in the GarageBand window; the sound comes into GarageBand already digitized into audio information in the form of a sampled analog wave, just as if you had ripped the music from a CD. You can't adjust each note or transpose notes to other keys with excellent results, as you can with Software Instrument tracks. And although you can tweak the sound of an instrument after recording it (making a vocal sound like it came through a megaphone, for example), you can't easily make a Real Instrument sound like another instrument (such as making a guitar sound like a drum).

- **Software Instrument tracks:** These are used for performances and loops recorded with MIDI (Musical Instrument Digital Interface) instruments, like the onscreen keyboard or an external USB MIDI keyboard. The notes you play on such keyboards are actually MIDI instructions to an instrument sound generator. That generator can create any sound you want, so you can switch instrument sounds at will: if you recorded a drum part into a Software Instrument track, you can change it later to a guitar or piano. You can also adjust and transpose the notes you played to other keys.

Sounds like fun, right? Let's get started.

The minimalist Mac musician

A minimalist artist needs very little to make art, and so it is with music. You could use GarageBand's royalty-free loops, recording vocals right through your Mac's internal microphone, without any further equipment or software.

Besides creating loops, GarageBand also simulates instruments and makes every kind of sound you'd care to make, providing a means, albeit primitive, for making wholly original music: the onscreen keyboard. You may know that digital synthesizers can sound like nearly any type of real instrument (as well as a good many imaginary ones). Because GarageBand and the Mac support MIDI, your Mac can act like a digital synthesizer using GarageBand's onscreen keyboard.

That said, the onscreen keyboard leaves a lot to be desired. Although you can simulate playing the piano keys harder or softer with your mouse — clicking lower in a key plays the note harder, while clicking higher in the key plays the note softer — you can't click more than one note at time. What about chords? What about trying to play faster than a snail?

▼ Tip

Run, don't browse, to the Version Tracker download site (www.versiontracker.com/dyn/moreinfo/macosx/16702) and get MidiKeys, a free and very useful alternative to the onscreen keyboard. Written by Chris Reed (http://www.manyetas.com/creed/midikeys_beta.html), MidiKeys uses an onscreen piano keyboard similar to the one provided with GarageBand to simulate a real MIDI keyboard. The big difference is that you can also type on your alphanumeric keyboard and press several keys at once to play chords. MidiKeys is especially useful with a PowerBook when you're on the road because all you need is the PowerBook's keyboard. To read more about MidiKeys, see Chapter 6.

Get your MIDI mojo working

To play the Software Instruments provided with Garage-Band, you need a keyboard of some kind: either the onscreen keyboard (or MidiKeys), or a real MIDI keyboard. Fortunately MIDI keyboards are easy to buy, and the newest ones connect to your Mac using the USB connection, as shown in Figure 1-1. You can connect a USB MIDI piano keyboard directly to your Mac through USB, or through an audio interface device that offers a MIDI connection. (You can also use the same audio interface device to connect real electric instruments and microphones and record directly into GarageBand, as described in Chapter 7.)

Like any USB device on a Mac, a USB MIDI keyboard is literally plug-and-play — just plug it in, start GarageBand, and play your piano and organ riffs to have them translated into Software Instruments. Just follow the same instructions you'd use for the onscreen music keyboard.

One popular model is the M-Audio Keystation 49e, available from the Apple Store. You can find a list of compatible MIDI devices on the Apple Web site at `www.apple.com/ilife/garageband/compatibility.html`.

One good reason to get a USB MIDI keyboard such as the M-Audio Keystation is to use the pitch bend wheel, as shown in Figure 1-2. The pitch bend wheel bends a note up or down. Press and hold a key while moving the wheel to hear the effect.

You can use the pitch bend wheel to simulate a slide guitar or pedal steel guitar, as well as those spacey sliding sounds from electric keyboards and synthesizers. Although you can use the Track Editor to do just about anything to a Software Instrument note played on a software keyboard emulator (such as MidiKeys), bending pitches as smoothly as with a pitch bend wheel on a MIDI keyboard is way too much work.

Figure 1-1
New band takes form in garage using a USB MIDI keyboard

Figure 1-2
Getting spacey sounds with the pitch bend wheel on a USB MIDI keyboard

You don't have to use just one keyboard on your USB connection, or even a keyboard at all for that matter, for GarageBand to receive MIDI input. If you are already a MIDI wizard, know that any MIDI instrument or device can be connected through an *audio interface*, which is a box of input and output ports for connecting various types

LUDWIG WAS NOT A LUDDITE: INSTRUMENTS AND TECHNOLOGY

There's no good reason to be snobbish about synthesizers and computer-made music. Primitive societies used brass, animal horn, bone, ivory, even gold; the oldest extant lyre is Sumerian and made of gold, with gold and silver strings. Technology marches on, and instruments change with the times. In the 16th century many "new" instruments were made of wood, and by the 18th century the technologies of woodworking and metalworking made the piano possible and Ludwig van Beethoven inevitable. By the 19th century, Adolphe Sax was so brazen as to combine a wind instrument and a brass horn to invent the instrument that now bears his name, the saxophone. Not surprisingly the technology of electricity, and eventually the microprocessor, would change musical instruments, thereby changing the music itself, forever.

MOOG AND ARP SYNTHESIZERS OF THE '60s AND '70s

In the '60s and '70s, synthesizers were large, odd-looking and odd-sounding machines based on analog electronics that used electric voltages to create and control sounds. Higher voltages made higher notes and lower voltages made lower notes, and musicians used special keyboards to play them. Early synthesizers played only a single note at a time: to get more notes, you either had to buy more synthesizers, or record parts on tape. Moog and ARP synthesizers bent quite a few ears by the mid-'70s with bands such as Emerson Lake & Palmer and Genesis. Musicians like Keith Emerson and Rick Wakeman used extravagant multikeyboard configurations in which each instrument was set up to produce a single sound per show. Joe Zawinful of Weather Report developed a unique technique for playing on two keyboards simultaneously, placing himself between a pair of ARP 2600 synthesizers, one of which had its keyboard electronically reversed, going from high notes on the left to low notes on the right.

Over time these devices were equipped with programmable memory; sounds the musicians created earlier could be stored and recalled later for live performances. The layering of sounds upon sounds became an important tool and almost a trademark for many artists. The next big step came in 1979: New keyboards were equipped with computer interface plugs so that they could be connected to other synthesizers. Development moved swiftly as more companies got into the act. The diversity of keyboards, drum machines, sequencers, and other musical devices grew rapidly.

of audio equipment. The Emagic Multichannel Interface A62 m is a good example: it connects to your Mac's USB port and offers six audio inputs (for line-in music, electric instruments, or microphones), two audio outputs (for speakers or preamps), and MIDI input/output (for connecting MIDI devices). Apple provides a utility called Audio MIDI Setup that works with audio devices connecting via FireWire, USB, PCMCIA, or PCI. Read more about this type of device in Chapter 6.

THE MIDI PROPHET

To move up another notch in technology and accessibility, the synthesizer industry decided to learn a lesson from the computer industry and develop a standard for interconnectivity. As electronic instruments began to go digital, a number of manufacturers — including Roland, Oberheim, Sequential Circuits, and Fender Rhodes — developed digital interfaces that allowed their own digital instruments to work together. But these proprietary interfaces did not permit interworking between devices developed by different manufacturers.

Dave Smith and Chet Wood, then working for a company called Sequential Circuits, devised — probably with some input from Roland — a Universal Synthesizer Interface to overcome this problem. Their proposal was presented to the Audio Engineering Society in autumn of 1981, and provided a starting point for the development of the MIDI standard.

MIDI stands for Musical Instrument Digital Interface, and is now an international standard that specifies how musical instruments with microprocessors can communicate with other microprocessor-controlled instruments or devices. The first synthesizer to speak MIDI was the Sequential Prophet 600 in 1983, played by some of the greatest keyboard players in jazz and rock.

MIDI TODAY

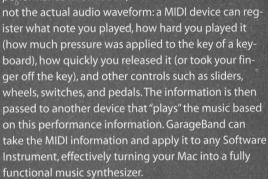

MIDI communicates performance information, not the actual audio waveform: a MIDI device can register what note you played, how hard you played it (how much pressure was applied to the key of a keyboard), how quickly you released it (or took your finger off the key), and other controls such as sliders, wheels, switches, and pedals. The information is then passed to another device that "plays" the music based on this performance information. GarageBand can take the MIDI information and apply it to any Software Instrument, effectively turning your Mac into a fully functional music synthesizer.

The newest development in MIDI devices is compatibility with USB (Universal Serial Bus) cables. Now you can plug the MIDI keyboard directly into your Mac, transmitting not only MIDI information, but also supplying power to the keyboard from your Mac through the USB cable, making it super easy to play music in any location with a PowerBook and a USB MIDI keyboard.

The M-Audio Keystation 49e is typical: It's a 49-note, full-size, velocity-sensitive USB MIDI keyboard with modulation and pitch bend wheels. You can shift the pitch of its keys up or down in octave using the Octave buttons, bend notes with the pitch bend wheel, and modulate the sound with the modulation wheel. Although you can use an optional power adapter, the keyboard draws so little power that your Mac can power it through the USB connection.

Instruments and microphones

You can also connect to a Mac an electric instrument, such as your favorite Stratocaster guitar, or use a microphone with your Mac to record acoustic instruments as well as vocals, using settings and effects designed for real instruments called, appropriately, *Real Instruments*.

You can also use microphones to record acoustic instruments that have no electric pickups. I play harmonica using a microphone connected directly to an iMac line-in connection. You can sing with a microphone connected the same way, to get a better vocal sound than you would from the Mac's internal microphone (which picks up everything in the room, including the sound of the Mac itself).

Most Mac models offer a line-in connection that accepts a cable with stereo miniplug, which is common in many music lovers' households. You can connect any kind of mono or stereo audio source, such as a CD or DVD player; an electric instrument, such as an electric guitar; a mono microphone; or a stereo set of microphones.

For connecting home stereo gear, find the jack (or jacks) marked "Line Out" on your stereo system, and connect it with a cable that uses either left and right RCA-type plugs or a stereo miniplug. If you use RCA-type plugs, you need to use a male RCA-to-stereo miniplug converter, or a cable that offers a stereo miniplug on the other end.

For electric instruments such as guitars, and for microphones, you need a phono-to-mini plug converter such as the Monster Instrument Adapter — a short cable that has a mono ¼-inch phono connection on one end and a stereo ⅛-inch miniplug on the other — to connect to your Mac's line-in connection.

 Tip

If your Mac doesn't offer a line-in connection, you can purchase a USB audio input device, such as the Griffin iMic or the Roland UA-30, and use it with the Mac's USB connection.

If you intend to connect more than one instrument or microphone at the same time, get an audio interface. An *audio interface* is a device that lets you connect multiple

audio sources to your Mac. Audio interfaces connect to your Mac via several formats including USB, FireWire, PC card, and PCI. You may already need a MIDI-compatible audio interface to use a MIDI keyboard, as described earlier in this chapter. Many audio interfaces offer both MIDI connections and connections for other audio devices; the Emagic Multichannel Interface A62 m, for example, connects to your Mac's USB and offers six audio inputs (for line-in music, electric instruments, or microphones), as well as MIDI connections.

Although I don't recommend it, you can use the Mac's built-in microphone if you have no other choice. It picks up sound from the room, so be aware that your recording may sound like just what it is: a recording made in a room with a single microphone.

We recommend using external microphones for vocals and acoustic instruments because you can place them closer to the person singing or the instrument playing. Of course, singing in a completely quiet room or a coat closet, if not an actual soundproof vocal booth, is best. Nevertheless, the Mac's internal microphone can be useful on the road with a PowerBook, especially when recording sound effects or ambient sound.

WELCOME TO YOUR NEW STUDIO

The icon that looks like the giant guitar at the Hard Rock Café in Las Vegas — yes, that's the one — should be in your Dock and ready to click. If you don't see it, you can always find GarageBand in the Applications folder — double-click it to launch it.

When you first start GarageBand, you have a choice of creating a new song or opening an existing song, as shown in Figure 1-3.

Figure 1-3
Your first choice: to create or to open

When you first create a song, you set the song's parameters, which include the tempo, time signature, and key. We explain these in "Starting a New Song Project" in this chapter.

Opening a song

The iLife installation DVD contains GarageBand songs you can open and use for whatever purpose. To open a song project, click Open Existing Song, and use the Open dialog box to browse to the GarageBand Demo Songs folder on the DVD, which contains folders of sample songs. Select a song such as Shufflin' Guitar Blues.band, Daydream.band, Half Dome.band, or Shufflin' Piano Blues.band (song project file names all end with the extension .band).

The GarageBand window, shown in Figure 1-4, shows a timeline of horizontal tracks with regions representing music. We clicked the open eye icon (to the right of the "i" icon) to show the prerecorded Apple Loops you can use in your songs, described in detail in Chapter 2 of this book.

Here's a quick overview of the sections of the GarageBand window (refer to Figure 1-4):

- **Track header:** A track contains the music from a single instrument or set of instruments. Each track has a header that shows the instrument icon and name. Click the mute button (with the speaker icon) to

mute the track, or click the solo button (with the headphone icon) to hear only that track.

- **Track mixer:** Drag the pan wheel to adjust the left-right placement of the track in the stereo field, and drag the volume slider to adjust the track's volume. The level meters show the track's volume level as you record and play.

- **Tracks with sound regions:** The track's audio information appears here as a region within a track, with its duration measured by the timeline beat ruler. A region is the colored rectangle that indicates the duration of a particular track in the timeline. The region shows a waveform representing a Real Instrument sound, or a set of notes representing a Software Instrument sound. Tracks are where you record performances and drag loops; each performance or loop is a region. You can drag the regions within the track to arrange the music.

- **Timeline beat ruler:** The timeline area of the GarageBand window offers a beat ruler with a playhead you can drag to different locations within the song. You can also use the ruler to align regions to specific beats and measures.

- **Zoom slider:** Use this slider to zoom into the timeline and get a closer view of the regions at a particular time in the song.

- **Function buttons:** You can add a new track (+ icon), open the Track Info window ("i" icon), open the Loop Browser (the open eye icon), or open the Track Editor (which occupies the same space as the Loop Browser when open).

- **Transport controls:** Use the record (red) button to start recording, or use the CD player-style controls to play at the point of the playhead, go to the beginning, fast backward, or fast forward.

Track headers   Track mixer   Timeline beat ruler   Tracks with sound regions

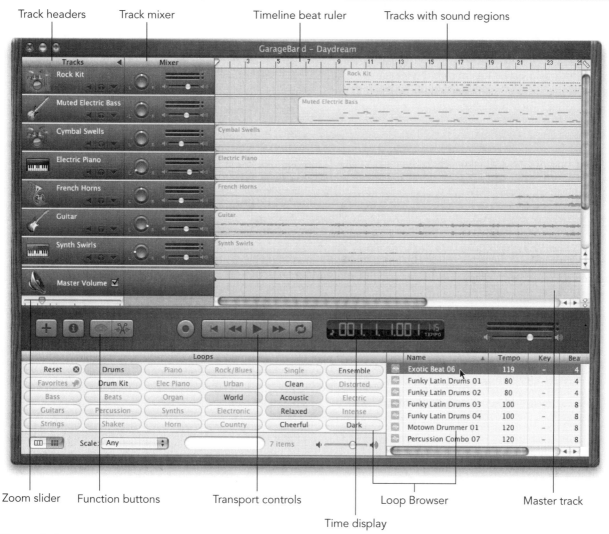

Zoom slider   Function buttons   Transport controls   Loop Browser   Master track

Time display

Figure 1-4
Welcome to the machine

- **Time display:** This indicator tells you the playhead position measured in musical time (using musical measures, beats, and ticks) or absolute time (hours, minutes, seconds, fractions of a second), and the tempo. It also provides buttons to change the tempo or the time measure.

- **Loop Browser:** This section offers either a grid of keyword buttons to refine your search for a loop, or a column view that lets you browse to a loop. After choosing a Software Instrument, you can scroll the matching list of loops on the right, or click more buttons to the right of the instrument button to refine your search. You can hear a loop by clicking on the loop, or drag a loop directly to the timeline to create a track.

- **Master track:** This track controls the master volume and lets you adjust the overall volume by dragging the volume slider. Adjust the volume of sections of the song by dragging points of the volume line in the track.

Playing a song

The timeline offers a playhead (represented by a vertical line) showing the location of the song's point of playback. A beat ruler appears at the top of the timeline showing beats and measures (units of musical time).

To play music, use the transport control buttons (from left to right, as shown in Figure 1-4):

- **Back to beginning (rewind):** Moves the playhead back to the beginning.

- **Fast backward:** Moves the playhead quickly back in time.

- **Play (or spacebar):** Starts playing at the point of the playhead (you can also use the spacebar on your alphanumeric keyboard as a substitute for the Play button). Play an entire song by clicking the back-to-beginning button to move the playhead back to the beginning, and then clicking the play button or pressing the space bar to start playback.

- **Fast-forward:** Moves the playhead quickly ahead in time.

- **Cycle:** Plays the entire song or a cycle region over and over as a loop. See Chapter 8 of this book for details on how to record into a cycle region, using it as an overdub region.

You can also drag the playhead in the timeline to a specific region or time in the song, and then click the play button or press the space bar to play from that point in the song to the end.

To raise or lower the volume of playback, drag the master volume slider (below the lower-right corner of the timeline) to the right to raise it, or to the left to lower it. See Chapter 4 for more details on controlling the master volume.

 Tip

The volume setting in GarageBand does not override the setting you choose in the Sound pane of System Preferences. The volume in GarageBand can only be equal to or less than the output volume set in the Sound pane.

STARTING A NEW SONG PROJECT

To start a new song project, click Create New Song when you first start GarageBand (refer to Figure 1-3), or choose File ➜ New.

 Tip

Before deciding to create a new song project, be sure you have enough disk space. Each minute of stereo audio recorded into GarageBand uses about 10 megabytes (MB) of space. The audio is not compressed as it is in iTunes, because you are still working on the song and you need the highest quality.

In the New Project dialog box that appears, as shown in Figure 1-5, define your song's tempo, key, and time signature, and then click Create.

You don't have to know how to read music to define these basic parameters, which characterize a song's rhythm and the range of notes played. But you have to start somewhere, and these parameters are the most important pieces of information for loops and recordings of Software Instruments. When you add a loop, or record with a Software Instrument, GarageBand automatically adjusts the loop or performance to the key, tempo, and time signature. The default settings — 120 beats per minute (bpm), in the key of C, with a time signature of ¾ — are typical for popular songs and jingles.

Figure 1-5
Setting the tempo, key, and time signature

▼ **Tip**

Of course, you can choose settings and then change them later. When you change the tempo and key, you can choose to have all recordings and loops made with Software Instruments change automatically to reflect the new settings. We describe how to change these settings for loops in Chapter 2, and how to adjust Software Instrument loops and recordings in Chapter 9.

Setting the tempo

You know what a *beat* is: it's the basic rhythmic unit in a piece of music. Every song has a beat; in fact, the beat is often used to justify the labels we affix to music, from

reggae to rhythm and blues (R&B). The *tempo,* measured in beats per minute (bpm), is a way of measuring the speed of a song.

Most songs stay in the same tempo from beginning to end. A high tempo usually translates into a faster song, at least in terms of beats per minute. You can set the tempo to any speed between 60 bpm, which is slow at one beat per second, up to 240 bpm, which is a pretty quick 4 beats per second. Most pop songs and popular rhythms are in the range of 100-130 bpm. In the New Project dialog box (refer to Figure 1-3), you can drag the Tempo slider left to slow it down and right to speed it up.

Although you can change the tempo at any time, setting the tempo first can help you record a performance accurately. GarageBand includes a *metronome* that indicates the exact tempo by playing a short blip for each beat. (The first metronome was a pendulum device invented by Maelzel in 1816 to indicate the exact tempo of a composition.) You can hear the "ticks" of the metronome while recording if you turn on the Metronome option in the Control menu; the sound of the metronome itself is not recorded. The metronome helps you stay in tempo while you perform with your instrument. See Chapter 8 to learn about recording a performance.

Setting the time signature

Counting beats would be a waste of time if you couldn't use them to determine when to play notes with an instrument, and when not to. Music is about repetition: by dividing the beats into measures you can more easily see the repeating musical phrases in a song.

The *time signature* is a way of dividing up the beats into measures and notes. For example, with a time signature of ¾, you have two beats in every measure, with each beat having the value of a quarter note (4). A *measure* is simply a handy metric device that separates music into pieces; sometimes a measure is called a "bar" (as in the 12-bar blues).

The most common time signature is ¼, used in such classics as "Yesterday" and "Get Back" by the Beatles — but check out the Beatles' "In My Life" for an example of a ½ time signature. While you are hunting down Beatles songs, "Norwegian Wood" is in ¾, and you can really hear the difference in time signature when "All You Need is Love" switches from ¼ (while Lennon sings "There's nothing you can do that can't be done") to ¾, then back again (when he sings "Nothing you can sing that can't be sung").

You can set the time signature to ½, ¾, ¾, ¼, ¼, ⅝, ⅞, ⅞, or ¹²⁄₈ (used in the Beatles' "Oh! Darling" and, along with ⅝, in "You've Got to Hide Your Love Away") in the Time pop-up menu (refer to Figure 1-5). The time signature defines how the timeline beat ruler is divided into beats and measures.

Setting the key

We explain a bit of music terminology in this section, but if you want the quick answer to, "What do I set the key to?" just pick one that sounds right. If you play a musical instrument or sing a lot, you already know that a song is played in a particular key. Singers often have preferences on what keys to sing in.

(As a harmonica player who didn't read music, I learned quickly that all I needed to do was ask the guitar player or piano player: their charts usually say what key the song is in. Some instruments are locked in a certain key; harmonica players use different harmonicas tuned to each key.)

To start with, the *pitch* in music is the property of sound that changes with the variation in the frequency of

vibration — giving Brian Wilson and the Beach Boys the ability to tell the difference between good vibrations and bad vibrations. A *note* is a notation representing the pitch and duration of a musical sound. Each note is separated from the next by a *semitone*, which is the musical interval between adjacent keys on a keyboard instrument. Two semitones make a *whole tone*. Although it's never that simple.

In Western music, a *scale* is a collection of notes arranged in either ascending or descending order. Ignoring atonal music for a moment, the *key* is the note on which a scale begins, ends, or around which a song is centered. There are 24 keys in Western music representing major or minor diatonic scales (a diatonic scale is one that has eight notes). You have 12 keys available for defining your new song: C, C# (pronounced "C-sharp"), D, D#, E, F, F#, G, G#, A, A#, and B.

By default, a new song is set to the key of C unless you change it in the Key pop-up menu (refer to Figure 1-5). The key of C (referred to as the "people's key" by leftists with a sense of humor) is popular for pop music, urban and rural folk songs, country ballads, classical music, Latin music, jazz, reggae, funk, R&B, and Southern rock. The key of D is often used for hard and soft rock, country, jazz, and bluegrass, and the key of A is often used for blues, R&B, and hip-hop. There are, of course, many exceptions; don't bother writing us angry emails that we are clueless about music.

You should choose a key you feel comfortable with, especially if you intend to sing. Often a band will change the key of a song to accommodate a singer who can't reach the high notes (or can't hold the low notes). The way to find out if you are comfortable with a particular key is to choose the key and experiment with loops, as described in Chapter 2.

STACY PARRISH: PRODUCING ARTISTS WITH GARAGEBAND

GarageBand is simple to use and therefore quite useful even to professional music producers. "With the artists I'm working with, I like to create music on a platform, so to speak, where everything is already set up and readily accessible," says Stacy Parrish, a producer and engineer for artists as diverse as Doyle Bramhall, Fee Waybill, and Rock and Roll Hall of Famers George Clinton and Jack Casady. He is equally at home working at world-class studios like Abbey Road, The Plant, and Criteria as he is in his home studio, Water. "With GarageBand and a laptop, I don't have to carry masters around with me. I can tinker with rhythm tracks, a groove and a feel, and seed the artists with a lyrical idea to see where they might take it on their own. They can sing right into the microphone and try things out. I can work in a number of different locations, with or without the artists, and I always have the same sounds with me — the same instrument settings, key and tempo settings, and so forth. There is continuity in the creative process."

▼ Tip

Whatever key you use, the Software Instruments you play automatically play in that key. Apple Loops with melody and harmony instruments are recorded in a specific key, but when you add them to a new song, as described in Chapter 2, the loops are automatically transposed to play in the new key: each note changes to reflect its relationship to the new central note. You have to hear this to believe it. You don't have to change your Software Instrument performances either; GarageBand transposes them to the new key for you, as I show in Chapter 9.

Of course, GarageBand keeps track of the key, tempo, and time signature for your song project when you save it. Don't be shy about choosing File ➜ Save to save your project as you work. You can also choose File ➜ Save As to save it as a different song.

Adding Prerecorded Loops

In This Chapter

Browsing and choosing Real Instrument and Software Instrument loops

Limiting loop results to those that match the song's key and scale

Marking loops as favorites and sorting loops

Extending a loop in a track • Playing multiple loops in tracks

Modifying the tempo and key of a song with loops

No talent? No problem! GarageBand offers a wide variety of loops you can use to build songs without ever having to play a note. Electronica, jungle, bass-and-drum, and ambient music samples are ready to roll. Rock guitar riffs are available for those slasher moments. Sing along to an R&B or funk rhythm. Rappers take note: All you need to do is select some loops and rap to your Mac's microphone (or connect a separate microphone).

Loops — prerecorded samples of sound that repeat — were used in the avant-garde music of the 1940s and 1950s, and eventually in popular music in the 1960s in Beatles songs such as "Tomorrow Never Knows" (the sounds of birds and backwards-played guitar licks) and "Being for the Benefit of Mr. Kite" on *Sgt. Pepper* (in which loops of pump organs and circus sounds were literally cut into pieces and thrown into the air, and then reassembled at random in the studio). Vocal loops appeared at the end of "I Am the Walrus" with "Everybody's got one" mixed with "Stick it up your oompah" and other phrases. The Beastie Boys paid homage to the Beatles 20 years later by including a loop in "The Sounds of Science" (on *Paul's Boutique*) that repeated part of the Beatles song "The End" (from *Abbey Road*). By then, sampled sounds, instruments, and vocals were used extensively in popular music, especially in hip-hop and rap.

You can hear in today's music many of the guitar licks, keyboard riffs, horn phrases, and drum rolls that made past musicians famous. These sequences that play exactly the same notes over and over in exactly the same way are called *loops*. Sometimes a loop is used over and over consistently throughout a song, and some loops occur only a few times or even just once. With GarageBand, you have more than a thousand loops created by professional musicians at your disposal — almost as if the musicians were recruited just for your song. You can purchase or obtain free loops from many sources, including Apple.

This chapter describes how to use the high-quality prerecorded loops that GarageBand offers right out of the box. In the process, we also explain the basic things you need to know to find the right loop, add more loops, and use them in songs. In particular, we explain the difference between Software Instrument loops and Real Instrument loops.

WISDOM OF IHNATKO: MY DOG HAS FLEAS, AND A PARASITE THAT WE'RE GIVING HIM THESE ORANGE PILLS FOR

Actually, I can't just stand by and be a passive bystander in this chapter. What about the oath I took when I accepted the position of Beloved Industry Pundit? I lost the leatherette guide they gave me, but I'm pretty sure this sort of situation was covered. It'd be a blow to my personal honor and there's a chance that it may mess up my BIP Guild Dental Plan.

So I'm going to add a bunch of sidebars to get you acquainted with a musical instrument that's undergoing a true renaissance: the ukulele. I'd never played any sort of stringed instrument in my life, but an hour after picking up my first uke, I was hooked. "Spread the love" is my motto, so sit tight and receive the Gospel of Uke, on a convenient installment plan.

TYPES OF LOOPS

A loop is essentially a piece of sound that sounds good when repeated. Loops can be recorded by performing with either a Real or Software Instrument. Both types of loops in the Apple Loop format for GarageBand repeat exactly as they should, note for note, in exactly the same tempo, so that you can repeat the loops over and over seamlessly. The loops Apple provides can be used free and clear of any royalties or licenses. GarageBand includes thousands of these prerecorded Apple Loops and a Loop Browser that categorizes them, so that you can find the ones you want for a particular mood or genre — everything from Acoustic Noodling 02 (guitar) to RnB Horn Section 09.

Get a thousand more loops from Apple in the extra GarageBand Jam Pack, or use prerecorded loops from other sources in the Apple Loop format, both free and purchased. (While loops obtained through other sources may be royalty-free, they may have other restrictions. Consult the fine print when you obtain them.)

When you play an Apple Loop or drag it to a track in the timeline, the loop automatically matches the tempo you've set for the song and the notes are automatically transposed into the key set for the song. No worries about being out of tune or totally incapable of keeping time — just let GarageBand do it.

Real Instrument loops

A *Real Instrument loop* is really a sound *sample*. The sound is recorded as a waveform by taking audio "snapshots" of the sound at regular intervals and storing the information in an audio file, just like a song from an audio CD. A Real Instrument loop has a waveform icon next to it, as shown in the bottom right corner of Figure 2-1.

There is really no difference between a Real Instrument loop and a Real Instrument performance recorded directly

Figure 2-1
Selecting a Real Instrument loop after clicking the Guitars keyword button

into GarageBand, other than the fact that a Real Instrument loop is saved in the Apple Loop format and available in the Loop Browser.

▼ Cross-Reference

See Chapter 7 to read about choosing a Real Instrument sound and Chapter 8 about recording a performance with one.

After adding a Real Instrument loop to a track, you can change its sound just by changing the sound of the Real Instrument track, as described in Chapter 7. You can also edit a Real Instrument loop in a track, as described in Chapter 9, in the same way as editing a Real Instrument performance.

A Real Instrument loop automatically matches the tempo you've set for the song, and the notes are automatically

transposed into the key set for the song (set the tempo and key as described in Chapter 1). However, not all Real Instrument loops sound good in every key — only the loops that would sound good transposed into the key you set are listed in the Loop Browser if you chose a key. You can also set a GarageBand preference to list only the Real Instrument loops that were recorded in the key you set (see the section "Matching the song's key" later in this chapter).

Software Instrument loops

A *Software Instrument loop*, on the other hand, is a set of MIDI instructions for playing back the sound, not the sound waveform itself. A Software Instrument loop has a musical note icon next to it, as shown in Figure 2-2.

There is really no difference between a Software Instrument loop and a Software Instrument performance recorded directly into GarageBand, other than the fact that a Software Instrument loop is saved in the Apple Loop format and available in the Loop Browser.

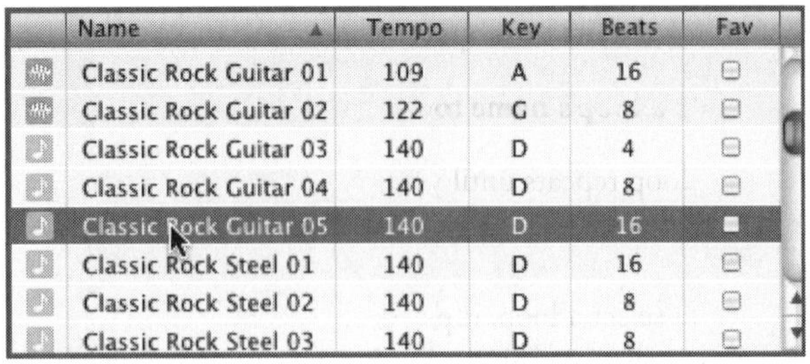

	Name ▲	Tempo	Key	Beats	Fav
	Classic Rock Guitar 01	109	A	16	☐
	Classic Rock Guitar 02	122	G	8	☐
	Classic Rock Guitar 03	140	D	4	☐
	Classic Rock Guitar 04	140	D	8	☐
	Classic Rock Guitar 05	140	D	16	☐
	Classic Rock Steel 01	140	D	16	☐
	Classic Rock Steel 02	140	D	8	☐
	Classic Rock Steel 03	140	D	8	☐

Figure 2-2
Selecting a Software Instrument loop after clicking the Guitars keyword button.

▼ Cross-Reference

See Chapter 6 to read about choosing a Software Instrument and Chapter 8 about recording a performance with one.

After adding a Software Instrument loop to a track, you can change not only its sound characteristics but also the instrument itself, as described in Chapter 6. You can also edit a Software Instrument loop in a track, as described in Chapter 9, in the same way as editing a Software Instrument performance.

A Software Instrument loop automatically matches the tempo you've set for the song, and the notes are automatically transposed into the key set for the song (set the tempo and key as described in Chapter 1). Software Instrument loops are far more flexible than Real Instrument loops. You can switch instruments, edit individual notes, and transpose loops into different keys, or change their tempos with no loss in sound quality.

BROWSING FOR LOOPS

The Loop Browser in GarageBand offers access to thousands of loops. Because it would take a while to listen to every loop in order to select the ones you want for your song, the browser offers ways to narrow your search. GarageBand offers two ways to browse loops: *browse view*,

WISDOM OF IHNATKO: WHY THE UKULELE?

At one time, *Guinness World Records* listed the ukulele as the World's Easiest-To-Learn Instrument. I suppose if you're *that* drunk, you can easily forget about the kazoo, but there's truth to that statement. The Uke is in a class of its own. Unlike a guitar, a ukulele has only four strings — not six or 12 — and most chords can easily be formed using three fingers. Plus, it has a very short neck, and you rarely have to move your hand anywhere up or down the fingerboard; most chords are formed in the same spot, up high by the tuners.

You'll find that most chords are flavors of the same three you learned with your first song (C, G7, and F) with just a finger added or different strums used to inject variations without really having to learn anything new. The uke is oddly addicting, and most of the folks I've talked to had the same early experience I did: they didn't *intend* to spend a half hour practicing every day, but (thanks to its small size) the uke was just *there* on the nightstand or the end table, and what with the consistently poor quality of prime-time television these days, you find that you need something to keep you from getting bored while watching *Law & Order*.

which lets you browse by clicking buttons in different categories, and *column view*, which provides an organizational view of loops in columns just like the Finder. You can choose whichever view you like.

Browse view

Browse view lets you browse loops by instrument, and for each instrument, you can narrow the search by genre, mood, and type. Follow these steps to browse loops:

1. **Open the Loop Browser by clicking the open-eye icon or choosing Control ➜ Show Loop Browser.**

2. **If you have already used browse view to browse loops, click the Reset button on the far left side to reset browse view.**

   Browse view, shown in Figures 2-1 and 2-2, lets you choose an instrument and refine your search, but once you have already chosen an instrument, the only way to choose a different one is to click Reset first.

3. **Click an instrument button (on the left side) to choose an instrument.**

   Loops for that instrument appear in the scrolling results list on the right. You can scroll this list to select a loop or continue to narrow your search with the following step.

4. **Click one button each for genre, mood, and/or type.**

   To narrow your search, you can reduce the number of loops in the list and use the grid of keyword buttons. After clicking a button for an instrument, the browser highlights more buttons to the right that you can click to narrow your search by genre, mood, and type. For

example, you can narrow the search by picking a musical genre (World), and then a mood (Relaxed), and/or a type (Electric). You don't have to use all three types of buttons. For example, you can select a genre and scroll through all the loops in that instrument that match the genre.

5. **Scroll the list of loops on the right.**

6. **Click a loop's name to hear it.**

   The loop repeats until you click the loop again to stop it or click another loop.

When you select a loop, it plays automatically. You can adjust the volume of playback by dragging the volume slider in the Loop Browser (in the center near the bottom).

Column view

With column view, as shown in Figure 2-3, you can browse to a loop in a fashion that is similar to browsing for a file in the Finder. With so many loops from which to choose, column view offers a quick way to find the loop you want, especially if you are already familiar with the way loops are categorized.

After clicking a keyword in the left column, you have a choice of matching categories in the middle column. Click a category in the middle column to show matching keywords in the right column. Click a keyword in the right column to show matching loops in the results list.

Marking favorite loops

It's late. Your eyes are dim from squinting at the long list of loops. What *was* that one you heard just a few hundred loops ago?

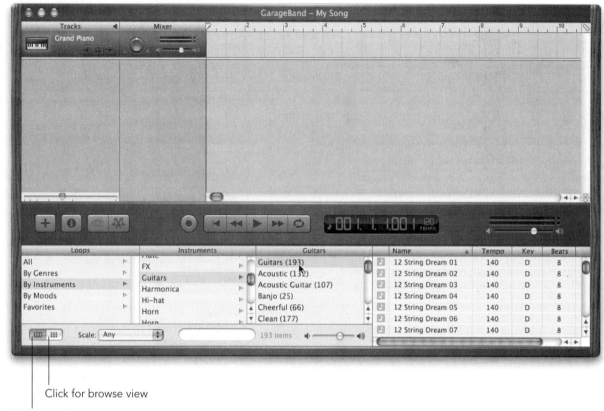

Click for browse view

Click for column view

Figure 2-3
Displaying a set of instrument loops in column view

You can mark your favorite loops to recall them later. Marking and unmarking loops is as simple as clicking the tiny checkbox in the Fav column of the scrolling list of loops, as shown in Figure 2-4. If you can't see the Fav column, scroll the list horizontally by clicking and dragging the scroll bar along the bottom, or widen your Garage-Band window by dragging the lower-right corner of the window.

To recall the list of favorite loops, click the Reset button in the far-left side of the Loop Browser, and then click the

Favorites button. Your favorites appear in the scrolling list on the right, as shown in Figure 2-5.

Matching the song's key

You may have noticed by now that loops, with the exception of drums and percussion, are prerecorded in different keys. The Key column in the scrolling list of loops indicates the loop's key. Software Instrument loops recorded in any key can match any other key and fit within any scale.

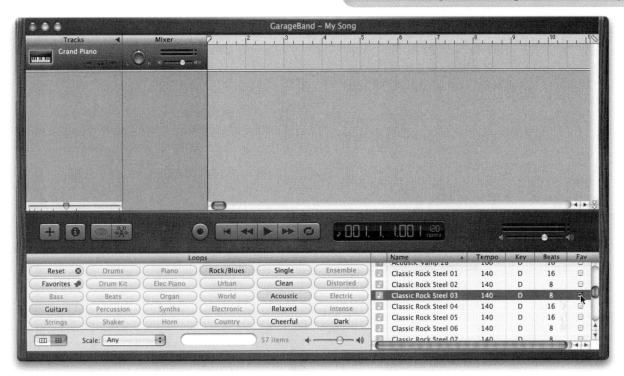

Figure 2-4
Marking a loop as a favorite

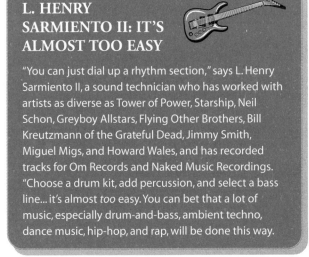

L. HENRY SARMIENTO II: IT'S ALMOST TOO EASY

"You can just dial up a rhythm section," says L. Henry Sarmiento II, a sound technician who has worked with artists as diverse as Tower of Power, Starship, Neil Schon, Greyboy Allstars, Flying Other Brothers, Bill Kreutzmann of the Grateful Dead, Jimmy Smith, Miguel Migs, and Howard Wales, and has recorded tracks for Om Records and Naked Music Recordings. "Choose a drum kit, add percussion, and select a bass line... it's almost *too* easy. You can bet that a lot of music, especially drum-and-bass, ambient techno, dance music, hip-hop, and rap, will be done this way.

For example, you can throw any Software Instrument loop at a song set to the key of D, and the loop is automatically adjusted for that key.

But Real Instrument loops are, by definition, pre*recorded* in a certain key. Because they are waveforms, they can't adapt so easily to different keys. Loops that are recorded in a different key might sound distorted after being automatically transposed, which is what happens when you use the loop in a song set to a different key. Consequently, you may not want to have to see all the Real Instrument loops that don't fit the song you are currently working on.

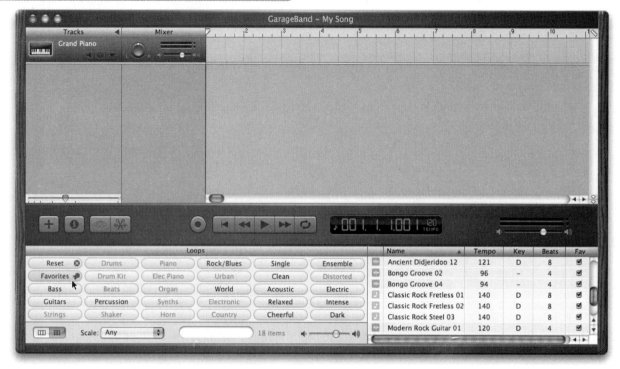

Figure 2-5
Browsing only the loops marked as favorites

To limit your loop choices to a particular scale or key so that you are not overwhelmed with choices that make no sense for your song, you can refine your search for loops by scale (major, minor, neither, or both) and set preferences to show only the loops that are relevant for the key of the song.

Most loops (except for drum and percussion loops) are recorded in either a minor or major scale. Defined in terms of Western music, a *scale* is a collection of pitches arranged in either ascending or descending order. Ignoring atonal music for a moment, the key is the tone on which a scale begins, ends, or around which a song is centered, and

defines the interrelationships of the seven pitches within that scale.

A *major scale* is when the intervals between the third and fourth notes and the seventh and eighth notes are semitones (a half step between notes), and all the other intervals are whole tones. The harmonies within the scale are based on these notes and the spacing between these intervals. A lot of uncomplicated rock and pop songs use a major scale.

A *natural minor scale* has a semitone between the second and third notes and the fifth and sixth notes; all the other intervals are whole tones. Some orchestrated blues and a lot of jazz is set in a minor scale.

Note

Most blues songs use a major scale, but with "blue" third and seventh notes that change from major to minor and back again.

The Scale pop-up menu in the bottom-left corner of the Loop Browser lets you narrow your results to Any, Major (in a major scale), Minor (in a minor scale), Neither, or Good for Both (loops that could be used in major or minor scales). To limit your choices of loops by scale, click one of these options from the Scale pop-up menu.

You can go one step farther: To show only loops that are relevant for the key of the song, follow these steps:

1. **Choose GarageBand → Preferences.**

   The Preferences window appears, as shown in Figure 2-6.

2. **Click the General button.**

3. **Click the "Filter for more relevant results" option.**

While this option is selected, GarageBand's Loop Browser displays only loops that are in the same key as the song or are in major or minor scales that are related to the key of the song.

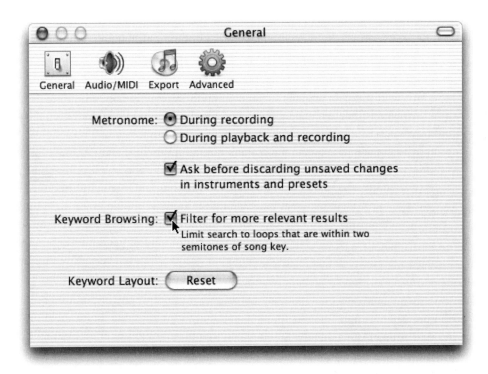

Figure 2-6
Setting the option to filter more relevant results

Sorting loops

You can quickly sort the loops in the scrolling list on the right side of the Loop Browser. Each column heading — Name, Tempo, Key, Beats, and Fav — can be used to sort the list of loops you are browsing.

Click once in the Name heading to sort the list by loop name in alphabetical order, from A to Z. Click it again to sort it in the opposite order, from Z to A. The tiny arrow in the heading shows whether the sort is A to Z (pointing up) or Z to A (pointing down). The same type of alpha sort works with the Key heading, sorting loops by key. In the Tempo heading, the tiny arrow shows whether the sort is from lowest to highest (sorting up, the arrow is up), or highest to lowest (sorting down, the arrow is down).

Sorting by key is a great way to find the loops that were recorded in a specific key. Sorting by Tempo helps you find loops recorded at specific tempos.

▼ **Tip**

In general, a loop sounds best when it plays at the tempo and key it was recorded in.

PLAYING LOOPS

As you probably know, when you click on a loop's name, you hear it. The loop repeats until you click the loop again to stop it, or until you click another loop to hear what that loop sounds like.

What you really want to do is hear a loop set against other loops. You probably want to set down a rhythm track and then listen to loops in that context. We cover adding tracks in Chapter 3, but you can create a track very simply by clicking and dragging a loop to an empty space in the timeline. Follow these steps:

WISDOM OF IHNATKO: YOUR FIRST UKE

Ukuleles typically come in three different sizes. The "soprano" uke is what most people are familiar with. It's too big to swallow whole, but only just. Most grownups find a "concert"-sized uke easier to play. It has a longer neck and there's more room for your fingers. "Tenors" are larger still, plus they're louder and have greater projection, but they're close to guitar-size and you lose that pleasant Ukulele-ish plinky-plinky sound that makes playing one such a fun undertaking.

So which model? Few local stores even carry ukes (unless you live in Hawaii, in which case life has cut you a pretty sweet break as it is), so you'll probably have to go online. eBay shows a number of dealers selling new student ukes for anywhere from $20–$50. A real cheap model is an appealing way to test the waters, but if and when you decide that this whole Ukulele hobby is going to work out, you'll want to upgrade. The cheap ones sound like hell and don't hold their tuning well.

I can't recommend the ukes of Flea Market Music highly enough. They sell two very popular models: the Flea (soprano, $119) and the Fluke (concert, $179). Both are available in a range of fashionable colors from www.fleamarketmusic.com. These ukes have a reputation as the sweetest-sounding and best-built ukes you can buy for less than $500, but my favorite feature is the fact that they have flat bottoms. My Fluke stands up on its own and I keep it on my desk right next to my Mac's keyboard, so that when I can't come up with my next gem of perfect truth, beauty, and wisdom, I can pick it up and strum out a couple of tunes (instead of walking away and turning on the Playstation).

For this reason, I insist that my Fluke is a critical piece of office equipment and thus, fully tax-deductible.

1. **Select a loop in the Loop Browser.**

2. **Turn on the Snap to Grid feature (if it isn't already on) by choosing Control ➜ Snap to Grid.**

   You know if the Snap to Grid feature is active because a check mark appears next to it in the Control menu. Although not necessary, the Snap to Grid feature makes it easier to line up *regions* (the colored rectangles that indicate the duration of a particular loop) in the tracks.

3. **Click and drag the loop to an empty space below the timeline beat ruler, as shown in Figure 2-7, and drop it into the timeline.**

   As you drag, you may notice that a vertical line appears lining up the loop with the beat. The loop snaps to different points in the timeline — points defined by the tempo and time signature (the beat) — if you have the Snap to Grid feature turned on. Drop the loop into the timeline by releasing your mouse button.

Figure 2-7
Dragging the Exotic Beat 05 loop to the timeline

After dropping a loop onto a track, GarageBand creates a region in the track showing a waveform for a Real Instrument or a set of dashes that look like notes for a Software Instrument.

After dropping a loop to a track, the loop's region takes up only a few measures of the song. To loop a region so that it plays repeatedly and smoothly, follow these steps:

1. **Move the pointer over the upper-right edge of the region.**

As you move your pointer to the upper-right edge of the region, the pointer changes into the loop pointer (an icon with a circular arrow).

2. **Click and drag the edge of the region to extend it.**

Drag the edge to the point where you want it to stop playing, as shown in Figure 2-8. The notches at the top and bottom of the region show where the loop ends and begins again — you can drag to the end of a loop or have it end anywhere in the middle.

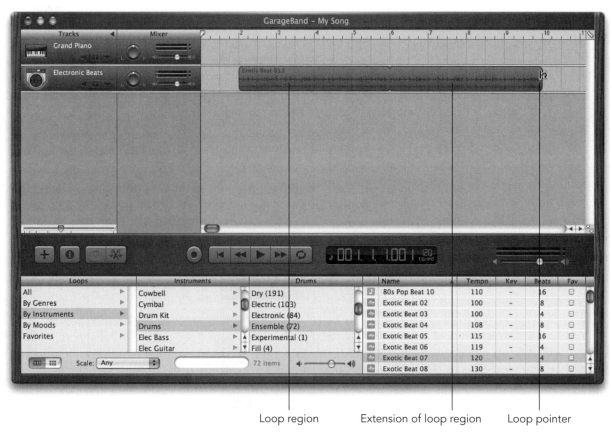

Loop region   Extension of loop region   Loop pointer

Figure 2-8
Extending a loop so that it repeats seamlessly

To hear the looping region, click and drag the playhead in the timeline back to the beginning, or to where the new recorded region starts, and then click the Play button.

Drag-and-drop as many loops as you want into the timeline. Each time you drop a loop into the space beneath existing tracks, you create a new track, as shown in Figure 2-9. The Snap to Grid option makes it easy to line up loop regions in the same time to play them simultaneously. You can also use existing tracks for more than one loop — you can drag-and-drop a Real Instrument

loop into a Real Instrument track, and a Software Instrument loop into a Software Instrument track.

Tip

If you have already assembled some tracks for a song, as described in Chapter 3, you can preview a loop along with the rest of your song. The loop automatically plays in the same key and tempo. Click the Rewind button to return the playhead to the beginning, click the Play button to play the song, and click the loop to hear it at the same time. The loop automatically plays along with the beat of the song.

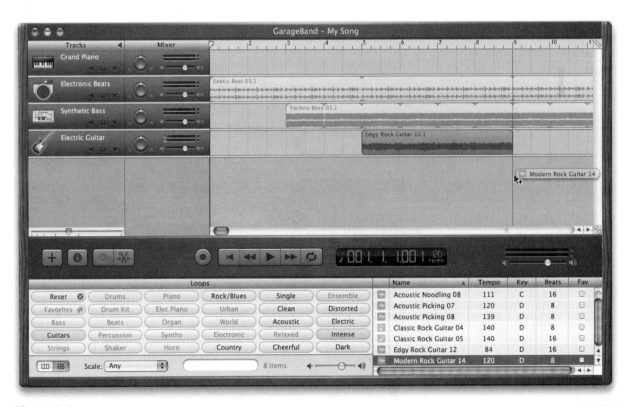

Figure 2-9
Adding another loop track to a song that has three loop tracks going simultaneously

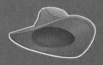

WISDOM OF IHNATKO: YOUR FIRST UKE SESSION

I'll throw in another plug for Flea Market Music (www.fleamarketmusic.com) because they also have a wide range of ukulele books and videos that'll get you up to speed with your new instrument toot sweet.

Just three bits of advice that I wish I had when I started out:

- First, there are two different ways of strumming the strings (actually three, if you count strumming with a pick, but nobody does that). When you just start out, you'll probably want to use the pads of your thumb and index finger. Strum *down* with your thumb, and then strum *up* with your index. The second method is to use the tops of the same two fingernails, though that's really tough to master when you're starting out. You'll be a little frustrated because when you hear uke players tear out fast, loud riffs, they're using their nails, or plucking the strings directly. But remember: Baby steps to start with.

- Second, when you're working through the little instructional booklet that came with the uke, or your first tutorial, you'll look at some of these chords and think it's *insane* that the neck of a uke can be gripped that way with human hands, which, alas, are all you're equipped with. Have faith. And if the chord diagram tells you to put your fingers someplace uncomfortable and you want to tell the book's author to put *his* fingers someplace uncomfortable, try using different fingers, or squeezing two strings down with the same finger.

- Third, the key to getting a nice, pure, and accurate tone is to press the string down precisely *between* the frets (the raised strips of the fingerboard) and press them right down to the fingerboard. This'll be tough at first, but you'll pick up the knack soon enough.

Start with a "C" chord (which is just one string). Just keep strumming until you can nail it consistently and play with rhythms. *Baby steps.*

MODIFYING TEMPO AND KEY

You may want to experiment a bit before you find the right tempo or key for the song. This is the mind-blowing part of GarageBand for many old-timers: When you change the tempo or key, the loops in all of the tracks adjust to the new settings automatically. You can speed up or slow down the tempo, and your loops play right on the beat.

Whatever key you set for a song when you create it, your loops automatically play in that key. Apple Loops with melody and harmony instruments are recorded in a specific key, but when you add them to a new song, the loops are automatically *transposed* to play in the new key; that is, each note changes to reflect its relationship to the new key. This is also true when you change the key of a song.

You can change the tempo, time signature, and key of a song at any time by following these steps:

1. **Select any track by clicking the track header.**

2. **Click the *i* button to open the Track Info window.**

   The Track Info window appears, showing the type of instrument (real or software).

3. **Choose Master Track from the pop-up menu at the top of the window.**

   The Master Track Info window appears, as shown in Figure 2-10.

4. **Change the tempo, time signature, or key signature by using the Tempo slider, the Time pop-up menu, or the Key pop-up menu, respectively.**

5. **Close the Master Track Info window, and play the song to hear the change.**

Close the Master Track Info window by clicking the red button that appears in the upper-left corner of the window.

Automatic transposing is handy if you already arranged a song with loops and then discovered that the vocal part you want to add doesn't sound good at that key (the singer finds it too high or too low). You can quickly change the key without having to change anything else to accommodate the vocals, and the loops change automatically.

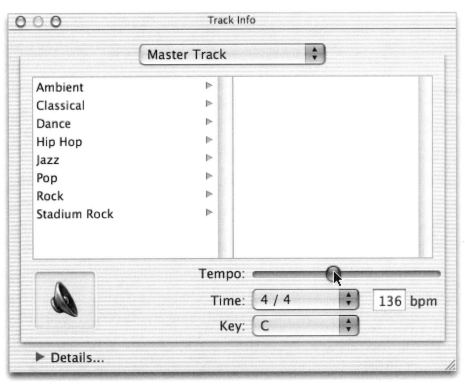

Figure 2-10
Changing the tempo in the Master Track Info window

INSTALLING MORE LOOPS

You can never have enough loops, but you can always add more. GarageBand Jam Pack, an optional software package from Apple, adds more than 2,000 prerecorded loops and more than 100 new instruments.

GarageBand Jam Pack comes on DVD. Just double-click the installer package. The pack is installed in the Garage-Band folder inside the Application Support folder in the Library folder at the root level. You need Mac OS X version 10.2.6 or newer with at least 256MB of RAM and a 600 MHz PowerPC G3 processor or faster; a G4 or G5 is required for some instruments. You also need a DVD-ROM drive and 3GB of disk space just to install the pack.

You can install more loops from third parties by dragging and dropping loop files or an entire folder of loop files into the GarageBand Loop Browser. The new loops are copied to the Loops Library and automatically indexed so that they appear in the Loop Browser.

LOOPS ON BROADWAY

You can find lots of great loops on the Internet. Most are audio files in a format such as WAV or AIFF that can be dragged into GarageBand as a Real Instrument track (see Chapter 3). Here are some places to look for loops:

- **Bitshift Audio (www.bitshiftaudio.com/).** This site offers free electro/breakbeat drum and synth loops.

- **Directions in Music (www.directionsinmusic.com/news.html).** This site offers free drum and percussion loops played by Michael Blair (ex-Lou Reed, Tom Waits, Elvis Costello, Ryan Adams, etc.) and recorded, mixed, and produced by Chris Bell.

- **Drums on Demand (www.drumsondemand.com/).** A commercial site offering loops in the Apple format, with nearly 900 live, acoustic drum loops.

- **House of Samples free samples page (www.mtlc.net/freesamples/freesamples.php).** Stop by and download a new sample every day — you won't find these sounds anywhere else. The free samples are provided by Northeastern University's Music Technology Program in cooperation with House of Samples.

- **Pro Loops (www.proloops.com/).** Pro Loops offers over 10,800 professional loops and samples, with free updates for active members, an online store, and hundreds of free loops and samples.

- **Sample Arena (www.samplearena.com/download.htm).** Loads of free royalty-free samples are available on this site.

- **Samples4.com (www.samples4.com/catalog/).** This site offers an extensive catalog of commercial samples for GarageBand.

- **Sound-Effects Library (www.sound-effects-library.com/free/mp3.html).** This site is one of the world's largest sound effects, music samples, and music tracks libraries.

Making Music Tracks

In This Chapter

Adding tracks and regions • Recording a region of music into a track
Moving, copying, and pasting regions • Splitting and joining regions
Adding a song or song sample as a track

In the '60s, the state-of-the-art recording equipment consisted of four separate tracks. The Beatles had to put their vocals, guitars, bass, and drums on three of the four tracks, reserving the fourth for tape loops. Recording and then playing back the tape loops on different tape machines and feeding the result into that fourth track was even more complicated. Today, studios have an unlimited number of tracks, with at least one track for each instrument.

With GarageBand, you can use as many tracks as you need (up to the limit of what your computer can handle) for both recordings and loops. When you're finished with your song, you can then mix all the separate tracks into two stereo tracks without any loss in sound quality.

An *arrangement* is a description in writing of how to play a song, much like a recipe. Because it describes notes played in a sequence over time, an arrangement has to show information about the song over time. Arrangers put together charts, sometimes with meticulous musical scores, to produce an arrangement. GarageBand offers a visual depiction of the song using a timeline, with instruments separated into tracks that extend from the beginning to the end of the song, with each track containing a separate musical instrument or voice.

This chapter shows how to create new tracks and add loops and recorded performances to them. It provides a brief overview of the timeline view of the tracks, and shows how to copy and move regions of music within the tracks and to other tracks.

ADDING TRACKS AND REGIONS

The main part of the GarageBand window shows a time-line of horizontal tracks with different regions representing music. Each track has a header that shows the instrument icon and name. To the right of the header you find the Mixer section of the track, and after that, the timeline area of the window. The timeline area offers a beat ruler with a playhead you can drag to different locations within the song; you can also use the ruler to align regions to beats and measures.

The track's audio information appears as a region within a track, with its duration measured by the timeline beat ruler. A *region* is the colored rectangle that indicates the duration of a particular track in the timeline. The region shows a waveform representing a Real Instrument sound, or a set of notes representing a Software Instrument sound. Tracks are where you record performances and drag loops; each performance or loop is a region. You can drag the regions within the track to arrange the music.

Creating and deleting a track

To create a track, follow these steps:

1. **Click the + button under the track headers to create a new track.**

   You can also choose Track ➜ New Track. The New Track dialog appears, as shown in Figure 3-1, with two tabs: Real Instrument and Software Instrument.

2. **Click the Real Instrument or Software Instrument tab.**

LININ' TRACK TO TRACKS OF MY TEARS

There are a lot of train songs in rock music, but that has nothing to do with the origins of the word *track* in music. A phonograph needle tracked its way around a groove in the vinyl record disc that became the first popular medium for music. Songs on a record were referred to as tracks way back in 1941 when Muddy Waters was first recorded on his back porch in Mississippi by John Work and Alan Lomax from the Library of Congress, using the first portable recording machine ("portable" indeed at 500 pounds) that engraved a sound on big acetate discs. "By making it possible to record and play back music in remote areas, away from electrical sources, [the portable recording machine] gave a voice to the voiceless," wrote folklorist Alan Lomax in *The Land Where Blues Began* (Delta/Dell Publishing, New York, NY; 1993). "[It] put neglected cultures and silenced people into the communication chain."

As soon as it became possible to record separate performances and join them together in a single recording, the idea of a *recording track* was born. The reason was simple: The sound engineer wanted to isolate the sound of one instrument (such as drums) from the sounds of others (such as vocals and guitars), so that one could be made louder or softer than the others. By using multiple tracks, an orchestra or band could record all the instrumental parts, and the singer could add a vocal track afterwards.

Figure 3-1
Creating a track with a Software Instrument

You can use either a Real or Software Instrument to define a track. Apple Loops come in both flavors. To record a performance with the onscreen keyboard or a USB MIDI keyboard, choose a Software Instrument. To record vocals (or anything else) through the Mac's built-in microphone, choose a Real Instrument such as a one from the Vocals category. Chapter 6 provides more detail about recording with Software Instruments; Chapter 7 describes how to record with Real Instruments such as guitars, and how to use the Mac line-in and microphone options.

3. **Select the type of instrument.**

   Select a category from the list on the left, and then select an instrument sound from the list on the right.

4. **Click OK.**

   A new track with the name of the instrument you selected appears in the timeline.

After creating a new track, you can drag a loop from the Loop Browser and drop it into the track: a Real Instrument loop into a Real Instrument track, or a Software Instrument loop into a Software Instrument track. The loop takes on the audio characteristics of the instrument you choose for the track.

To delete a track, select the track by clicking the track header, and choose Track ➜ Delete Track. Poof, it's gone.

 Tip

> You can undo just about any action in GarageBand by choosing Edit ➜ Undo.

The next section describes the basics on how to record into a track, but to learn more about recording a performance with a Real Instrument, see Chapter 8.

Recording a region of music

To record a performance with a Software Instrument using your onscreen music keyboard, the MidiKeys onscreen keyboard, or a USB MIDI keyboard, or to record your vocals using the Mac's built-in microphone, follow these steps:

1. **Click the track header for the track you want to record into.**

   You can record into a new track or an existing track. To record using the onscreen keyboard or a USB MIDI keyboard, use a Software Instrument track; for vocals, use a Real Instrument track.

2. **(Optional) To have the metronome and the Count In option play one measure before starting to** record, choose Control ➜ Metronome and Control ➜ Count In, respectively.

3. **(Optional) Vocalists should check their microphone input before singing into your computer.**

   Choose System Preferences from the Apple menu and click the Sound icon to open the Sound pane. Click the Input tab, and in the list of sound input devices, select the internal microphone (see Figure 3-2). As you sing or speak, you should see purple highlighted indicators that show the input level. Make sure you have highlighted indicators extending to the right but not so far as to reach the right edge. If the indicators reach the edge, the sound is clipped.

 Cross-Reference

> For more details on recording with your internal microphone, see Chapter 8.

IT'S ABOUT TIME

GarageBand includes a metronome that plays a short blip (not recorded with the music) for each beat of the measure to help you keep time while playing an instrument. You only hear it when you are recording. You can turn it on or off by choosing Control ➜ Metronome (a check mark means it is on). If you use the metronome, you might also want to turn on the Count In option by choosing Control ➜ Count In. Just like a bandleader counting in, "1-2-3-4," to prepare the band for a song, GarageBand plays the metronome one full measure before starting to record so that you can get ready to perform along with the beat.

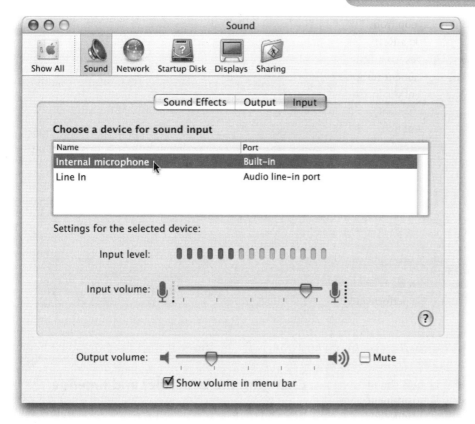

Figure 3-2
Checking the internal microphone input level

4. **Click the red Record button to start recording, and then start performing using your onscreen keyboard, USB MIDI keyboard, or Mac's internal microphone.**

   GarageBand starts recording in the track while playing any other tracks, and it lays down a new region in the track's timeline, as shown in Figure 3-3.

5. **When you're done performing the new music, click the red Record button *again* to stop recording, and click the Play button to stop playback.**

You can press the spacebar to stop recording and playback simultaneously.

To hear your recording, drag the playhead in the timeline back to the beginning, or to where the new recorded region starts, and then click the Play button or press the spacebar. (The timeline area of the GarageBand window offers a playhead you can drag to different locations within the song.)

GarageBand represents the music with a region in the timeline showing graphically what the sound looks like:

Figure 3-3
Recording a performance with the onscreen keyboard into a Software Instrument track for a Grand Piano

- **Real Instrument regions:** Loops are blue regions showing waveforms, and recordings are purple regions showing waveforms.

- **Software Instrument regions:** Both recordings and loops are green regions showing dashes in a musical scale, with dashes in the upper part of the region signifying higher pitches.

▼ **Tip**

As building blocks for your song, regions help you define pieces of music that may change, depending on the arrangement. For example, you may record a part into a separate Software Instrument track, and then copy the region of that one performance to several places in the timeline, so that you only need to perform the part once.

Changing the beat ruler and timeline

The timeline beat ruler indicates how musical time is broken up into beats and measures. You can use the beat ruler to align musical regions precisely. The timeline offers a grid to snap these segments into place: to turn it on, choose Control ➔ Snap to Grid.

You can set the grid to different note values in the time measure, such as quarter notes, eighth notes, sixteenth notes, thirty-second notes, quarter-note triplets, eighth-note triplets, and so on. To set the grid to a different note value, click the grid button in the upper-right corner of the timeline, as shown in Figure 3-4, and then choose a grid value from the menu. In addition to the note values, you can set the grid to Automatic so that the grid becomes more precise as you zoom in or out with the timeline zoom slider (located under the track names).

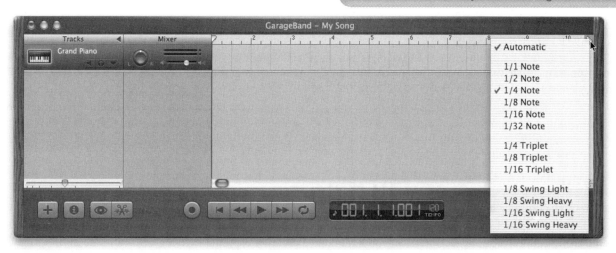

Figure 3-4
Setting the timeline grid to a different note value

WISDOM OF IHNATKO: DON'T BE EYEBALLIN' THAT UKE, BOY!

This isn't so much a tip as a piece of advice. One of the reasons I wanted to learn the Uke was because it seemed to be ideally suited as a computer accessory. Every now and then you have to restart your Mac, or wait for something to download, or you're sitting there reading a long Web page or piles of email. That's time you could be *doing* something, so why not strum a Uke? It's small and handy and it fits nicely in the crook of your arm, in the dead space between your chest and the desk.

So I intentionally determined *not to look at the uke* while I played. I tried to make my fingers "feel" their way on the strings. The idea was to be able to play without taking my eyes off my Mac's screen so I could strum while working my way through a couple of thousand emails. But it was actually a brilliant idea. If you break yourself of the habit of watching yourself play, you get the only feedback that matters: *it sounds right.* You're also not intellectualizing what you're doing. ("OK, I strum this three more times but then I have to get ready to move my fingers *here.*") More to the point, you can look at your music while you play, which means that you don't get whiplash by glancing at the music then your hands and then the music and then...

WORKING WITH REGIONS

The reason why you may want to record pieces of performances into separate regions, rather than performing a part for an entire song, is that you can move and copy the regions as well as edit them in the Track Editor (described in Chapter 9).

You can move regions easily within tracks, make copies of regions, and place copies anywhere you want. You could perform a piece of music once and use it thousands of times. You can even copy multiple regions in different tracks at once; for example, if a set of regions for bass and drum tracks are perfect for a few measures, and you want to use them throughout the song, select the regions and then copy and paste them to another place in the song.

Moving, copying, and pasting regions

Click a single region to select it. To move a region within a track, changing its starting point in the song, simply drag it to the left or right. You can even drag a region up or down from one track to another if you want the region to take on the characteristics (sounds and effects) of the destination track.

Note

Real Instrument regions can be moved only to other Real Instrument tracks, and Software Instrument regions can be moved only to other Software Instrument tracks.

When you drag a region over another region in the same time slot, as shown in Figure 3-5, the region underneath is shortened to the edge of the region you are dragging over

it. If you completely cover a region with another region, the region underneath is deleted.

Shift+click each region to select multiple regions. Select multiple regions at once by dragging a selection rectangle around all the regions you want to select; as you drag from a point in the timeline, any regions intersecting your rectangle are highlighted to show that they are selected, as shown in Figure 3-6.

To copy or cut a region, select the region by clicking it, and then choose Edit ➜ Copy (or press Command+C) to copy, or Edit ➜ Cut (or press Command+X) to cut. To paste the copy at a different location in the timeline, move the playhead to the point where you want the copied region to start, as shown in Figure 3-7, and then choose Edit ➜ Paste (or press Command+V).

Tip

To automatically make a copy of the region, drag it while holding down the Option key; dropping the copy is just like pasting it into the new location. Delete a region by selecting it and then pressing Delete on your keyboard or by choosing Edit ➜ Delete.

After pasting one or more regions, the playhead moves to the end of the first pasted region. This is convenient because you can choose Edit ➜ Paste again (or press Command+V again) to paste another copy right next to the first one.

To delete regions from one location and paste them into another, choose Edit ➜ Cut instead of Edit ➜ Copy. However, it may be faster to just drag the selected regions to the new location in the timeline.

Figure 3-5

Moving a region over the end of another region

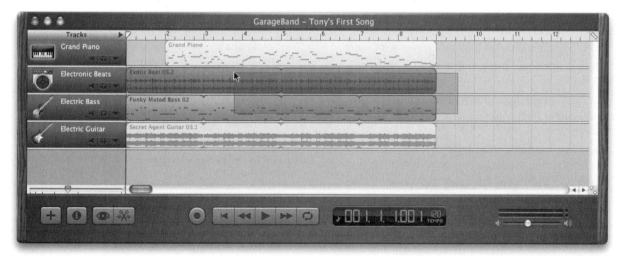

Figure 3-6

Dragging around multiple regions in the timeline to select them

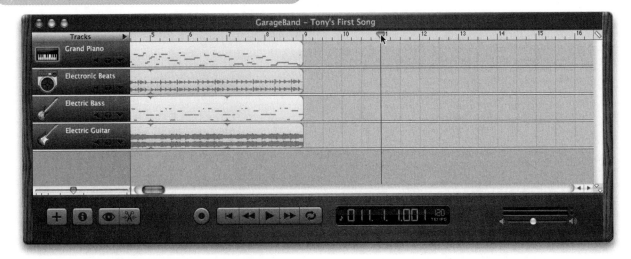

Figure 3-7
Setting a new position to paste the copied regions

Looping, shortening, and extending regions

Although pasting over and over quickly repeats a region over time, GarageBand makes looping a region a lot easier with the loop pointer. When you loop a region, it repeats without any seams in between. You can loop anything: Real Instrument recordings, Software Instrument recordings, and loops of both types.

To loop a region within a track, follow these steps:

1. **Move your pointer to the upper-right edge of the region.**

   The pointer changes to the loop pointer (a circular arrow), as shown in Figure 3-8.

2. **Drag the loop pointer to extend the region.**

   Drag the region to the point where you want it to stop looping, as shown in Figure 3-9. The notches at

the top and bottom show the beginning and end of the piece of music. You can drag to extend the entire looping region, so that the entire region repeats, by extending to an end notch. You can also extend to the middle of a looping region, stopping the loop anywhere you want.

You can shorten a region so that only the visible part of the region plays. You can also lengthen a Software Instrument region, adding silence — but only to Software Instrument regions; Real Instrument regions can only be shortened or returned to their original lengths.

To resize a region, follow these steps:

1. **Move your pointer over the lower half of the region's right or left edge.**

   The pointer changes to the resize pointer, as shown in Figure 3-10.

2. **Drag the edge of the region to shorten or lengthen it.**

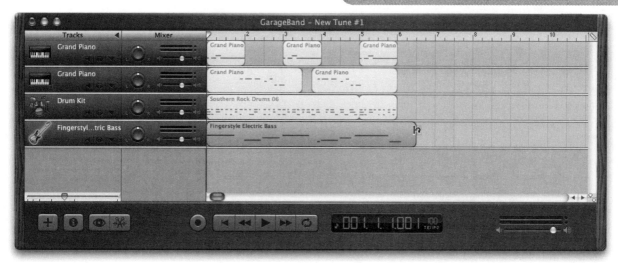

Figure 3-8
Display the loop pointer by moving the mouse pointer to the upper-right edge of a region

Figure 3-9
Dragging with the loop pointer to loop the region

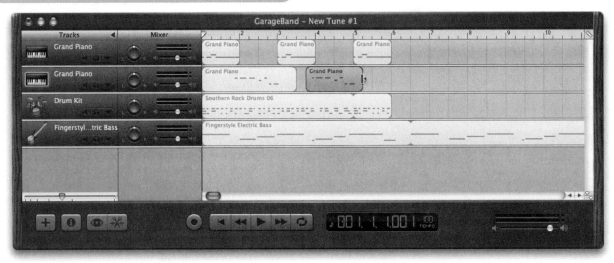

Figure 3-10
Dragging with the resize pointer to shorten or lengthen a region (not looping)

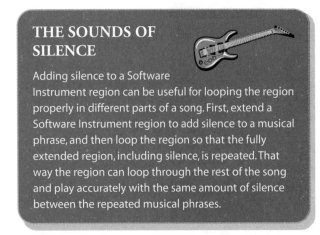

THE SOUNDS OF SILENCE

Adding silence to a Software Instrument region can be useful for looping the region properly in different parts of a song. First, extend a Software Instrument region to add silence to a musical phrase, and then loop the region so that the fully extended region, including silence, is repeated. That way the region can loop through the rest of the song and play accurately with the same amount of silence between the repeated musical phrases.

Splitting and joining regions

Splitting and joining regions may seem like a bit too much, but what if you recorded a great performance at the beginning and end of a region, but stank up the place in the middle? You can split the region into three parts — the good one, the stinky one, and the final good one — and then join the first and last parts into one region. Nice.

You can join regions together as long as they are already adjacent to one another on the same track, and have no space between them. Software Instrument regions (green) can be joined only to other Software Instrument regions, and Real Instrument recordings (purple) can only be joined to other Real Instrument recordings. Real Instrument loops (blue regions) can't be joined to other regions.

To split a musical region into two or more parts, follow these steps:

1. **Select the region.**

2. **Move the playhead to the point in the region where you want the split to occur, and choose Edit → Split.**

   The selected region is split into two regions at the playhead; any notes at the split point in a Software Instrument region are shortened so that they don't extend past the split point.

To join two or more regions, follow these steps:

1. **Select the regions to be joined.**

2. **Choose Edit → Join Selected.**

When you join Real Instrument regions, a dialog box appears, asking if you want to create a new audio file. Click Create to do this, so that the regions are joined into one. Otherwise the joining is cancelled.

ADDING A SONG AS A TRACK

Jamming with a prerecorded song is so easy with Garage-Band that you can experiment all you want, and then lay down a track along with the real song and merge the two into your own creation. We've done this many times, such as adding a harmonica solo to a song that never had one, or adding vocals to an instrumental song. You can even mix several songs or song samples together to make a sound collage.

GarageBand can take an AIFF, WAV, or MP3 audio file and give it its own Real Instrument track in the timeline. For example, you can drag a song converted to AIFF or MP3 directly from iTunes to your desktop to make a copy of the song as an audio file, and then drag the file from the desktop into the GarageBand timeline, as shown in Figure 3-11. Drag the song into an existing Real Instrument track, or create a new track by dragging into an empty space in the timeline.

Figure 3-11
Dragging a song from the Finder desktop into the timeline

As you drag the audio file into GarageBand, a vertical line appears, lining up the beginning of the audio file with the beat. If you have the Snap to Grid option turned on (choose Control → Snap to Grid), the beginning of the audio file snaps to the beat in the timeline just like a loop. To move the audio file within the timeline, just drag the region for the audio file left or right within the track. You can control the volume and apply Real Instrument sounds and effects to the song like you can with any other Real Instrument track.

When you bring an MP3 audio file into GarageBand, the audio is converted to the AIFF format and stored with the song project, just like a recording of a Real Instrument performance. In fact, that's what it is: a waveform, just like any other Real Instrument performance or loop. You now have the makings of a great song. But remember, don't steal music: do not use copyrighted songs or parts of songs in your own compositions. With so many free loops you can use, why bother with the older material?

IMPORTING A MIDI SEQUENCE

You are not limited to the loops in GarageBand, songs from iTunes, and performances you record yourself (although that's quite a bit of choice already). You can also import any MIDI file, such as a drum loop, a bass track, or an entire song in MIDI format.

All you need is a handy free program called Dent du Midi that you can download from `http://homepage.mac.com/beryrinaldo/ddm/`. Pronounced "don do midi" and named after a 10,600-foot-high mountain in the Swiss Alps, Dent du Midi takes standard MIDI files and generates separate files for each track containing MIDI note data. These files are suitable for dragging and dropping into Software Instrument tracks.

To add a MIDI file to GarageBand, follow these steps:

1. **Download a MIDI file from the Web.**

   To find MIDI files on the Web, try Google (search for something like "MIDI loops"), or better yet, use MIDI Explorer (`www.musicrobot.com/`), a MIDI-specific search engine.

2. **Launch Dent du Midi and drag the file you downloaded into the upper portion of the window.**

   The program extracts the various MIDI tracks that make up the song and stores them in a folder.

WISDOM OF IHNATKO: RECORDING A UKE

Well, making my first GarageBand uke recording gave me fits. I had two different kinds of microphones and neither kind seemed to work very well. I finally turned to a friend of mine (a professional audio engineer) for advice and he told me the awful truth: he doesn't know where to put the microphones, either. Not just for a uke, but for *any* instrument. With experience, an engineer will have learned the best place to mike a guitar, or an acoustic piano, or a saxophone, or that thingamabob that looks like a bent coat hanger with a tennis ball on it and when you twang the tennis ball it goes *chkhkhkhkhrrrrhrrhrrrrrrr!* I'm not sure the thing actually has a name, but even so, it takes lots of trial and error.

So if you're having no luck, just keep moving your microphone around until you've accidentally placed it smack-dab in the middle of the instrument's invisible and elusive sweet spot.

3. **Open the tracks folder and double-click Report.txt.**

   The Report.txt file tells you the tempo of the track. Knowing the tempo helps a lot, because if you import into a song with a different tempo, the beats may not line up.

▼ **Cross-Reference**

You synchronize songs using the Track Editor, as described in Chapter 9.

4. **Quit Dent du Midi, and then launch GarageBand.**

5. **Create a new song, and set the tempo for the song to the tempo reported in Report.txt.**

   Set the tempo in the New Project dialog box. If you are importing a MIDI sequence into an existing song, see Chapter 2.

6. **Drag each file created by Dent du Midi over to the GarageBand window and into a Software Instrument track.**

   Drag the song into an existing Software Instrument track, or create a new track by dragging into an empty space in the timeline.

As you drag the MIDI file into GarageBand, a vertical line appears, lining up the beginning of the MIDI file with the beat. If you have the Snap to Grid option turned on (choose Control ➜ Snap to Grid), the file's beginning snaps to the beat in the timeline just like a loop. To move the MIDI file within the timeline, just drag the region for the file left or right within the track. You can control the volume and apply Software Instrument sounds and effects to the MIDI sequence you imported, just like you can with any other Software Instrument track.

Mixing the Tracks

In This Chapter

Adjusting track volume with the Track Mixer

Setting the pan position for each track in the stereo field

Controlling the volume of all tracks using the master track

Setting the master track volume and effects for all tracks

Mixing is an art form unto itself. It's the process of controlling and balancing the volume of all the tracks and adding track effects while combining all the tracks into the final song. You've probably bought past albums that were *remixed* as well as *remastered* for CD. These terms simply mean that the tracks of the songs were recombined in such a way as to bring out the subtleties in the music.

Mixing engineers know how to make a performance of nine instruments sound good when you hear it in two stereo channels, balancing the loud and soft instruments. Bands have been known to split up over the handling of their album mixes; Paul McCartney cited Phil Spector's mix of the *Let It Be* album as a major reason for the arguments that led to the demise of the Beatles, while Skip Spence of Moby Grape got so mad with an album mix that he sunk a hatchet into the door of the studio and had to be escorted off the premises.

Nothing like that is likely to happen to you, because this chapter shows you how to mix your tracks into a song quickly and easily.

USING THE TRACK MIXER

You can add and edit as many tracks to your song as you want, but eventually you have to balance the volume in all the parts so that they blend into two tracks for stereo playback. You do this by controlling the volume and stereo pan position for each track.

It's surprising what you can hide or reveal in a mix just by adjusting the volume for each track — for a mind-blowing example, play an old LP version of Frank Zappa's *Hot Rats*, and then play the newly remixed and remastered CD version that brings out entire sets of instruments previously lost in the mix.

In the GarageBand window, the Mixer section of each track appears between the section with the track name and the timeline; if it is not visible, click the triangle next to the word Tracks at the top of the window, or choose Track ➜ Show Track Mixer.

Adjusting volume

In the Mixer section of a track, you can click and drag the track's volume slider to the left to lower the track's volume or to the right to raise it, as shown in Figure 4-1. The volume for each track can be raised or lowered so that you can achieve a balance of sound across all the tracks.

Creating a mix of the song is not always complicated. You may simply need to raise or lower the volume of the individual tracks using the track volume sliders. If it sounds good after doing so, you are well on your way to finishing the mix. However, you may need to refine the volume for each track to get a good mix by setting the track volume curve, as described in Chapter 11.

WISDOM OF IHNATKO: HOW MANY TRACKS, THEN?

GarageBand is *awfully* powerful, considering that it's only one component of a $49 software suite. Out of the box, you can work with up to 64 individual tracks at once. And that's not even the top limit. If you happened to have the Boston Pops over at the house for Monday Night Football, the cable went out, and you all figured that while you all were waiting to get the picture back it'd be fun to record the NFL "Are Your Ready For Some Football?!?" song on your PowerBook as a full orchestral arrangement, you could do it all in GarageBand by going into the Preferences panel, upping the max number of tracks to 255, and having each musician record their bits as separate tracks.

The caveat: it's possible that you can set GarageBand to use far more tracks than your Mac can possibly handle. GarageBand is probably the most interactively resource-intensive app of the whole iLife suite, and unless you have a nice, peppy G5 or dual-processor G4, you're going to bang your head on the performance ceiling. In that case, you'd probably want to record the brasses, the woodwinds, the string section, and so on, in individual groups. The good news is that the number of tracks is limited by RAM, not necessarily by processing power, though the CPU limits how many notes the app can handle at once.

HISTORY OF RECORDING 101: THE MAGNETIC MIX

Magnetic tape recording, introduced in the early 20th Century, radically altered the making of music at that time, and contributes to this day to the interfaces — the sliders, faders, and other controls — we use in software for digital recording. The basic techniques of editing — cutting and splicing to remove, rearrange, or compile pieces of recordings; mixing two or more sound sources into one recording; and fading sound in or out — were all innovations that were made easier with tape.

As engineers reduced the size of tape recorder heads, it became possible to record multiple simultaneous tracks on a single tape. Musicians or singers could be separated into two or three groups, such as recording the rhythm section and the rest of the band separately. If there was a flub on one or the other of the tracks, it could be rerecorded without reassembling the whole band. The tracks were then mixed into two stereo tracks or one mono track. In the '50s, most rock and roll records were mono recordings. "The 'mix' was the acoustical result of the distance between the microphone and the singer, the microphone and the drummer, the microphone and the bass player, and so on," wrote Frank Zappa in his autobiography, *The Real Frank Zappa Book* (Poseidon Press, New York, NY; 1989). "How far away you were from the microphone determined how 'important' you were in the mix. What qualified as an 'acceptable drum sound' on a '50s recording seems laughable today."

Figure 4-1
Raising the volume for the Digital Horns track relative to the other tracks

Setting the pan position

If you ever listened to an early Pink Floyd or Moody Blues song, you might remember how the sound seemed to fly from one speaker to the other, or actually come from somewhere in the middle.

A song can be mixed for stereo playback so that you might hear vocals coming from the left speaker and guitars coming from the right, but also drums and bass coming from somewhere in the middle. Stereo speakers can create a field of sound, also known as the *stereo field*, in which instruments and vocals are balanced in volume across the two stereo channels — not set to full volume in one channel. Your brain interprets the audio information as more like a three-dimensional sound panorama.

TRY THAT WITH TCHAIKOVSKY

Extreme stereo panning, with instrument sounds bouncing around from left to right, can be useful in certain types of recordings, possibly not in others. "On the *Sergeant Pepper* album we did all sorts of things with the stereo effect," wrote Beatles producer Sir George Martin in his autobiography, *All You Need Is Ears* (St. Martin's Press, New York, NY; 1979). "We had things in absurd positions. We had movement, with an instrument floating from one side to the other, giving the listener the impression that it was almost flying over his head. On the other hand, taste would prevent you from trying something like that if you were recording Rachmaninov's Piano Concerto. People do like to listen to their favourite works recorded in a way that evokes the concert hall. They don't want the piano, in the middle of its cadenza, floating through the roof and traveling across to the other side of the platform."

In the Mixer section of a track, you can set the *pan* (short for "panorama") position for the track. This means that you get to place the track right where you want it in the panorama of the sound field — to the far left side, closer to the middle, or on the right.

To set the pan position of a track, click on the simulated pan wheel in the Mixer section of the track, as shown in Figure 4-2. Then drag down to pan to the left channel or drag up to pan to the right; the wheel's white dot indicates the position. Press Option+click the pan wheel to return it to the center position.

You may want to put the drum and bass tracks in the middle (balanced between left and right stereo fields), and place the vocals, lead instruments, and supporting instruments in either channel.

Figure 4-2
Setting the pan position for the Digital Horns track to the right side

USING THE MASTER TRACK

The master control knob on an amplifier controls the volume. Similarly, in GarageBand the *master track* oversees all the tracks and controls their volume and effects.

No matter how high you set the volume of each track, the master track decides the *uppermost volume* of all the tracks and turns on the crucial *reverb* and *echo* for all the tracks. The echo effect copies and plays back the original sound later in time and lower in volume (enough to be heard distinctly from the original). Reverb re-creates the sound of an acoustic space by playing back many copies of the original signal at slightly varied times and volume levels. (*Reverb* is short for "reverberation.") The master track turns these effects on for the rest of the tracks and sets the upper limit for the tracks.

Every song has a master track, which is usually hidden until you explicitly show it. You can show the master track by choosing Track ➜ Show Master Track. The master track appears with the heading Master Volume at the bottom on the timeline as the last track, as shown in Figure 4-3.

Figure 4-3
Showing the master track, which is labeled Master Volume

You don't have to show the master track to adjust the volume for all the tracks, but you can use the master track to make very detailed sound adjustments using the master track volume curve, and turn on other useful effects that work across all the tracks, as described in Chapter 11.

Setting volume for all the tracks

The master volume slider (located below the lower-right corner of the timeline) actually works with the master track to control the volume for the entire song. It sets the uppermost limit for the output volume, which is also the volume used when exporting the song to iTunes. This slider is similar to the track volume sliders, except that it controls the master track (which does not have a Mixer section).

 Tip

The master volume slider sets the upper limit of volume, while the master track volume curve can be used to adjust the volume within that limit.

To adjust the master volume, which sets the upper limit for all tracks, click and drag the slider to the right to raise it or to the left to lower it, as shown in Figure 4-4.

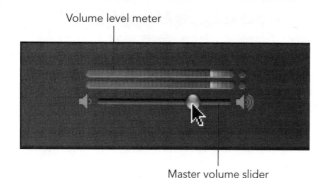

Volume level meter

Master volume slider

Figure 4-4
Adjusting the master volume for the song

While rock music should be played loud, be sure not to make the volume so high as to cause *clipping* (a distortion that sounds like a sharp, crackling sound that is caused by volume overload). As the song plays, watch the level meters above the master volume slider. The meters are the two narrow grooves — one for each channel of stereo sound — immediately above the master volume slider. The meters show green, then orange, and then red as the volume level increases. The red part, at the far right, appears only when the volume is at its highest. If the red dots to the right of the meters appear (see Figure 4-4), the volume is way too high. These *clipping indicators* stay on to remind you that clipping occurred in the song. You can reset these indicators by clicking them. Before exporting a song, you should lower the volume to a point where clipping is not occurring on playback.

Setting standard effects

The master track offers effects that work on the entire song — including echo, reverb, equalizer, and compressor.

These effects are also available for each track. I describe all of the effects in Chapter 10.

The standard echo and reverb effects should be turned on in the master track. If you turn them *off* in the master track, they do not work in the individual tracks, either. You can apply the effects across all tracks or turn off effects for all tracks.

To add or change effects in the master track, follow these steps:

1. **Select the Master Volume track.**

2. **Click the Track Info button (with the *i* icon), or choose Track ➜ Show Track Info.**

   The Track Info window for the master track appears, offering preset effects settings for various music genres (Ambient, Classical, Dance, and so on).

3. **Select a genre in the left column and a preset for that genre in the right column.**

   As shown in Figure 4-5, the master track offers presets for each genre. I chose Rock as the genre and Live Gig as the preset.

4. **Click the triangle next to Details to reveal the detailed section.**

   As shown in Figure 4-6, the master track settings are already turned on.

5. **Make sure the options for Echo, Reverb, or Equalizer are turned on in the Master Track Info window if you want to have those effects in your song or in individual tracks.**

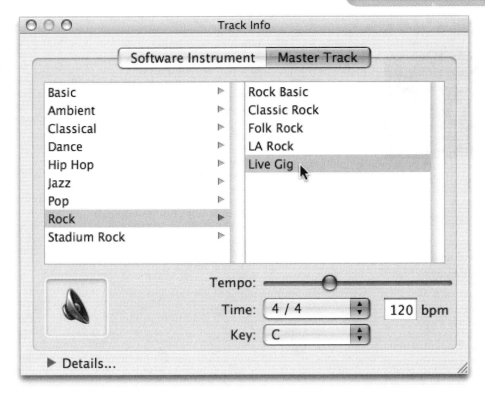

Figure 4-5
Choosing a master track effect preset for the song

6. **Close the Master Track Info window by clicking the red button that appears at the top-left corner of the window.**

   The settings are saved automatically with the song when you save the song (by choosing File ➜ Save).

You can add more effects or make changes to the effects that affect the entire song. These settings establish the upper limit for the same effects used in individual tracks. For more information about effects, see Chapter 10.

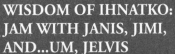

WISDOM OF IHNATKO: JAM WITH JANIS, JIMI, AND...UM, JELVIS

Try this: locate an MP3, AIFF, or WAV file in the Finder and then drag it into GarageBand's timeline. Hey, cool! The file has now been added as a new track! So it's now easy to see how your fourth grader's saxophone rendition of "Voodoo Child" stacks up to the real thing, or more practically, to integrate tracks recorded by folks who don't use GarageBand or even Macs, necessarily.

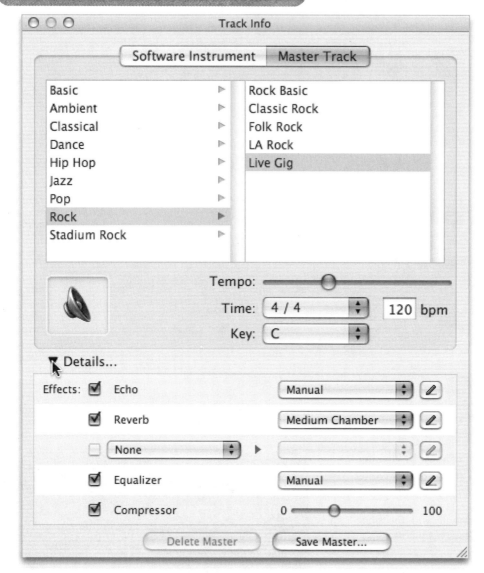

Figure 4-6
Setting the master track effects that affect all tracks

Playing in iTunes

In This Chapter

An overview of your iTunes music player ● Setting up your GarageBand song information
Exporting your GarageBand song to iTunes
Converting your song to other formats for computer, iPod, and CD
Customizing your encoder settings ● Playing your GarageBand song in iTunes

Ever been to a juke joint? More than half a century ago, jukeboxes were the primary and most convenient way for people to select the music they wanted to hear — especially newly released music — and share it with others. Juke joints were hopping with the newest hits every night.

Today, you can use iTunes to create a digital jukebox, and then conveniently click a button to play a song. Connect your Mac to a stereo amplifier in your home, or connect speakers to your Mac, and suddenly your Mac is the best jukebox in the neighborhood.

iTunes is already on your Mac: it's part of the iLife '04 suite of applications that includes Garage-Band. With iTunes you can listen to a new song on the Internet and download it immediately. You can also buy music online at the iTunes Music Store. iTunes downloads music from the store and puts it in your library, making it immediately available for playing, burning onto a CD, or transferring to an iPod. You can even listen to Web radio stations using iTunes and add your favorite stations to your music list.

Transferring songs from CD to your computer is called *ripping* a CD. Ripping an entire CD's worth of songs with iTunes is quick and easy, and track information, including artist name and title, arrives automatically over the Internet. iTunes gives you the power to organize songs into playlists and *burn* (record) CDs of any songs in your library, in any order. You can even set up dynamic smart playlists that reflect your preferences and listening habits. iTunes offers an equalizer with preset settings for all kinds of music and listening environments, and it gives you the ability to customize and save your own personalized settings with each song.

This chapter provides a quick overview of iTunes and how to get your GarageBand song into your iTunes library. You can preserve your music virtually forever without any loss in quality, and you can also use your music in a variety of creative projects made possible by the iLife suite.

GETTING TO KNOW YOUR NEW JUKEBOX

The first time you run iTunes, the Setup Assistant appears, as shown in Figure 5-1.

You need to set up iTunes so that it can use your Internet connection to download song information, such as artist name and song titles. Follow these steps:

1. **Launch iTunes.**

   Double-click the iTunes application, or click the iTunes icon in the Dock.

2. **If this is the first time you've used iTunes, click Agree for Apple's License Agreement.**

Figure 5-1
Using the iTunes Setup Assistant

Apple's License Agreement appears only when you start iTunes for the first time. It's always fun to read, and you can click Save to save the license agreement as a document, Print to print it, Decline to quit iTunes immediately (and run off to talk to your lawyers), or Agree to move on to iTunes Setup Assistant.

The Setup Assistant takes you through the process of setting up iTunes for the Internet.

3. **Click Yes or No for the following options:**

   ◫ **"Yes, use iTunes for Internet audio content," or "No, do not modify my Internet settings":** I suggest clicking Yes, because iTunes offers more features than you typically find with browser plug-ins from other companies. On the other hand, if you are happy with your plug-ins and helper applications, you can click No and leave your Internet settings untouched.

   ◫ **"Yes, automatically connect to the Internet," or "No, ask me before connecting":** If you use an always-on broadband Internet service, you probably want iTunes to connect automatically, so you can click Yes. If you use a dial-up modem, if your Internet service is intermittently off, or if your Internet service charges when you use it, you probably don't want this connection to be automatic. Click No to make iTunes ask you first.

4. **To go to the next screen, click Next.**

   The Setup Assistant also asks if you want iTunes to search your home folder for music files.

5. **Click Yes or No to find music files on your hard drive.**

   If you already have music files on your hard drive, you may want to click Yes to organize them in iTunes.

On the other hand, you may want to click the No button for now, because iTunes may find files you don't want to add to your library (such as music for games, if you have installed games on your hard drive). You can add music files later by dragging them to the iTunes window.

6. **Click Next to go to the iTunes Music Store screen of the Setup Assistant.**

   The assistant asks if you want to go straight to the iTunes Music Store. I suggest clicking No for now, until you get to know iTunes.

7. **In the Setup Assistant window, click Done.**

   The iTunes window appears, as shown in Figure 5-2. You can drag the bottom-right corner of your iTunes window to make it larger or smaller on your screen.

The iTunes window offers a view of your music library and other sources for music, such as CDs and iPods, as well as controls for organizing, importing, and playing music, as follows:

◉ **Source pane:** This pane lists the sources of your music: Library (your music library), Radio (Web radio stations), Music Store (the iTunes Music Store), your iPod (see Chapter 13 for updating your iPod), and your playlists (see Chapter 12).

◉ **Song list/Browse view:** Depending on the source selected in the Source pane, this view displays the songs in your music library, your playlist, your iPod, the iTunes Music Store, or Web radio stations. For information on browsing the songs in iTunes, see Chapter 12.

◉ **Status window:** Displays the name of the artist and song (if known), and the elapsed time.

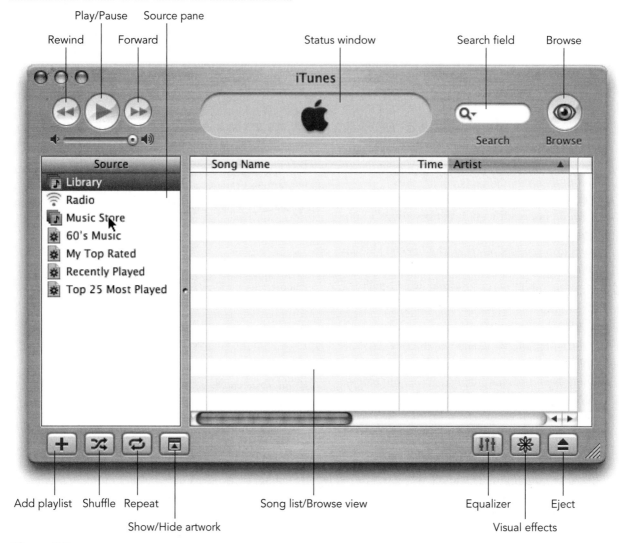

Figure 5-2
An empty iTunes library ready for your songs

- **Search field:** Use this to search your music library (see Chapter 12).

- **Player buttons — Forward/Next, Play/Pause, and Previous/Rewind:** These work just like CD player controls.

- **Playlist buttons — Add, Shuffle, Repeat:** Add playlists, and shuffle or repeat playback of songs in playlists or other selected sources.

- **Show/Hide buttons — Artwork, Equalizer, Visual effects:** Use to display or hide song artwork (supplied with purchased songs), the equalizer, or visual effects.

- **Eject, Browse:** Eject performs a CD or iPod eject, and Browse turns browse view on or off.

iTunes is indispensable for music. Purchase music from the online iTunes Music Store and from other sources and download directly into iTunes. Listen to Web radio broadcasts through iTunes. It gives you the power to organize songs into playlists — even "smart" playlists that fill with songs automatically based on song information. Use the EQ to fine-tune the sound; use presets for all types of music and listening environments, creating your own presets; or even assign different presets to different songs.

And when you organize your music library with fine-tuned versions of your favorite songs and GarageBand compositions, get yourself an iPod or burn a CD and you will find that your music follows you everywhere. iTunes is where it's at, and it's where your songs should be. After your songs are in iTunes, you can play them on your Mac and on your iPod, burn them to CD, and use them with projects in iPhoto, iMovie, and iDVD.

When you export songs, GarageBand takes all your tracks, mixes them automatically according to the settings you

selected, and exports the songs as two-track stereo audio files to iTunes in AIFF (Audio Interchange File Format), which is the highest-quality uncompressed format. You can then use iTunes to convert the songs to a compressed format such as MP3.

EXPORTING TO ITUNES

Before exporting your GarageBand composition, you might want to save a copy of the song under a different name. Although this move takes up more hard drive space, you'll have two versions of the song: one version mixed a certain way with effects used on the tracks, and another version without effects (ready for exporting to a professional audio program, as described in Chapter 11). Choose File ➜ Save As, and give the song a name it deserves.

Setting up the song info

If you set up your song information in advance in GarageBand, right before exporting, iTunes uses the information to place the song in the iTunes library under the appropriate artist name so you can find it easily. iTunes even creates a playlist or uses an existing playlist based on this information.

After you save the song in GarageBand, type the name for an iTunes playlist as well as the artist or composer in the Export pane of the GarageBand Preferences window, as shown in Figure 5-3. (iTunes playlists are described in Chapter 12.) Choose GarageBand ➜ Preferences, click the Export tab, and type the playlist name in the iTunes Playlist field. You can also enter the name of the composer and album in the Export pane. The composer name is used for both the artist and composer fields in iTunes.

Figure 5-3
Setting the song and playlist information in GarageBand before exporting to iTunes

After you have the song in iTunes, you can find it with the information you set in the Export pane of the GarageBand Preferences window. For example, songs by "Bove, Tony" show up in iTunes under the artist name "Bove, Tony" and also in the playlist set in GarageBand — so you can click the playlist in the iTunes Source pane to see the songs you've exported.

Mixing down

To export your song in GarageBand, choose File ➜ Export to iTunes. GarageBand creates a *mixdown*, as shown in

Figure 5-4 (the final mix into two stereo channels), and exports the song automatically to iTunes in the uncompressed AIFF format.

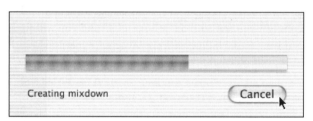

Figure 5-4
Exporting a song from GarageBand to iTunes

GarageBand exports the song from the very first measure to the end of the last region in the song, or exports just a cycle region if the cycle region option is turned on (see Chapter 11, "Creating the Final Mix," for more information about using a cycle region when exporting).

iTunes automatically places the song in its library according to the playlist title, album title, and composer name, and uses the composer name for both the artist and composer fields, as shown in Figure 5-5.

The song is now in your iTunes library; you can edit the song information further if you need to, burn the song to CD, or convert the file to another format. GarageBand exports the song in the AIFF format, which occupies a lot of hard drive space (and uses way too much space and power in an iPod), but AIFF is the ideal format to burn to CD for audio CD players that do not support the MP3 file format. You should use iTunes to convert the song to a compressed format such as MP3 for use in an iPod or on your computer.

Figure 5-5
Selecting the song in the iTunes library

ON BECOMING A COMPOSER

What is music? If the famous avant-garde composer John Cage decided to record himself gargling mouthwash, would it be music? In fact, if a set piece can be executed as music, and can be perceived by an audience as music, then that's what it is. A composer can write down a recipe for the music, which is called a score, and an arranger can arrange the piece with an orchestra, deciding who plays what. But the score is not the music, any more than the recipe is the meal. "Music, in performance, is a type of sculpture," wrote Frank Zappa in his autobiography, *The Real Frank Zappa Book* (Poseidon Press, New York, NY; 1989). "The air in the performance space is sculpted into something. This 'molecule-sculpture-over-time' is then 'looked at' by the ears of the listeners... A composer is a guy who goes around forcing his will on unsuspecting air molecules, often with the assistance of unsuspecting musicians." Want to be a composer? Just follow Frank Zappa's simple instructions:

"1. Declare your intention to create a 'composition'.

2. Start a piece at some time.

3. Cause something to happen over a period of time (it doesn't matter what happens in your 'time hole' — we have critics to tell us whether it's any good or not, so we don't worry about that part).

4. End the piece at some time (or keep it going, telling the audience it is a 'work in progress').

5.   Get a part-time job so you can continue to do stuff like this."

CONVERTING THE SONG FORMAT

When converting your GarageBand songs from the AIFF format using iTunes, the encoding format and settings you choose affect sound quality, hard drive space (and iPod space), and compatibility with other types of players and computers. Some encoding formats compress the music and others do not. Compression reduces the sound quality because it throws away information to make the file smaller. The amount of compression depends on the bit rate you choose, as well as the encoding format and other options.

In general, more compression means smaller files but poorer music quality. Less compression means better quality, but larger files. You can therefore trade quality for space, and have more music of lower quality, or trade space for quality, and have less music of higher quality.

Power is also an issue. Playing large, uncompressed files in an iPod takes more power because the hard drive has to refresh its memory buffers more quickly to process information as the song continues to play — you might even hear hiccups in the sound.

I prefer a high-quality sound overall, and I typically don't use the low-quality settings for encoders except for voice recordings. I can hear differences in music quality at the high compression levels, and would rather go out and buy another hard drive if necessary to store more music. But iTunes gives you the choice of audio quality in the Import Using pop-up menu in the Importing dialog box (which you get to from the Preferences dialog box). This is perhaps the most important choice to make before converting a song's format.

To set your encoder and quality settings in iTunes before converting a song, follow these steps:

1. **Choose iTunes → Preferences, and then click Importing.**

   The Importing dialog box appears; make changes to the encoding format and settings, as shown in Figure 5-6.

2. **Choose the encoding format you want to convert the song into and select the settings for that format.**

Use the pop-up menus to make your changes. The Setting pop-up menu offers different settings depending on the encoder you select in the Import Using pop-up menu. Choose one of the following encoders from the Import Using pop-up menu depending on what you need:

- **AAC Encoder:** The online iTunes Music Store uses a protected form of this format, but you can use the unprotected form and make copies as you wish. I recommend AAC for all uses. There are always exceptions, of course, such as ripping

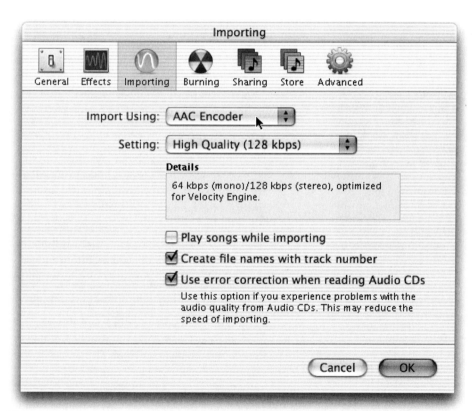

Figure 5-6
Choosing an encoder in the Importing preferences in iTunes

TO COMPRESS OR NOT TO COMPRESS: THAT IS THE QUESTION

When GarageBand mixes down songs into the AIFF format, the songs are not compressed and are therefore perfect in quality. You can use these versions to rip CDs, and the resulting digital music files can then be burned onto another CD with absolutely no loss in quality. AIFF and WAV are the preferred formats for copying music tracks from one CD to another, and for saving music that you intend to edit or alter in some way.

Too much compression can be a bad thing; compressing an already-compressed music file reduces the quality significantly. Every time you compress something, you lose *even more* information than before. Not only that, but once your song is compressed, you can't uncompress the song back to its original quality. This is bad. Don't compress something that is already compressed. You can convert uncompressed AIFF or WAV files to MP3 or AAC, but not the other way, and you should not convert compressed MP3 to AAC or vice versa.

iTunes gives you the choice of encoders with the Import Using pop-up menu, located in the Importing Preferences window.

CDs in order to burn your own CDs (see AIFF Encoder). Technically known as MPEG-4 Advanced Audio Coding, AAC is a higher quality format than MP3, comparable to CD quality (MPEG stands for Moving Picture Experts Group, a body that recognizes compression standards for video and audio). Choose the High Quality setting from the Setting pop-up menu, or choose Custom

and see the sidebar on customizing your encoder settings.

- **AIFF Encoder:** Select AIFF if you plan on burning the song to an audio CD; AIFF offers the highest possible quality, but it also takes up lots of space. Choose the Automatic setting from the Setting pop-up menu.

- **Apple Lossless Encoder:** The Apple Lossless encoder is a compromise between the lower-quality encoding of AAC or MP3 that results in lower file sizes, and the large file sizes of uncompressed, high-quality AIFF or WAV audio. Apple Lossless provides CD quality sound in a file size that is about 60 to 70 percent of the size of an AIFF or WAV encoded file. The virtue of this encoder is that you can use it for songs you intend to burn onto audio CDs, and for playing in iPods — the files are just small enough that they don't hiccup on playback.

- **MP3 Encoder:** The MPEG-1, Layer 3 format, also known as MP3, is supported in many players and applications. The MP3 format offers many different compression and quality settings, so you can fine-tune the format to get better quality, sacrificing hard drive (and iPod) space as you dial up the quality. Choose the High Quality setting from the Setting pop-up menu, or choose Custom and see the sidebar on customizing your encoder settings.

- **WAV Encoder:** WAV is the high-quality sound format used on PCs (like AIFF), and also takes up a lot of space. Use WAV if you plan on burning the song to an audio CD, or if you plan on using the music with PC-based digital sound- and video-editing programs, which import and export WAV files. Choose the Automatic setting from the Setting pop-up menu.

3. Click OK to accept the changes.

After changing your importing preferences, and until you change them again, iTunes uses these preferences whenever it imports or converts songs.

▼ Tip

Converting an uncompressed song to a compressed format is so quick and easy that you can do it painlessly. Go ahead and convert the AIFF version to AAC to play it in your Mac and iPod. Convert the AIFF version again to MP3 to send it to other people who use other types of music players.

To convert a song to another file format, select the song(s) you want to convert in the iTunes library, and then choose Advanced → Convert Selection. The encoding format you chose in the Importing preferences window appears in the menu: Convert Selection to MP3, Convert Selection to AAC, Convert Selection to AIFF, or Convert Selection to WAV. Choose the appropriate menu operation to perform the conversion. iTunes creates a copy of each song and

converts the copy to the new format. Both the original and the copy are stored in your music library (with the same artist and song name so they are easy to find).

CUSTOMIZING YOUR ENCODER SETTINGS

Listening pleasure depends entirely on the listener and the way the song itself was recorded. Some people can hear qualitative differences that others don't hear or don't care about. Some people can also tolerate a lower quality of sound in exchange for the convenience of carrying more music in their iPods. And sometimes the recording is so primitive sounding that you can get away with using low-quality settings to gain more disk space.

Everyone hears the effects of compression differently. You may not hear any problem with compressed audio that someone else says is tinny or lacking in depth. I prefer a high-quality sound overall, and I typically don't use the low-quality settings for encoders except for voice recordings. I can hear differences in music quality at the higher compression levels, and I'd rather go out and buy more hard drives and larger-capacity iPods if I can afford them.

Before converting your GarageBand songs, you may want to change your import preferences depending on what type of music they are, and whether or not you plan to copy the songs to your iPod or burn an audio or MP3 CD. The encoders offer general quality settings, but you can also customize the encoders and change those settings to your liking. iTunes remembers your custom settings until you change them again.

To customize your encoder settings, choose Custom from the Setting pop-up menu when you set your Import preferences. The AAC Encoder offers only two choices: High

MORE ABOUT ENCODERS

Choose the right encoder for the job. I use the AAC Encoder because it sounds better than the MP3 Encoder (to my ears, anyway) and offers basically the same or better file compression, freeing up more space on my hard drive and iPod.

However, other computers and music players don't support AAC yet. To share your music with your poor cousin who uses an MP3 player other than an iPod, convert using the MP3 Encoder. But as an iPod user, you can use either the higher-quality AAC Encoder or the MP3 Encoder.

Quality and Custom. Use the High Quality setting for most music, but for very complex music (such as jazz and classical), you may want to fine-tune the AAC Encoder settings.

For either the MP3 or AAC encoders, iTunes lets you set the *bit rate* more precisely for importing. This determines how many bits of digital music information can travel during playback in a given second. Measured in kilobits per second (Kbps), you use a high bit rate (such as 192 or 320 Kbps) for higher quality, which of course increases the

file size. 320 Kbps is the highest-quality setting for this format; 128 is considered high quality by some, but it's only medium quality in my humble opinion. So, with the bit rate setting, you can trade quality for more space by specifying a lower bit rate, or trade space for more quality by specifying a higher bit rate.

The MP3 Encoder custom settings are shown in Figure 5-7. The MP3 Encoder offers Variable Bit Rate Encoding (VBR), which varies the number of bits used to store the

Figure 5-7
Customizing the settings for the MP3 Encoder

music depending on the complexity of the sound. While the quality of VBR is endlessly debated, in my opinion it's only useful at the Highest setting, because VBR can encode at up to the maximum bit rate of 320 Kbps in those rare cases where the sound requires it, while keeping the rest at a lower bit rate.

iTunes also lets you control the sample rate, which is the number of times per second the sound waveform is captured digitally (or *sampled*). High sample rates yield a higher quality of sound and larger file sizes.

 Tip

Never use a higher sample rate than the source. CDs use a 44.100 kHz rate, so choosing a higher rate simply wastes space.

Another setting to consider is the Channel choice. Stereo, which offers two channels of music for left and right speakers, is what we all hear most of the time. However, mono — monaural or single channel — was the norm for pop records before the mid-1960s. (Phil Spector was known for his high-quality monaural recordings, and the early Rolling Stones records are in mono.) When digitized, monaural recordings take up half the space of stereo recordings. Choose Auto to have iTunes determine the appropriate setting for the music, so that Spectorized recordings are saved in mono and everything else in stereo.

PLAYING SONGS

To play a song in your iTunes library or playlist, or from a CD or iPod, just double-click the song, or click the song and then click the Play button. Either way, the Play button turns into a Pause button while the song plays.

When the song finishes, iTunes continues playing the songs in the list in sequential order until you click the Pause button (which then turns back into the Play button). You can skip to the next or previous song using the arrow keys on your keyboard, or by clicking the Forward or Back button next to the Play button. Pressing the Space bar of your keyboard performs the same function as clicking the Play button; pressing it again is just like clicking the Pause button.

The status display above the list of songs tells you the name of the artist and song (if known), and the elapsed time of the track. Click the artist name, and the name disappears and the song title is displayed; click the title, and it is replaced by the artist name. If you click the Elapsed Time status, the status changes to the remaining time and then, with another click, to the total time (one more click brings you back to the elapsed time).

To read more about organizing your music in iTunes, see Chapter 12. Chapter 13 describes how to update your iPod with iTunes, and Chapter 14 provides all the information you need to burn your own CDs from iTunes.

PART II

Careful with That Axe, Eugene

Using Software Instruments

In This Chapter

Choosing a Software Instrument • Using a MIDI keyboard, MidiKeys,
or the onscreen keyboard • Setting Software Instrument effects
Saving effects presets and custom Software Instruments

One of the first popular groups to use a synthesizer in live performances was, surprisingly, the Beach Boys. In the late 1960s, the group performed "Riot in Cell Block #9" and used the Moog analog synthesizer to produce the sound of a police siren. Today's digital synthesizers can sound like nearly any type of sound, including real-life instruments and a good many imaginary ones.

This chapter shows how your Mac can act like a digital synthesizer with GarageBand's *Software Instruments.* Software Instruments are synthesized instrument sounds whose performance you control using the onscreen keyboard or a USB MIDI piano-style keyboard connected to your Mac. I also describe in this chapter the free MidiKeys software, which is a useful alternative to the onscreen keyboard provided with GarageBand.

RECORDING WITH MIDI

MIDI is the universal language of synthesizers and sequencing programs. A *sequencing program* records the details of your performance as you play on a MIDI instrument or device, such as a MIDI keyboard, or the onscreen keyboard that comes with GarageBand (or an alternative, MidiKeys). In a sense, GarageBand is a sequencing program, but it does not offer MIDI output or a synchronizing clock, so it can't act as a sequencer for other MIDI hardware devices. You use MIDI to perform with a Software Instrument.

PETE SEARS: ON THE ROAD WITH MIDI

"Most of us (professional musicians) already know that you can use a MIDI keyboard with software such as Pro Tools, and you can reproduce just about any type of synthesized sound," says Pete Sears, who has played keyboards for decades with acts such as Rod Stewart, Jefferson Starship, and Hot Tuna. "With GarageBand, you can use that MIDI keyboard without a full Pro Tools setup and still reproduce just about any sound you like. Not only that, GarageBand is particularly useful on the road in a laptop. You could sit in an airplane with headphones and compose music, right on your laptop keyboard, which is quite useful for a traveling musician." To use your laptop keyboard, see "Playing the MidiKeys keyboard" in this chapter.

MIDI information is *performance* information, not digitized audio data. Each note you play is converted to an instruction, which, like the holes on a piano roll for a player piano, tells the synthesizer what note to play. Each MIDI instruction includes information such as what type of sound (or in GarageBand, what type of Software Instrument) to use, the note's pitch and duration, its velocity (how hard the note was struck), whether a pitch bend wheel was used to bend the note, and so on.

The advantage you have with a MIDI recording (that is, using a Software Instrument) is that you can change the note's pitch, length, and so on, almost as if you were changing typos with a word processor. GarageBand offers the Track Editor to make such changes. You can therefore record a performance that's less than perfect (even sloppy), and easily fix it.

Another advantage is that you can record short performances and easily join them into a seamless longer performance. You can get each part right, even at a slower tempo, and then join the parts and speed up the tempo without having to rerecord anything.

Software Instrument tracks, which are comprised solely of MIDI instructions, can be automatically transposed to other keys as well as slowed down or sped up in tempo. For example, if you set the key to C when you create a new song in GarageBand, and then change the key later to D in the Master Track Info window, any tracks already recorded with Software Instruments are automatically transposed to the new key. You don't have to rerecord them.

Choosing a Software Instrument

GarageBand provides a wide variety of Software Instruments — Electric Piano, Smokey Clav, Cathedral Organ, Orchestral Strings, Dub Horns, Electric Tremolo guitar, Steel String acoustic guitar, you-name-it guitar, and synthesizer sounds with weird names like Martian Lounge and Modern Prophecy.

To choose a Software Instrument, you can either create a new track or use an existing track (for example, you can change an existing Software Instrument track from one type of instrument to another). To create a track, follow these steps:

1. **Click the "+" button under the track headers to create a new track.**

   You can also choose Track ➔ New Track. The New Track dialog box appears, with two tabs: Real Instrument and Software Instrument.

2. **Click the Software Instrument tab.**

   For example, to record a performance with the onscreen keyboard or a USB MIDI keyboard, choose the Software Instrument tab.

3. **Select the category and type of instrument.**

   Instrument categories appear in the list on the left, as shown in Figure 6-1, where Woodwinds has been selected. Instrument types, such as Soprano Sax, from each category are listed on the right.

4. **Click OK.**

   A new track with the name of the instrument you selected appears in the timeline, as shown in Figure 6-2.

The Software Instrument track is now selected (if not, click on its header). If you have already connected a MIDI keyboard, or if you opened the onscreen keyboard or MidiKeys window (described later in this chapter), you should already be able to hear notes from your keyboard without having to record anything. You can then hear the sound of the instrument you selected. To learn how to connect a MIDI keyboard or to make sure you have everything connected properly, see the section "Using a MIDI keyboard or instrument" later in this chapter.

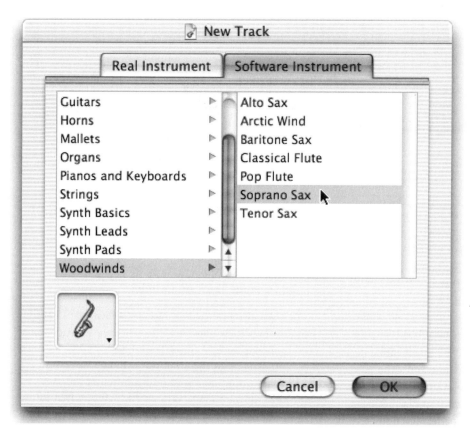

Figure 6-1
Choosing a Software Instrument while creating a new track

Figure 6-2
A Software Instrument track ready for recording

 Tip

You can play along with a song in iTunes with your onscreen or MIDI keyboard and any Software Instrument. Start a song in iTunes, and then switch to GarageBand and play along. Both the iTunes output and the GarageBand output are mixed automatically so that they play on your Mac's speakers simultaneously. You can figure out the song's melody lines by playing along in GarageBand. Even better, you can import the song into GarageBand, as described in Chapter 3.

Although you can change the Software Instrument for a track to experiment, a track can have only one instrument for the length of a song. If you want to add more instruments, you need to create a track for each instrument.

Switching a track's Software Instrument

To change the instrument for a Software Instrument track, follow these steps:

1. **Open the Track Info window.**

   Double-click the Software Instrument track's header (or click the track, and then click the *i* Button, or choose Track ➜ Show Track Info) to open the Track Info window, shown in Figure 6-3.

2. **Choose Software Instrument from the pop-up menu.**

   The pop-up menu at the top of the Track Info window lets you switch from a Software Instrument track to the Master Track. Make sure the pop-up menu says "Software Instrument."

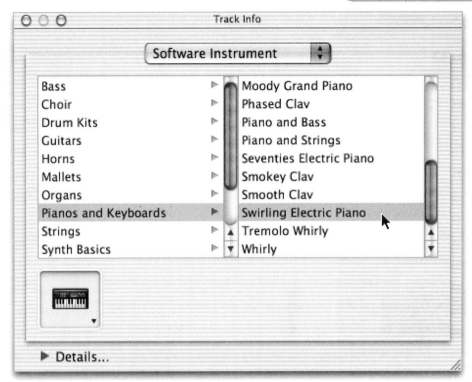

Figure 6-3
Changing the instrument for a Software Instrument track

3. **Select the category and type of instrument.**

   Select a category from the list on the left, and then select an instrument type in the list on the right.

4. **Click the red button in the top left corner of the Track Info window to close the window.**

   Move your cursor over the blank buttons to see their colors, and click the red one. After closing the window, the name of the instrument (and its icon) for the track changes to your new choice.

Whatever instrument sound you're looking for, you'll probably find it or something like it that you can modify (as described later in this chapter in "Setting Instrument Effects") until it sounds just right. If you still can't find it,

try the optional GarageBand Jam Pack, which offers 100 more Software Instruments and over a thousand more loops.

▼ **Note**

When you are done recording a Software Instrument's performance based on an existing loop instrument, you can delete the loop if you no longer need it.

Whether you created a new Software Instrument track or you want to use an existing one, your next step is to click the track's header to select it, and start playing. Your choice for musical input is the onscreen keyboard (or an alternative such as MidiKeys) or a MIDI keyboard.

CLONING SOFTWARE INSTRUMENTS

If you find a Software Instrument loop that has a sound you want, but can't find the Software Instrument used for it (or you don't know the special settings for the instrument), you can use the loop to define your Software Instrument. First, add the loop to your song, as described in Chapter 2, just to define the Software Instrument track's sound. Then either edit the loop's notes, as described in Chapter 9, to turn the loop into the performance you want, or record a fresh performance into the same track (after the loop). For example, I liked the Electric Guitar sound of the loop World Muted Guitar 07, so instead of trying to duplicate it by changing settings, I simply created a new track by dragging that loop to the timeline. I then recorded my performance (with MidiKeys) into that track. My performance sounded exactly like the guitar in World Muted Guitar 07.

Playing the onscreen keyboard

The onscreen music keyboard supplied with GarageBand offers a tiny window with simulated piano keys you can click with your mouse. If you don't see an onscreen piano keyboard window, choose Window ➜ Keyboard to display it. The onscreen keyboard is titled Grand Piano or the name of the Software Instrument chosen for the selected track (in this example, the Soprano Sax chosen in Figure 6-2).

You can move the onscreen music keyboard to any location you want on your screen by clicking the space between the keys and the side of the keyboard and dragging it. To expand the keyboard, increasing the number of keys shown, click and drag the expansion triangle on the lower-right edge of the keyboard, as shown in Figure 6-4. You can simulate louder or softer playing by using your mouse. Clicking lower in a white or black key plays the note louder, and clicking higher in the key plays the note softer.

To change the range of notes you can play, click the small triangles to the left or right of the keys — the left one lowers the keys by an octave, while the right one raises them an octave. By expanding the keyboard and changing its range of notes, you can play every note that you could possibly want.

The onscreen music keyboard is primitive — you can't play more than one note a time, and you have to click your mouse to play. You can use it to experiment with different instrument sounds and effects, and to add notes when editing a track in the Track Editor, but it is not likely you would use it to record anything more than a short performance.

If you don't hear music as you click the onscreen keyboard, make sure you click first on a Software Instrument track. When you start a new song in GarageBand, a Software Instrument track labeled Grand Piano opens automatically. Make sure that this track is still selected by clicking the track header, and then click inside the onscreen keyboard window to start playing the keyboard. You can also change the Software Instrument for the track, as described in "Switching a track's Software Instrument" in this chapter, and create more Software Instrument tracks to try different instrument sounds.

To play several notes at once (as in a chord) with your computer keyboard, use MidiKeys (see the next section, "Playing the MidiKeys keyboard"). To use a full-size piano-style keyboard, you can connect a MIDI-compatible music keyboard, as explained in the section "Using a MIDI keyboard or instrument."

Figure 6-4
Expanding the onscreen keyboard to show more keys

Playing the MidiKeys keyboard

This simple, free program makes it possible to use your computer's keyboard as a piano keyboard, with the ability to play chords. I have even used it on stage in performance situations, playing keyboard riffs on a PowerBook.

MidiKeys (version 1.6b3 as of this writing) is a free program written by Chris Reed (http://www.manyetas.com/creed/midikeys_beta.html) that simulates a MIDI keyboard with an onscreen piano keyboard similar to the one provided with GarageBand. You can download it from the Version Tracker site (www.versiontracker.com/dyn/moreinfo/macosx/16702). MidiKeys unpacks as a disk image; open the disk image icon, and drag the MidiKeys application to your hard disk (typically to your Applications folder). Double-click the MidiKeys application to run it.

MidiKeys sends MIDI instructions to GarageBand just like an external MIDI keyboard and can be used to play any Software Instrument. It displays a miniature keyboard on your screen in a separate window, just like the Garage-Band onscreen keyboard — clicking the keys sends notes to GarageBand, as shown in Figure 6-5. The huge difference is that you can also use your computer keyboard and press several keys at once to play chords.

To play MidiKeys with your computer keyboard, press any of the following keys separately or at the same time to play a chord (assuming you have not changed the key map in the MidiKeys Preferences window, as described later):

- First row of keys (from Z to /) for the white piano keys. The Z key is the same as middle C on a MIDI or piano keyboard. The X key is the same as D on a piano keyboard. To play a C major chord (C-E-G), you can press Z-C-B simultaneously.

- Second row (from S to ;) for the black piano keys (sharps and flats). The S key is equivalent to C-sharp.

- Third row (from Q to O) for white piano keys one octave lower. The Q key is equivalent to the A key on a MIDI or piano keyboard.

- Fourth row (from 2 to 9) for black piano keys (sharps and flats) one octave lower.

Use Octave Up and Octave Down commands in the Keys menu for higher or lower notes. You can switch up to four octaves up or down; a ghost arrow over the keyboard indicates an octave displacement (to the right, an octave up; to the left, an octave down). You can adjust the octave from your computer keyboard using the left and right arrow keys, and adjust the velocity using the up and down arrow keys. The Velocity slider controls the volume of the note, which is equivalent to how hard you pressed it.

Figure 6-5
Playing multiple keys at once (a chord) using MidiKeys

▼ **Tip**

You can change the way the notes map to keys on your computer keyboard. Choose MidiKeys ➜ Preferences to change the key mapping for your computer keyboard using the Key map pop-up menu. The Full choice maps just over two octaves onto your computer keyboard. The Single choice maps just rows ZXCV and ASDF on your computer keyboard (the notes are the same, but only one octave is available). The Upper Single choice maps to the same octave as the Single choice, but uses the QWER and 1234 rows instead. The Reversed Full choice simply swaps the octaves mapped by the Full choice.

MidiKeys does not produce any sound — you have to use it with a Software Instrument track already selected. When you start MidiKeys, its destination pop-up menu is set to Virtual source, and you should leave it at that setting unless you use other MIDI hardware (see the section "Using a MIDI keyboard or instrument" later in this chapter).

The window for MidiKeys can easily get lost behind your GarageBand window if you click outside the MidiKeys window, so I suggest placing the MidiKeys window so that it overlaps with the edge of the GarageBand window, making it easier to switch back and forth. MidiKeys offers a way to float the MidiKeys window above all other applications, including GarageBand. Choose MidiKeys ➔ Preferences, and click the checkbox next to the Keyboard window is always on top option. You can set the transparency of the keyboard window with the slider below the option, as shown in Figure 6-6, so that you can see the GarageBand window while playing. The Opaque when MidiKeys is in front option turns off transparency when you make MidiKeys the active application, so that the window is solid. Even with this option set, when you bring Garage-Band to the front by clicking in the GarageBand window, MidiKeys goes back to being transparent.

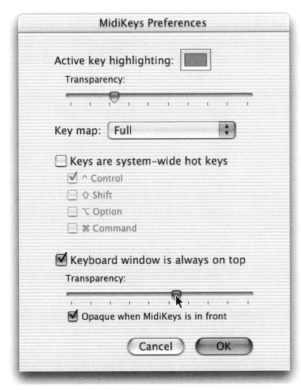

Figure 6-6
Setting preferences and options for MidiKeys

STACY PARRISH: FLYING WITH MIDIKEYS

"With GarageBand and MidiKeys, you could be coming up with really solid ideas while sitting on an airplane," says producer and engineer Stacy Parrish. "Just sitting there with a pair of headphones — it's easy, and you don't have to pull a guitar out and play for everyone on the plane like the Singing Nun. You're not bothering anybody. As simple as watching a DVD on an airplane, you could be recording your next album."

With MidiKeys, you can run your fingers up and down your computer keyboard like Little Richard or Leon Russell, but don't try using your feet like "The Killer" Jerry Lee Lewis — the keys of your computer keyboard are just too small. Still, MidiKeys opens the possibility of recording music using only your laptop.

If you don't hear music as you press your computer keys or click the MidiKeys keyboard, make sure you click first on a Software Instrument track. When you start a new song in GarageBand, a Software Instrument track labeled Grand Piano opens automatically. Make sure that this track is still selected by clicking the track header, and then click inside the MidiKeys window to start playing the keyboard. You can also change the Software Instrument for the track, as described in this chapter's section "Switching a track's Software Instrument," and create more Software Instrument tracks to try different instrument sounds.

Using a MIDI keyboard or instrument

MIDI has been around since the early 1980s, so there are a lot of MIDI keyboards and instruments on the market.

PETE SEARS: GET COMFORTABLE WITH YOUR INSTRUMENT

"I usually feel I'm compromising something when I have to use rented keyboards on the road," says Pete Sears, who has played keyboards on the road as a member of Jefferson Starship, Hot Tuna, and many other bands. "While rented keyboards are adequate as pianos, they often don't perform certain functions that I am used to working with, especially in the area of MIDI. To a guitar player, it's like having to get used to an unfamiliar guitar that doesn't quite have the sound you need. If there is any rule about performing music, it's that you must get comfortable with your instrument and your gear. But you always get by somehow."

More professional keyboards offer smoother pressure sensitivity and weighted keys for playing.

MIDI keyboards can either be *controllers* that don't make sound by themselves (they must be connected to your computer and played through GarageBand) or synthesizers that can produce sound apart from GarageBand or any other software synthesizer. MIDI controllers are generally less expensive because they don't need much of the internal circuitry of the synthesizers.

Connecting MIDI devices

Some new MIDI controllers and synthesizers have built-in USB connections for connecting directly to your Mac with a USB cable. The M-Audio Keystation 49e, for example, is an inexpensive MIDI controller (under $100) that plugs directly into your Mac and derives its power from the Mac through the USB cable.

Most MIDI controllers and synthesizers use MIDI-format inputs and outputs, and you need a separate box called a *MIDI interface* (dig that — a Musical Instrument Digital Interface *interface*), to connect the MIDI device to your Mac.

MIDI interfaces come in different sizes and configurations and with a variety of extra options, including multiple In/Out ports and possibly also audio recording capabilities (in which case the box is usually referred to as an *audio interface*, combining audio recording and MIDI support). For example, the Emagic Multichannel Interface A62 m connects to your Mac's USB and offers six audio inputs (for line-in music, electric instruments, or microphones), two audio outputs (for speakers or preamps), and MIDI input/output (for connecting MIDI devices).

For something simpler that connects an older MIDI device to your Mac, try a 1x1 MIDI interface, which offers only one channel of MIDI data in and one channel out, but is sufficient for using a MIDI device with GarageBand. Examples are the M-Audio MIDISport Uno 1x1 and the Edirol UM1SX. Both are under $40 and are simple to use.

Whatever type of interface you pick, make sure the manufacturer provides an appropriate software driver for the newest version of Mac OS X. You'll need to install the latest driver before using the interface with GarageBand. The best place to get the appropriate drivers is directly through the support Web sites of the manufacturer. Mac OS X will not recognize your MIDI device unless you restart after installing.

Troubleshooting MIDI device connections

Whether you use a USB MIDI keyboard or a MIDI inter-face device, you have to make sure GarageBand recognizes it. If you don't hear music from your USB MIDI key-board, make sure the keyboard is connected to the USB port and that the keyboard is turned on. When you first start a new song in GarageBand, a Software Instrument track labeled Grand Piano opens automatically — make sure that this track is still selected by clicking the track header.

To see if your MIDI keyboard is actually playing, watch the time display in GarageBand as you play — the MIDI status light to the left of the tempo should flash each time you play a note. If you are still not hearing music, make sure the volume slider for the track is not all the way to the left, and turn up the output volume for your computer's speakers or your external speakers.

If you still don't hear music, choose GarageBand ➜ Preferences and click the Audio/MIDI button to see the Audio/MIDI pane, as shown in Figure 6-7. The MIDI Status should indicate that your system detected at least one MIDI input; if not, you may have to troubleshoot your connection by using the Audio MIDI Setup utility.

Current versions of OS X come with MIDI support that is controlled by the Audio MIDI Setup utility (in the Utili-ties folder in your Applications folder). The Audio MIDI

Setup utility offers a visual representation of your MIDI setup, and it works with audio devices connected via FireWire, USB, PCMCIA, or PCI. You can use it to select audio channel input and output devices for your Mac and control volume levels and other characteristics. Follow these steps:

1. **Check your connections.**

   Make sure your MIDI interface box (or audio inter-face box) is connected properly to your Mac, and your MIDI instrument is connected to the interface box. If you are using a USB MIDI keyboard, make sure the USB cable is connected properly to the Mac's USB connection.

2. **Double-click the Audio MIDI Setup application (in Applications/Utilities) to open the Audio MIDI Setup window, and then click the MIDI Devices tab.**

   The MIDI device connected to your computer appears in the pane, as shown in Figure 6-8. If your MIDI device doesn't appear, click the Rescan MIDI button on the toolbar.

3. **Choose New Configuration from the Configura-tion pop-up menu.**

   In the dialog box that appears, give the new configu-ration a name, and click OK.

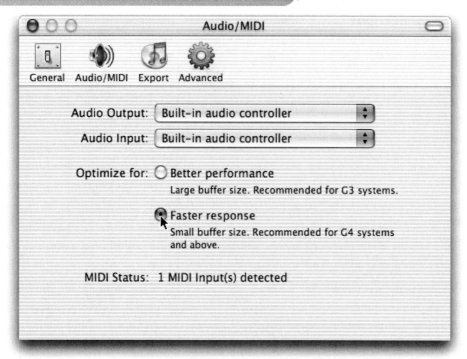

Figure 6-7
Checking to see if GarageBand recognizes your MIDI device in the Audio/MIDI pane of GarageBand preferences

4. **Double-click the icon for your MIDI interface device to describe the device.**

   The Audio MIDI Setup dialog for your device appears, enabling you to give the device a name. You can click More Information to change settings for the MIDI properties and ports for the device. Click Open Icon Browser to change the icon if you want.

5. **Click OK to finish making changes.**

6. **Optional: Add another MIDI device.**

   Note: You don't have to do this unless you want to control multiple MIDI devices connected to the interface using Audio MIDI Setup. To add another MIDI device to your new configuration, click the Add Device button on the toolbar. For each MIDI device connected

to your MIDI interface device that you want to include in the configuration, click the Add Device button. Double-click the icon for the device to name the device, select a different icon for it, and specify MIDI settings for the device. To specify the connection between the MIDI interface device and a MIDI device, drag from the output or input connectors above the device icon to the corresponding connector on the other device icon.

7. **When you're finished, choose Audio MIDI Setup ➜ Quit Audio MIDI Setup.**

Your MIDI device should now be working with GarageBand. To check, choose GarageBand ➜ Preferences and click the Audio/MIDI button (see Figure 6-7).

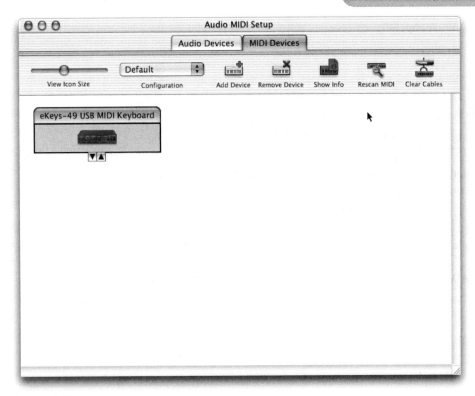

Figure 6-8
Using Audio MIDI Setup to configure MIDI devices

SETTING INSTRUMENT EFFECTS

You should now be jamming with your onscreen keyboard, MidiKeys, or MIDI keyboard. All you need to do is select a Software Instrument track and choose an instrument. You don't even have to record anything — you can play music just to hear the Software Instrument you've chosen. You can also change the Software Instrument by opening the Track Info window as described in "Switching a track's Software Instrument" earlier in this chapter, and the sound changes on the fly immediately after selecting the other instrument.

You can also play with effects this way, with the Track Info window open. The effects are your ticket for getting a unique sound — for example, you can simulate amplifier settings with a software guitar, add echo and reverb to the sound, or tweak the instrument generator itself to get any type of sound you want. You can learn more about effects in Chapter 10.

To change Software Instrument effects for a track, follow these steps:

1. **Open the Track Info window.**

   Double-click the Software Instrument track's header (or click the track and then click the *i* Button or choose Track ➜ Show Track Info) to open the Track Info window.

2. **Click the Details triangle to reveal the settings for effects.**

   The Track Info window provides a more detailed view of settings for each Software Instrument. Click the Details triangle to reveal these settings, as shown in Figure 6-9.

3. **Click a general effect, or choose a special effect from a pop-up menu on the left side.**

   In the Track Info window's Details section, the instrument Generator and all the Effects (such as a compressor, an equalizer, echo, reverb, and so on) are on the left side. To turn on the Echo effect, for example, click the checkbox next to Echo on the left side to put a check mark in the box.

4. **Adjust the settings for the effect using a slider or pop-up menu on the right side.**

   The settings for the Generator and all the Effects are controlled by sliders or pop-up menus on the right side. For example, to adjust the Echo effect chosen in Step 3, click and drag the slider on the right side of the Echo effect. The Compressor, Echo, and Reverb also have sliders that you can drag to adjust their settings; the other effects offer pop-up menus with presets you can select or modify. For a complete description of these effects, see Chapter 10.

Figure 6-9
Using Audio MIDI Setup to configure MIDI devices

5. **Repeat steps 3 and 4 for each effect you want.**

   For example, if you changed the instrument's Generator (the code that creates the Software Instrument) on the left side (the Generator pop-up menu on the left controls the sound source of the instrument), you can change the Generator preset on the right side (the preset controls on the right are specific settings for that sound source). In Figure 6-10, we changed the Generator to Guitar in the pop-up menu on the left, and chose the Clean Electric Guitar Generator preset from the pop-up menu on the right.

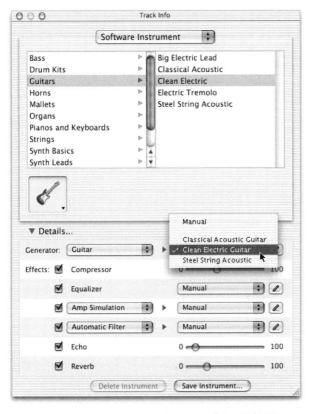

Figure 6-10
Using the Guitar generator with the Clean Electric Guitar preset

6. **Play your onscreen keyboard or MIDI keyboard as you adjust settings.**

   The sound of your Software Instrument changes immediately as you adjust the settings, so you can experiment with effects before closing the Track Info window.

7. **Close the Track Info window after making changes, or click Save Instrument, as described in the next section.**

   To close the window, click the red button in the top left corner. The changes you made are automatically saved with the Software Instrument's track in the song. You can save your settings as a custom Software Instrument, as described in the next section.

You can also modify the presets for the generator and each of the effects (except Echo and Reverb) and create custom presets for these effects by clicking the pencil button to the right of an effect's pop-up menu of presets. When you click the pencil button, a new window appears, as shown in Figure 6-11, with many options you can use to modify an effect preset.

When finished making changes to a preset, click the Close button to close the window. GarageBand shows a warning dialog that asks "Do you want to save the file before switching to a new one?" Click Save to save the settings, and in the subsequent dialog type a preset name and click OK. If you click Don't Save, you throw out the changes you made and revert back to the original preset.

In Chapter 10, I describe in more techie detail the effects you can apply to a Software Instrument.

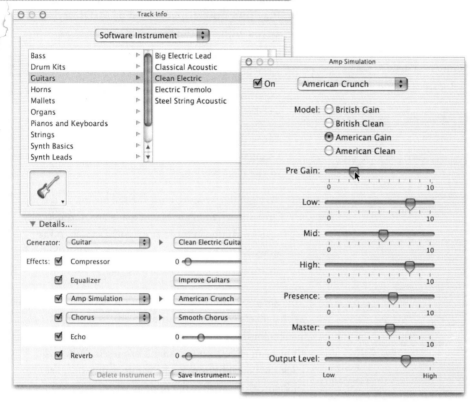

Figure 6-11
Modifying the American Crunch preset for the Amp Simulation effect

SAVING YOUR SOFTWARE INSTRUMENT

After getting the sound you want from a Software Instrument by adjusting the effects settings, you can save the settings as a custom instrument. Even though the changes you made to the effects and the sound of a Software Instrument are automatically saved with the Software Instrument's track in the song, you may want to save these custom settings so that you can use the identical instrument, sound, and effects settings in another song.

To save a Software Instrument that you customized, follow these steps:

1. **Double-click the Software Instrument's header.**

   The Track Info window appears.

2. **Click Save Instrument.**

   The Save Instrument dialog box appears.

3. **Type a new name for the instrument (such as "Tony's guitar").**

   Click OK when you're finished.

4. Choose an icon for your custom instrument by clicking the instrument's icon and dragging across the selection of icons to the one you want, as shown in Figure 6-12.

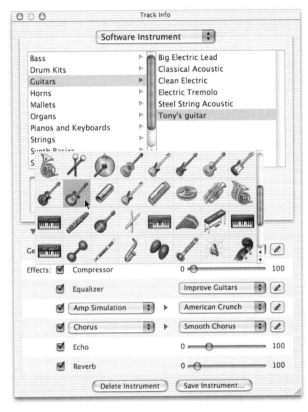

Figure 6-12
Selecting an icon for Tony's guitar, a custom Software Instrument

L. HENRY SARMIENTO II: CUSTOMIZING INSTRUMENTS FOR BAND MEMBERS

L. Henry Sarmiento II is a sound technician and producer at Herbie Herbert's Sy Klopps Studio in San Francisco. He finds a use for GarageBand even though he is an expert in Pro Tools and other Mac audio and MIDI programs. "One of the really cool things you can do as a production engineer for a band is create custom Software Instruments for the band and copy them to the band's computers so that they can take them home and create with them."

The instrument appears in the Software Instruments menu in the submenu of the category you already selected. For example, if you had already selected Organs on the left, your custom Software Instrument is saved in that submenu on the right; if you had selected Guitars on the left, your custom instrument is saved in the Guitars submenu. You can then use the new instrument in any song.

You can save as many custom Software Instruments as you want. Software Instrument settings are stored in a folder for the instrument type (such as Guitars) inside the Software folder, which is inside the Track Settings folder of your instrument library. You can find the Software folder in Macintosh HD/Library/Application Support/GarageBand/Instrument Library/Track Settings/Software. You can copy the file for a Software Instrument (or an entire folder of Software Instruments) to another computer and use them with that computer's GarageBand.

Using Real Instruments

In This Chapter

Connecting electric instruments and microphones • Setting up
a mixer or an audio interface for connecting instruments and mics
Choosing a Real Instrument sound and setting effects • Saving
a custom Real Instrument sound

No matter how you change the settings of a Software Instrument defined to sound like a slide guitar, you can't get the true sound of a slide guitar unless you actually play one. Professional musicians treat their favorite instruments like members of their families. "It's been through three wives," Waylon Jennings remarked about his Telecaster guitar. "To me, a guitar is kind of like a woman. You don't know why you like 'em, but you do."

GarageBand is more than accommodating to musicians who want to record with their own instruments; the software can simulate various amplifiers that would cost you a fortune to assemble yourself. For example, you can get that distorted guitar sound of the early Kinks records (as in "You Really Got Me") without having to do what guitarist Dave Davies had to do to get that sound: slashing the speaker in his amplifier. GarageBand offers virtual amps for Arena Rock, British Invasion, Clean Jazz, and so on. As we describe in this chapter, you can connect an electric instrument to your Mac, such as your favorite guitar, or connect a microphone (or use the Mac's built-in microphone) to record acoustic instruments as well as vocals, using Real Instrument settings and effects.

THE LIMITATIONS OF AUDIO INPUT

Before you plug your Stratocaster into the back of your laptop, know the limitations of input. Computers are typically set up for playing and recording audio with home stereos. Instruments are typically set up to plug into amplifiers that use different connectors and input levels than a home stereo.

You can bridge this gap with a professional-quality audio interface connected to your Mac that lets you plug a microphone, electric guitar, or other electric instrument in the interface and control the volume level of the input. We describe how to connect with an audio interface in this section.

If your electric instrument or amplifier offers *line-out* (a.k.a. *line-level*) output for connecting to a home stereo,

STACY PARRISH: REHEARSING WITH GARAGEBAND

"GarageBand is like a rehearsal stage, compared to recording software such as Digidesign's Pro Tools," says Stacy Parrish, producer and engineer for Rock and Roll Hall of Famers George Clinton and Jack Casady, as well as guitarist and vocalist with his own band. "GarageBand certainly makes it easy to dream up a riff, get it onto a CD, and send it out to the other musicians for them to check out. If I can get any kind of feedback from them in advance, it saves a lot of time. We don't waste time going through the concepts and arrangements while also paying for studio time. We can find out in advance if an arrangement doesn't work."

you don't need the interface: you can connect the line-level output directly into your Mac's Line In connection. Line-level microphones are available that can record professional-quality vocals, but they are typically very sensitive and may pick up other sounds in the room. You can also sing right into your Mac's built-in microphone, but you will no doubt pick up room sounds as well.

But let's get it straight right from the start: GarageBand is not a professional recording tool, any more than your garage is a professional sound studio. For example, to get the best sound quality with the widest frequency range from an electric guitar, you may consider using a real amplifier *before* sending the signal into the computer for recording. You would have to use a high-quality microphone with the amplifier, and perhaps phantom power, a compressor, and so on. For vocals, you need a silent vocal booth. If you go cheap on any of these components in the chain, you may as well be playing a $200 guitar through a $50 pocket amp.

The point is that GarageBand is more suited for rehearsal and composition with a real instrument than for recording a real instrument with studio quality. You can also use GarageBand to simulate effects and amplifier settings while performing live. And there's always a chance that what you record will transcend any limitations of the process; you don't really care that "Strawberry Fields" by The Beatles was recorded on a four-track tape machine with substantial generational loss, do you?

To record a Real Instrument track, you need at least 10MB of free hard drive space per minute of recording. You will also want headphones or speakers for high-quality stereo playback. Headphones are best for *monitoring* the recording — hearing yourself play along with the music.

CONNECTING INSTRUMENTS AND MICROPHONES

Most Mac models offer a line-in connection that accepts a cable with stereo miniplug. You can connect any kind of mono or stereo audio source, such as a CD or DVD player, or a home stereo that offers recording through a tape out or similar connection. Find the line out from your stereo system, and connect a cable that uses RCA-type left and right stereo plugs or a stereo miniplug to your stereo system. If you use RCA-type plugs, you need to use an RCA-to-stereo miniplug converter, or a cable that offers a stereo miniplug on the other end. You can then record anything that plays on your home stereo into a Real Instrument track.

Connecting your instrument or microphone to your home stereo is great: some stereos have a preamp that lets you connect a microphone and set the input volume level. However, running your instrument through a home stereo may not be an ideal setup.

To connect directly to your Mac and get the best sound quality, you want a line-level source of audio — your instrument, microphone, amplifier, and audio interface all offer line-level output. The stock line input on Macs (if your particular Mac has one) isn't designed to take a guitar or microphone signal that's lower than a line-level signal. To get the best sound quality, you want to get some sort of preamp (which boosts the input level to line level) or audio interface, as we describe in the next section.

The sound quality may not be at its highest, but you can still connect your electric instrument or microphone directly to the Line In connection on a Mac and get sound quality that's appropriate for experimentation. For example, I routinely connect my harmonica microphone (which, like many instruments and microphones, has a cable with

a ¼-inch phono plug for plugging into an amplifier or pre-amp) to a cable converter, and then directly into my PowerBook's Line In connection. All you need is a phono-to-miniplug converter such as the Monster Instrument Adapter (see Figure 7-1), which is a short cable that has a mono ¼-inch phono connection on one end, and a stereo ⅛-inch miniplug (that connects to your Mac's Line In connection) on the other. This provides one channel of input; for stereo input (two channels), you need a converter that offers two mono ¼-inch phono plugs on one end, and a stereo ⅛-inch miniplug on the other.

▼ **Tip**

If you have an XLR-style connector for your microphone or instrument, you need a converter to convert it to a phono plug.

▼ **Tip**

If your Mac doesn't offer a Line In connection, you can purchase a USB audio input device like the Griffin iMic or the Roland UA-30. If you intend to connect more than one instrument or microphone at the same time, we recommend that you use an audio interface.

To assign sound input to your Mac's line-in connection so that you can record from an external microphone or an electric instrument, follow these steps:

1. **Connect your instrument, microphone, or sound source to the line-in connection on your Mac.**

   If you don't have a line-in connection, you can use a USB audio input device like the Griffin iMic or the Roland UA-30.

2. **From the desktop of your system, choose System Preferences from the Apple menu.**

1/8-inch miniplug

1/4-inch phono connector   1/4-inch phono plug   1/8-inch miniplug connector

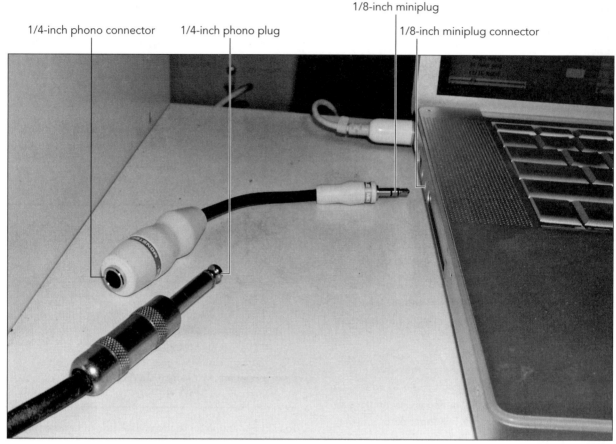

Figure 7-1
Setting up the Mac's Line In connection for recording

3. **In the System Preferences window, click the Sound icon to open the Sound pane.**

4. **Click the Input tab, and in the list of sound input devices, select Line In.**

   The list appears in the Sound pane, as shown in Figure 7-2.

5. **Make sure Mute is unchecked, and set the input volume level.**

To set the volume level for sound input, start playing (or singing). As you play, watch the input level meter. As the volume gets louder, the oblong purple dots light up highlights, from left to right. To adjust the volume, drag the slider underneath the input level meter. If all the dots are highlighted all the time, you're way too "hot." ("Hot" is studio tech talk for being too loud.) If the dots are not highlighted at all, you're way too low. (For some reason, studio techs don't say "cool" or "cold.") You want the dots to be highlighted about three-quarters of the way across

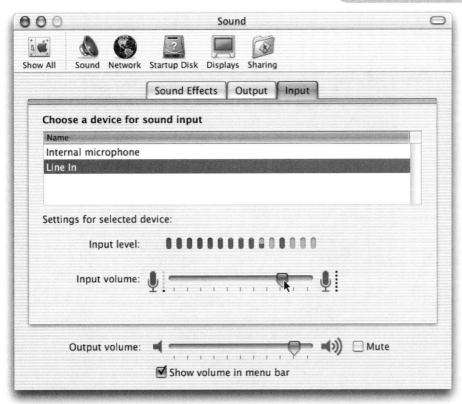

Figure 7-2
Setting up the Mac's Line In connection for recording

from left to right for optimal input volume. Note that the volume changes if you connect a different instrument, so you should adjust the input volume level whenever you change instruments.

6. **Quit System Preferences by choosing System Preferences ➜ Quit System Preferences to save your settings.**

That's it. You can now play your instrument, or sing into a Real Instrument track in GarageBand. You need to start GarageBand, of course, and do a few more things with your Real Instrument track — such as choose an instrument sound — as we describe later in this chapter.

Setting up a mixer or audio interface

When John Mayer entertained the Mac faithful at the January 2004 launch of GarageBand, his guitar seemed to be plugged directly into the Mac. But insiders say he most likely plugged into a small audio interface that was connected to the Mac, because the sound quality was so good.

If your electric guitar has active pickups, it may have enough juice to drive the Mac's input properly; because most electric guitars have passive pickups, however, their signals need a boost. With a preamp, mixer, or audio interface, you can control the input volume; otherwise, you have no way of controlling the analog *gain* (the volume of

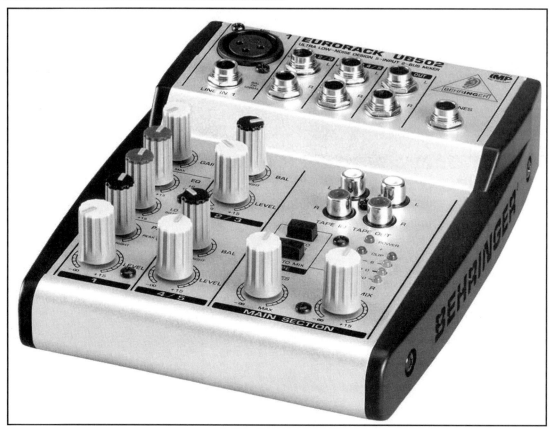

Figure 7-3
A standalone mixer for converting the input signal to line level for input through the Mac's line-in connection

an analog input device that makes sound waves) into the line input's analog-to-digital (A/D) converter. To control the input volume at the source, use a preamp with input trim control, an audio interface, or a standalone mixer, as shown in Figure 7-3. Behringer (www.behringer.com/) offers the Eurorack UB502 for under $60.

With line-level output from a mixer or preamp, you can connect the mixer or preamp to the Mac's Line In connection. You can then control the volume before it reaches the Mac. You must also adjust the volume in the Sound pane of your System Preferences, as described in the previous section.

An *audio interface* is an adapter or device that enables you to connect audio sources to your Mac. They come in several formats including USB, FireWire, PC card, and PCI. You may already need a MIDI-compatible audio interface to use a MIDI keyboard, as described in Chapter 6. Many audio interfaces offer both MIDI and connections for other audio devices; The Emagic Multichannel Interface A62 m, for example, connects to your Mac's USB port and offers six audio inputs (for line-in music, electric instruments, or microphones) as well as MIDI connections.

Digidesign's Pro Tools or Pro Tools LE is supplied with the Mbox audio interface, as shown in Figure 7-4. The Mbox connects to your Mac with a USB cable, which also provides power to the box. You can connect multiple signal sources — microphones, instrument cables, patch cords, and so on — to your Mbox.

To use an audio interface for input to your Mac, follow these steps:

1. **Connect your instruments, microphones, or sound sources to the audio interface.**

   Follow the connection instructions provided with your audio interface.

2. **Choose GarageBand → Preferences; in the Preferences window, click the Audio/MIDI Interfaces button.**

   The Audio/MIDI Interfaces pane appears, as shown in Figure 7-5.

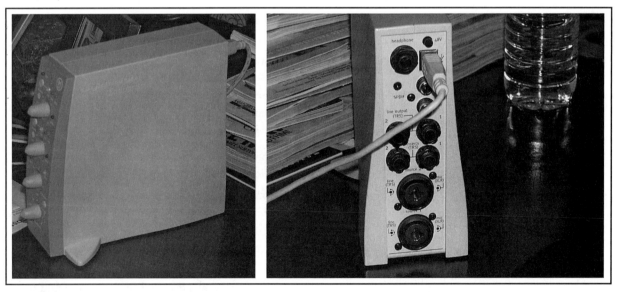

Figure 7-4
An audio interface (view from front and back) that connects to the Mac through its USB connection

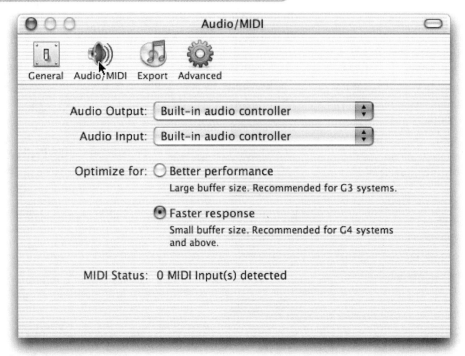

Figure 7-5
Setting up an audio or MIDI interface to input sound to GarageBand

3. **Choose the audio interface from the Audio Input pop-up menu, and then close the preferences window (click the red button in the upper-left corner of the window).**

You can configure your audio interface with more specific controls. Apple provides a utility called Audio MIDI Setup that works with audio devices connected via FireWire, USB, PCMCIA, or PCI.

To use an audio interface with one or more instruments, microphones, and audio devices, install the software that comes with the interface first, following the manufacturer's instructions. You can then use Audio MIDI Setup (in Applications/Utilities) to select audio input and output, control volume levels, and set other characteristics by following these steps:

1. **Connect the audio interface to your Mac, and then connect the instruments, microphones, or audio devices to the interface.**

Connect your audio interface device to your Mac, following the instructions that came with it. You should be able to connect your guitar, keyboard, microphone, or any other instrument that has an electric pickup.

2. **Double-click the Audio MIDI Setup application (in Applications/Utilities) to open the Audio MIDI Setup window, and then click the Audio Devices tab.**

The Audio Devices pane appears, as shown in Figure 7-6. You can change various settings depending on the audio device or instrument you are using.

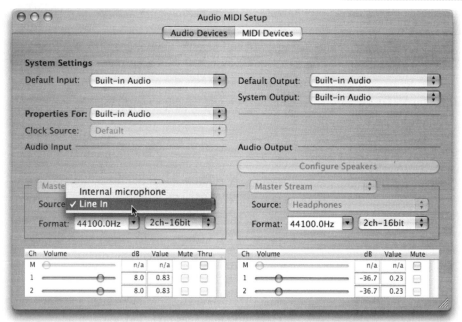

Figure 7-6
Using Audio MIDI Setup to change settings with an audio interface

WISDOM OF IHNATKO: SEE THOSE TWISTY PEG-THINGIES AT THE TOP OF THE GUITAR? THEY'RE NOT DECORATIVE

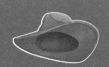

You've recorded seven tracks. Two lead guitars, two rhythm guitars, a bass, and a friend of yours contributed two acoustic riffs. So why don't they sound right together?

Because nobody tuned his or her instrument before recording. It sounds fundamental, tuning is an easy step to overlook in the rush to get results. It's especially problematic when lots of people are contributing tracks at different times and in different places. The same guitar doesn't sound the same in two sessions recorded three weeks apart. Not even your own. Changes in temperature and humidity can affect your instrument over a period of mere hours, making it impossible at times to stay in tune with *your own* tracks.

If you don't have a guitar tuner, go to www.emagic.de. On eMagic's downloads page you'll find a free software-based guitar tuner that works right within GarageBand as an Audio Unit plug-in. If musicians refuse to tune up even though they have a free tuner available, they're being colossal jerks (or typical bass players).

3. **Choose the name of the audio interface from the Default Input pop-up menu.**

4. **To configure the interface, choose it from the Properties For pop-up menu.**

5. **When you're finished, choose Audio MIDI Setup ➜ Quit Audio MIDI Setup.**

The audio devices and instruments connected to your audio interface are now ready to use with GarageBand.

Using a microphone

Microphones are quite versatile. I use a handheld microphone to play harmonica directly into GarageBand, connecting the microphone's cable to the line-in connection as described earlier. You can go on location and set up stereo microphones to record an acoustic performance of a band, nature sounds, or the music of native cultures. The quality of the recording depends almost entirely on the type of microphone you use and its placement near the source of the sound.

Use the Mac's built-in microphone if you have no other choice; it picks up sound from the room, so be aware that your recording may sound amateurish. We recommend using external microphones for vocals and acoustic instruments because you can place them closer to the person singing or the instrument playing. Of course, you'll get the best vocal recordings by singing in a completely quiet room, if not an actual soundproof vocal booth that doesn't produce echoes. The Mac's internal microphone can be useful, however, especially when recording sound effects or ambient sound on the road with a PowerBook.

To assign sound input to your Mac's internal microphone so that you can use it to record sound, follow these steps:

1. **Choose System Preferences from the Apple menu in Mac OS X.**

2. **In the System Preferences window, click the Sound button.**

3. **Click the Input tab, as shown in Figure 7-7.**

4. **Click the Internal Microphone option in the list of sound input devices.**

5. **To set the volume level for sound input, sing into your Mac's microphone (typically located near the display) or play whatever acoustic instruments you want to record.**

   The internal microphone is always on and detecting sound, so watch the input level meter in the Input tab. To adjust the volume, drag the Input volume slider; the purple oblong dots that simulate a level meter highlight from left to right as the volume gets louder. For a good input volume level, you want the dots to be highlighted about three-quarters of the way to the right, not all the way (which is too loud). If you don't have enough dots highlighted, the volume may be too low.

Compared to traditional microphones, the built-in microphones in PowerBooks and iMacs aren't all that great in my opinion. In fact, the PlainTalk mics that came with many older Macs were appreciably better; so were professional mics and USB microphones such as the iVoice (Macally Peripherals, www.macally.com) and the Verse-704 (Labtec, www.labtec.com).

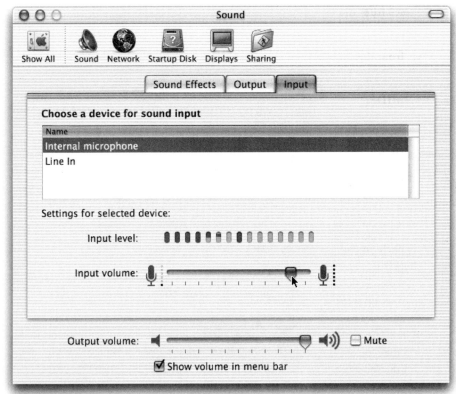

Figure 7-7
Setting up the Mac's internal microphone for recording

Many microphones come with foam covers that you should keep on when recording. Contrary to what you may think, their purpose isn't to protect the mic: they're wind guards that filter sibilant sounds, such as wind, and mitigate the presence of some popping sounds, such as the sound of a *b* or *p*.

Here are a few tips on what you can do before recording to improve your vocal performance:

- Clear your throat to make sure that you're really ready.

- Test the microphone to make sure it is turned on and operational.

- Eliminate background noises wherever possible. This includes closing windows and turning off electronic devices (such as TVs, radios, and stereos).

- Get close to the mic, but keep a few inches of separation between the mic and your lips.

- Practice before you record. Your first or second practice "take" is likely to sound somewhat stilted and artificial. You need to warm yourself up to the material.

CHOOSING A REAL INSTRUMENT SOUND

You can choose a Real Instrument sound and set as many characteristics and effects as you want *before* recording into a Real Instrument track. On the other hand, you can record without any effects or sound treatment, and then add effects and change the characteristics of the sound later (such as running the sound through a simulated amplifier, as described in detail in Chapter 10).

To record a Real Instrument performance, create a Real Instrument track and choose a Real Instrument sound, even if the one you choose is a Basic Track with No Effects. To create a Real Instrument track, start a new song or open an existing song, and then follow these steps:

1. **Choose Track → New Track to create a new track.**

   Alternatively, you can click the + button under the track headers to create a new track. The New Track window appears showing two tabs, Real Instrument and Software Instrument.

2. **Click the Real Instrument tab to show the list of Real Instruments.**

3. **Select a category and then an instrument sound.**

   On the left side, click on Bass, Guitars, Drums, or whatever type of instrument you want; the effects for that category are listed on the right. In Figure 7-8, for example, we selected a Real Instrument Guitar sound (Arena Rock) for a track to be used to record a live harmonica, effectively creating an entirely new sound.

4. **Set the input format and channel.**

   In the New Track dialog box, set the input channel (select an option from the Input pop-up menu) and

the input format (select the Mono or Stereo option). By default, the track is set to monophonic recording (one input), but if your electric instrument offers stereo output, you can switch to stereo.

5. **Turn the track monitor on or leave it off, depending on whether you want to hear your performance as you perform.**

   You can turn the track's monitor on or off in the New Track dialog box. Turn the monitor on to hear yourself and the other tracks of the song as you play your instrument or sing. You should use headphones if you are monitoring a microphone track.

6. **Click OK.**

   The New Track dialog box closes and your settings for the new track take effect.

▼ Caution

You may get a loud shrieking noise that sounds like Jimi Hendrix joined the band (only he's lost his mind). You're getting *feedback*: the microphone (or pickup) you're using is picking up the sound from the speakers. While it may sound cool some of the time, too much feedback can burn out your speakers and even damage your ears. Turn the monitor off, or use headphones rather than speakers when turning the monitor on. To turn off the monitor for any track, select the track, click the "i" button to open the Track Info window, and then deselect the Monitor option.

Before recording, make sure that your instrument or your microphone is connected and working. After selecting a Real Instrument sound, you can immediately hear the sound and its associated effects simply by playing the instrument (or by singing, if your track is for vocals).

Figure 7-8
Selecting a Real Instrument guitar sound (Arena Rock)

To change the sound for a Real Instrument track before or after recording, click its header and then click the Track Info button to open the Track Info window. For example, after playing harmonica for a while with a Real Instrument sound set to Arena Rock guitar (without actually recording), we changed the Real Instrument sound to a Solo Sax (in the Band Instruments category), as shown in Figure 7-9. The track icon changes to a sax, and the new setting takes effect for that track immediately. If we had recorded a

performance in that track, the sound of the performance would have changed automatically.

It doesn't matter whether you've already recorded a performance or not: you can change the Real Instrument setting and effects for the track in the Track Info window. That means you can choose almost any setting and effects to perform with (or just the Basic Track/No Effects setting), and change them later.

Figure 7-9
Changing the Real Instrument setting for the track to Solo Sax

▼ **Tip**

You may hear a hum when playing an electric guitar with pickups, even when using an audio interface. The hum may not be heard in all Real Instrument Guitar settings; for example, Clean Jazz has no hum, but Modern Rock has a lot. Most of the hum can be cancelled out by using the hum-canceling settings on your guitar pickup switch. If your guitar has three pickups, your pickup switch should have five positions (use position two or four). If your guitar has three pickups, you should have three positions (use the center position). While you are at it, turn off all fluorescent lights, as they introduce hum in guitar pickups.

CHANGING REAL INSTRUMENT EFFECTS

Rather than trying to discover your unique sound by spending a fortune on special effects boxes, pedals, and amplifiers, you can try out effects and amplifier settings in GarageBand. The Real Instrument choice you make when you create a Real Instrument track is actually a set of digital effects and settings saved with a name for easy selection. You can modify any of the characteristics of any Real Instrument choice, and even save your own custom Real Instruments. The Track Info window provides a more detailed view of settings for each Real Instrument sound.

To change the effects and amplifier settings for a Real Instrument track, follow these steps:

1. **Open the Track Info window.**

   Double-click the Real Instrument track's header (or click the track, and then click the "i" button or choose Track ➜ Show Track Info) to open the Track Info window.

2. **Click the Details triangle to reveal the settings for effects.**

   The Track Info window provides a more detailed view of settings for each Real Instrument. Click the Details triangle to reveal these settings, as shown in Figure 7-10.

3. **Click a general effect, or choose a special effect from a pop-up menu on the left side.**

   In the Track Info window's Details... section, the instrument effects (such as a Noise Gate, Compressor, Equalizer, Echo, Reverb, and so on) are on the left side, and the settings for the effects are in pop-up menus on the right side. To turn on the Echo effect, for example, click the checkbox next to Echo on the left side.

4. **Adjust the settings for the effect using a slider or pop-up menu on the right side.**

   The settings for the effects are controlled by sliders or pop-up menus on the right side. For example, to adjust the Echo effect chosen in Step 3, drag the slider on the right side of the Echo effect. The Gate, Compressor, Echo, and Reverb effects offer sliders you can drag to adjust their settings; the Equalizer and other effects offer pop-up menus with presets you can select or modify. For a complete description of these effects, see Chapter 10.

5. **Repeat Steps 3 and 4 for each effect you want.**

   For example, if you clicked the Equalizer effect on the left side (by clicking the checkbox to add a check mark), you can change the Equalizer preset on the right side (the preset controls on the right are specific settings for that effect). In Figure 7-11, we chose a Phaser from one of the effects pop-up menus on the left, and then chose the Circle Phases preset in the Phaser settings pop-up menu on the right.

6. **Play your instrument or sing into your microphone as you adjust settings.**

   As you change the characteristics and effects associated with a Real Instrument — such as changing the echo, reverb, noise gate, and other settings in the Track Info window — you can hear the difference in sound in real time by playing the tracks while you adjust the settings.

7. **Close the Track Info window after making changes, or click Save Instrument, as described in the next section.**

   The changes you made are automatically saved with the Real Instrument's track in the song. You can save your settings as a custom Real Instrument, as described in the next section.

You can also modify the presets for the effects (except Gain, Compressor, Echo, and Reverb), and create custom presets for these effects by clicking the pencil button to the right of an effect's pop-up menu. When you click the pencil button, a new window appears, as shown in Figure 7-11, with many options you can use to modify an effect preset.

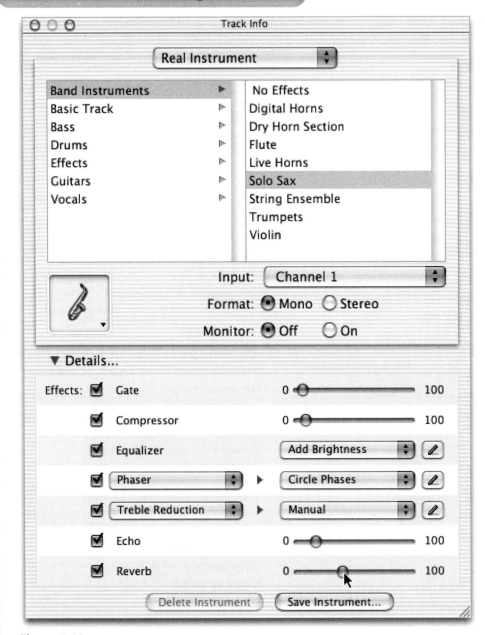

Figure 7-10
Changing the Reverb setting for the Solo Sax effect

Figure 7-11
Changing the Equalizer setting manually

The pop-up menu and the pencil button give you ultimate control over effects such as the Equalizer. You can customize any of the effects, including Amp Simulation, in the pop-up menus on the left side. All these effects and more are described in Chapter 10.

After changing settings, click the Close button to close the window. GarageBand pops up a dialog box that asks, "Do you want to save the file before switching to a new one?" Give the preset a name and click Save to save the settings as your own custom preset, or click Don't Save to discard the settings.

WISDOM OF IHNATKO: GARAGEBAND LIMITS

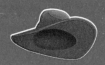

If you've gotten this far, you've probably been duly wowed by GarageBand's features. But there's one thing that (at this writing) limits the app's potential as a professional tool: the ability to export your work to other hardware and software.

Ideally, you'd be there on the front porch of your Nantucket cottage, plucking out a new anthem that will unite the hearts and minds of the world into one cogent and mutually supportive being (or, failing that, make you a bargeload of money and sell a lot of Mountain Dew). You would record and edit it in GarageBand and when your vacation's over, you'd walk into the studio with a CD-ROM. All of the MIDI tracks and loops you created on the beach would be loaded into your studio instruments and controllers, and barring some tweaking, world peace/your ability to *buy* a beach house instead of renting one would be in the bag.

Alas, GarageBand doesn't export MIDI. You can export your project as a high-quality AIFF. No worries there. But for now, as far as MIDI is concerned, what happens in GarageBand stays in GarageBand.

This particular note is more of a brief warning than a serious complaint. Again I say: 49 stinking dollars. And you get a free movie editor and free DVD mastering software and a free music library and a free photo manager with it!

▼ Tip

Before you learn all about effects, you can record something now, and apply the effects later. To get a clean, unaffected recording of your instrument or voice, choose Basic Track in the left column of the Track Info window, and No Effects in the right column. You can click the Details triangle to open the Details pane and verify that no other effects are applied, and that Echo and Reverb are set to zero. This setting is also useful if you are using an external amp simulator or synthesizer.

SAVING REAL INSTRUMENT SETTINGS

Although you can save presets for effects as described in the previous section (and in Chapter 10), you can also save all the settings (and presets) as a custom Real Instrument

sound. Even though the changes you made to the effects and the sound are automatically saved with the Real Instrument's track in the song, you may want to save these custom settings so that you can use them in another song. Here's how:

1. **In the Track Info window, click the Save Instrument button.**

   The Save Instrument dialog box appears.

2. **Give the instrument a new name (such as "Harmonica-soft"), and then click OK.**

3. **Choose an icon for it by clicking the instrument's icon and dragging across the selections to the one you want.**

The instrument appears in the submenu of the category you already selected. For example, if you had already selected Band Instruments on the left, your custom Real

Instrument is saved in the Band Instruments submenu on the right; if you had selected Guitars on the left, your custom instrument is saved in the Guitars submenu on the right. You can then use the sound for any Real Instrument track of any song.

You can save as many custom Real Instrument sounds as you want. Real Instrument settings are stored on your hard drive in a folder for the instrument type (such as Guitars) inside the Real folder. The pathname to the Real folder is Macintosh HD\Library\Application Support\GarageBand\ Instrument Library\Track Settings\Real. You can copy the file for a Real Instrument (or an entire folder of Real Instruments) to another computer and use them with that computer's copy of GarageBand.

Recording and Performing

In This Chapter

Setting the tempo and time signature for recording • Recording into a cycle
region for loops and overdubs • Tips on recording vocals • Performing
live using simulated amplifiers and effects

The moment of truth has arrived. You think you can't perform well enough to create a hit song? You think you don't have the best equipment to do it? If John Lennon had not had the courage, at age 15, to play a gig in front of an audience even though he didn't know how to tune a guitar, he might not have met Paul McCartney (or he might not have let Paul show him how to tune the guitar and play some chords).

You've got to take a chance. Had Elvis not gone to Sun Records on his own initiative to make a recording for his mother's birthday, Sam Phillips would never have met him and turned him into a star.

GarageBand makes a neat synthesizer with a MIDI keyboard. It also makes an excellent amateur recording studio, ready to make CD-quality tracks. And with amplifier settings and effects, you can turn your GarageBand-equipped Mac into the most comprehensive guitar "stompbox" yet — using your Mac (most likely a laptop) as an intervening digital effects generator between your instrument and your amp. To do all these things, you need to know all about recording and performing with GarageBand, the subject of this chapter.

TESTING 1, 2, 3. . . IS THIS THING ON?

If a garage band in Portland, Oregon, hadn't stumbled upon a cover version of a ridiculously simple song and not forked over $37 for a two-hour recording session, we would not have that classic record today known as "Louie Louie." What you may not know is that the studio, Old Northwest Recording, was not miked for rock music at that time, and the lead singer had to stand on his tiptoes and strain his voice, which is one reason why the lyrics are slurred.

SETTING THE TEMPO AND TIME SIGNATURE

GarageBand can record only one track at a time, unlike professional audio editing programs such as Digidesign Pro Tools. But that limitation also makes it easier for a single performer to record a musical piece in any tempo that is comfortable and add it to a composition that is set to a different tempo (try *that* with a band). A single performer can record piece after piece and build up layers to create a song, with each layer recorded in a different time signature. (Try *that*, Frank Zappa wannabes.)

Setting the metronome and Count In

You can hear the other tracks while recording a track, and you can also hear a metronome that plays a short blip for each beat of the measure to help you keep time while recording an instrument. (The blips are not recorded.) A more sophisticated metronome is used in professional studios as a *click track*; you can simulate a click track with GarageBand's metronome. You can turn the metronome

on or off by choosing Control ➜ Metronome (a check mark means it is on). You don't have to use it — it may be better to put down loops for a drum track, or both drums and bass guitar, and then record your performance using the drums and bass as your guide.

However, when you use the metronome, you can also turn on the Count In option by choosing Control ➜ Count In. This option reacts just like a bandleader counting in "1-2-3-4" to prepare the band to begin a song. GarageBand plays the metronome one full measure before starting to record so that you can get ready to perform along with the beat.

The number of beats in a measure is set by the *time signature*, which you define when you create a new project (as described in Chapter 1), along with the *tempo*, which defines the speed of a song in beats per minute (bpm). The tempo and time signature you set for a song determines the rate at which the metronome plays a blip. You should set the time signature and tempo for your performance before recording anything; make sure your metronome is turned on, so that the blips help you to keep on the beat while recording.

If you set the time signature to ¾ (typical for a rock song, with four beats in each measure) with the Count In option turned on, the metronome will play four blips to define a measure before starting to record, and then continue to play four blips per measure (measures are numbered in the timeline's grid). The speed — how fast these four blips play — is set by the tempo.

Changing the time signature

With GarageBand, you can record one piece of music in one time signature, and another piece of music in another time signature, and combine them in a song. The benefit is that GarageBand keeps your performances in time and on the beat for each time signature, so you don't get confused and perform poorly. You can also record a performance in any tempo that feels comfortable, and then change the tempo after recording to a tempo that is faster or slower — your performances stay in time and on beat.

The time signature is a handy way of dividing up the beats into measures and notes. For example, with a time signature of 2/4, you have two beats in every measure, with each beat having the value of a quarter note (4).

The most common time signature in rock music is 4/4. That does not mean you have to play only four notes in a measure — all it means is that those four beats anchor your notes to the music. You might intentionally play slightly before a beat to "slide into" the beat, or slightly after a beat to play a laid-back part. You might play eight notes inside a 4/4 measure.

76 TROMBONES PLAY IN 6/8 TIME

Lots of popular songs were composed in a 4/4 time signature, but other time signatures are also common. Popular songs composed in 3/4 include "Sunrise, Sunset" (Sheldon Harnick/Jerry Bock) from *Fiddler on the Roof*, "Norwegian Wood" (Lennon/McCartney) by the Beatles, and "Where the Streets Have No Name" (U2/Bono) by U2. "Seventy Six Trombones" (Meredith Willson) from *The Music Man* is in 6/8, while "Oh! Darling" (Lennon/McCartney) by the Beatles is in 12/8. Time signatures can also change in the middle of a song — "Strawberry Fields Forever" (Lennon/McCartney) by the Beatles changes from 4/4 to 6/8 when Lennon first sings "Strawberry Fields forever..." and back to 4/4 when he sings "Let me take you down..."

IN TIME WITH JORMA KAUKONEN

Rock and Roll Hall of Fame inductee Jorma Kaukonen, founder of Jefferson Airplane and Hot Tuna, and a fantastic guitar player, also teaches guitar camp when he's not on tour — the Fur Peace Ranch Guitar Camp (www.furpeaceranch.com). My band mates and I participated in a "band camp" with Jorma in charge, and one of many things he taught us was how to use the time signature effectively. During the instrumental break in the middle of a bluesy country song in 4/4 signature time, Jorma led the band into a faster riff in essentially 8/4 time. He explained why, tongue-in-cheek: "When you think you've done enough, and you can't go anywhere else with the song, that's when you go double-time."

Whatever time signature you select, the grid in the timeline (and in the Track Editor, described in Chapter 9) reflects the choice. For example, with a 4/4 time signature the grid shows four tick marks in each measure, with the measure's midpoint set to the second tick mark. If you choose 9/8, you'll see an unusual grid in the timeline with nine tick marks in each measure with the midpoint set at tick mark 4, as shown in Figure 8-1. The grid not only helps you align the start of your recording with another track, it also helps you align individual notes of a Software Instrument performance to the beat when using the Track Editor in the bottom half of the GarageBand window (as described in Chapter 9).

You can change the time signature just for recording a performance (and change it back to its original setting after the recording), without affecting regions in other tracks of the song. To change the time signature, follow these steps:

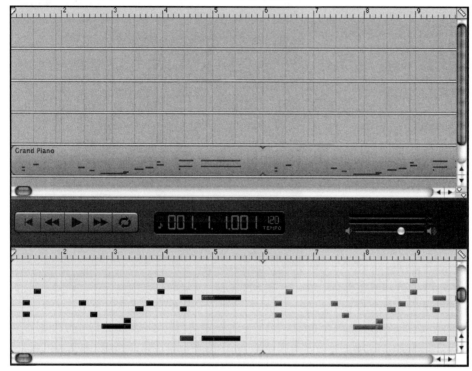

Figure 8-1
The grid in the timeline and the Track Editor show that the time signature is set to 9/8.

1. **Choose Track → Show Master Track.**

   As I explain in Chapter 4, every song has a master track, usually hidden until you explicitly show it. The master track appears with the heading Master Volume at the bottom on the timeline as the last track.

2. **Click the Master Volume track header to select it.**

3. **Click the Track Info button (the *i* button), or choose Track → Show Track Info.**

   The Track Info window for the master track appears, offering preset effects settings for various music genres (Ambient, Classical, Dance, and so on).

4. **Choose a time signature from the Time pop-up menu.**

   The Time pop-up menu, shown in Figure 8-2, offers a range of time signatures.

5. **Close the Track Info window.**

   Click the tiny red button in the top left corner of the window to close it.

▼ **Tip**

You can also reach the master track's Track Info window by clicking any track, choosing Track Info, and then choosing Master Track from the pop-up menu at the top of the window.

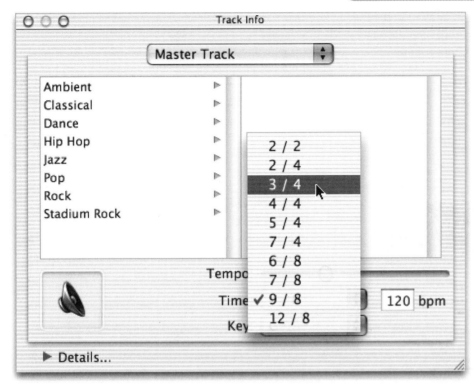

Figure 8-2
Changing the time signature in the master track's Track Info window

PLAYING RHYTHM GAMES IN THE BAND

You can use GarageBand to learn about rhythm and improvisational jamming by choosing a time signature, using the metronome and Count In option, and performing to the count or along with another drum or percussion loop. "Rhythm is just time, and time can be carved up any way you want," wrote Mickey Hart, percussionist and songwriter for the Grateful Dead, in his book *Drumming at the Edge of Magic* (HarperCollins, San Francisco, CA; 1990). Hart describes a rhythm game taught to him by master percussionist Alla Rakha in which Alla Rakha beat out a count of ten and then called out a number, such as 12, and Hart would try to lay down 12 beats within the span of his ten (for a 12/10 time signature). "His last beat and my last beat would meet — at the One. With this simple game, Alla Rakha destroyed my beliefs about rhythm... He showed me the obvious truth that 12 bars of 11 are the same as 11 bars of 12." Hart took Alla Rakha's rhythm games back to the Grateful Dead and spent months practicing. "Our song called 'The Eleven,' which explores a rhythmic cycle of 11 beats, dates from this period... We felt we were on the edge of a break-through, that somewhere in these rhythm games was the key to a new kind of music — polyrhythmic rock and roll.

You can also set the grid in the timeline (and in the Track Editor, described in Chapter 9) to different note values in the time measure, such as quarter notes, eighth notes, sixteenth notes, thirty-second notes, quarter-note triplets, eighth-note triplets, and so on. While these changes do not change the metronome's blip speed, they help you align regions in the track or notes in a Software Instrument region. To set the grid to a different note value, click the grid button in the upper-right corner of the timeline, as described in Chapter 3.

Changing the tempo

You can change the tempo of the song to record your performance with a Software Instrument at a slower tempo, and then increase the speed with no change in quality. You may even want to record at a faster tempo and then slow it down.

You can't do this with Real Instrument recordings, but when you change the tempo in a song, all of the loops (even Real Instrument loops) and all Software Instrument recordings adjust to the new settings automatically. You can increase or decrease the tempo, and your loops and Software Instrument recordings play right on the beat.

The Time Display indicator below the timeline view of the tracks tells you the playhead position in musical time (using musical measures, beats, and ticks) or absolute time (hours, minutes, seconds, fractions of a second), and the tempo. Click the tempo, and a pop-up slider appears to change the tempo on the fly, as shown in Figure 8-3.

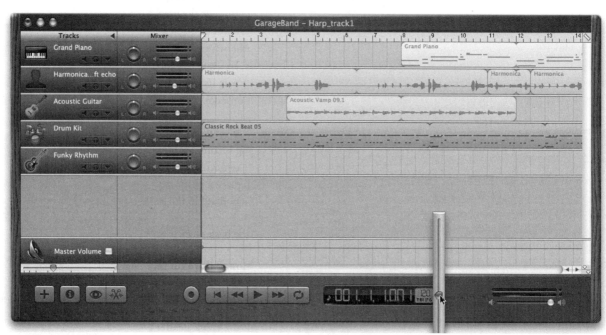

Figure 8-3
Changing the tempo to record at a different tempo

In Figure 8-3, I'm about to record a Real Instrument track (Funky Rhythm guitar), but I'm changing the tempo first. The Software Instrument tracks (Grand Piano recording and Drum Kit loop) and the Real Instrument loop track (Acoustic Guitar) all change their tempos automatically as we change the tempo, while the Real Instrument recording (Harmonica) does not change.

 Tip

Because all other types of tracks can change with the tempo except Real Instrument recordings, it makes sense to treat Real Instrument recordings differently. You might want to record Real Instrument tracks first, establishing a tempo, and then perform with Software Instruments in the same tempo to match the performances to the Real Instrument track tempo. Or you might do it in reverse: record the Software Instrument tracks at any tempo you want, then adjust the tempo appropriately for the final song, and then record your Real Instrument tracks.

RECORDING TECHNIQUES

Before the 1960s, recording studios were set up mostly for recording live performances in the studio. The band might record take after take of an entire song, and decide which take to use on the record. Some of the most popular and endearing artists made their records this way — the Beatles, Bob Dylan, and Joan Baez. *Overdubbing* — recording into one track while simultaneously monitoring (listening to) the other tracks, then combining the tracks — was a relatively new concept and involved rerecording onto tape, with loss of sound quality at each step.

Tape overdubbing ("sound on sound" recording), pioneered by guitar innovator Les Paul, made it possible to erase or record over a previous recording so that mistakes could be fixed. Another advantage of recording on tape was the ability to cut the tape and join it back together.

You could, therefore, *edit* the recording — pieces of the recording could be removed or rearranged.

Sounds like GarageBand, right? Regions can be recorded and then rearranged and edited. GarageBand accommodates the different styles of recording that have evolved since the early days of overdubbing, when John Lennon had barely enough tracks with a four-track tape deck to overdub a harmonica on "I Should Have Known Better" after singing the chorus. Much of today's music is recorded as separate tracks and built up by overdubbing, overlaying more tracks to enrich the sound. At the end of this process, the multiple tracks are mixed into the final song.

You can record each track separately in GarageBand, and build up a song with as many tracks as you need, up to the limit of what your computer can handle. You can overdub a section of a song by simply creating a new track and recording into it at the precise point in the song that you want the section to begin — click a starting point in a track or otherwise move the playhead to begin recording at that point. You can also correct a mistake this way: record the correct part in a new track, and edit the other track to delete the mistake.

However, you can reach your limit of tracks fairly quickly if your song is complex (or you need to correct a lot of mistakes). You can combine performances into a single track, or replace a portion of a track, by using a cycle region as described in the next section of this chapter.

Here are the basic steps for recording a performance:

1. **(Optional) Turn on the metronome by choosing Control → Metronome, and the Count In option by choosing Control → Count In.**

2. **Click the track header for the track you want to record into.**

To record using the onscreen keyboard, MidiKeys, or a USB MIDI keyboard, use a Software Instrument track; for real instruments or vocals, use a Real Instrument track.

3. **For a Real Instrument recording, turn the track monitor on if you want to hear your performance as you perform; leave it off if you don't want to hear your performance as you perform.**

You can turn the track's monitor on or off in the New Track dialog — choose Track ➜ Show Track Info, or just double-click the track header, to open the New Track dialog box. Turn the monitor on to hear yourself as you play your instrument or sing — you also hear the other tracks of the song as you sing or play. You should use headphones if you are monitoring a microphone track or you will no doubt hear screeching feedback.

4. **Move the playhead to the starting point.**

Click rewind to start recording at the beginning of the song, or click a point in the timeline to move the playhead to that point in the song. You can also click and drag the playhead to the point in the timeline where you want to start recording.

5. **Check your instrument connection and line-in input volume (or internal microphone volume) if recording a Real Instrument track.**

6. **Click the red Record button, or press the R key, to start recording, and start performing immediately or after the count in (if using the Count In option).**

GarageBand starts to record in the track while playing any other tracks, and it lays down a new region in the track's timeline. You can record in the track for the entire song or for only portions of a song.

FEED YOUR HEAD

Headphones, the least expensive way to listen to high-quality music, vary widely in quality. Circum-aural headphones have ear cups that totally surround the ear, and for my head are more comfortable than supra-aural headphones that sit directly on the ear. Supra-aural headphones may sound better because most are designed as "open" headphones that let the sound resonate more (as opposed to "closed" or sealed headphones that block out all sound but make you feel like you are inside a tin can). Earbuds are headphones you insert in your ear and also vary widely in quality. You may already have the pair of earbuds from Apple that came with an iPod, but Apple offers a better pair for $39 (the Apple In-Ear headphones) that offers a richer sound, better isolation from outside ambient noise, and rubberized earpieces for better comfort.

The only way to know if a certain pair of headphones is best for your ears is to try them. Frequency response specs don't help much — true sound quality is the most accurate reproduction of the music, which is not necessarily the case with headphones capable of reproducing sounds way above and below the range of human hearing. You might hear better music reproduction from headphones with a frequency response from 20 to 20,000 Hz than from a pair with a 10 to 30,000 Hz frequency response. Impedance and sound pressure levels matter a bit more depending on what source you are using to drive the headphones. High-end studio headphones usually need more power to drive them than the power derived from an iPod or similar player, but work fine with Macs. Make sure you turn the volume down before listening to a pair, then turn it up slowly, so that you don't damage your ears.

7. **To finish recording, do one of the following:**

 Click the red Record button, or press the R key. The song continues to play even though Garage-Band stops recording. You can click the Record button or press R again to continue recording later in the song. You can eventually click the Play button, or press the spacebar, to pause playback.

 Press the spacebar. The recording stops and the song pauses immediately.

Here are some keyboard shortcuts to remember:

spacebar	Play from the playhead, pause the currently playing song, or stop recording and pause
R	Start recording
→	Move playhead forward by one measure
←	Move playhead backward by one measure
Home or Z	Move playhead to the beginning

▼ **Tip**

After recording a performance, click the rewind button, or press the Home or Z keys, to move the playhead back to the beginning to listen to your performance. Listening carefully is an excellent way to improve your playing.

Recording into a cycle region

A *cycle region* is a section of the timeline that plays over and over like a loop. When you define a cycle region, the regions in the tracks you've created play over and over, no matter what you recorded before or after.

BILL PAYNE: LISTEN TO IMPROVE YOUR SOLOS

"Board tapes (of on-stage performances) can be helpful in evaluating your progress when it comes to constructing better solos," wrote Bill Payne, keyboard player, composer, and founder of Little Feat, in articles for Player Magazine. "Listening before trying again reinforces your conceptual thinking and gives you confidence or brings you back to how to construct a better solo." He added a word of caution: "Relative volumes may appear different — a guitar might sound softer on the board tape if the volume on stage is loud — so don't let that throw you. The art of improvisation is built on mastering your instrument and coming to grips with the language you want it to speak. It is a lifetime work."

When you *record* with a cycle region already defined, the cycle region limits your recording to that region of the selected track. The cycle region plays over and over as you perform. To make overdubbing easier, you use a cycle region to overlay or replace the sound in a single track, confining your changes to that track, so that you don't have to create new tracks. The cycle region limits your recording to that region so that you don't accidentally record over other regions in the track.

You can use a cycle region in different ways with Software Instruments and Real Instruments:

◉ With a Software Instrument track, you can record into a cycle region, *overlaying* each performance over the previous one, and layering the performances like a stack. This is useful for building up a loop. For example, you can use this technique to merge multiple performances of the same percussion instrument into a

THE DELAYED EFFECT

With Real Instrument tracks, you may find that that the sound you hear by turning on the Monitor option is delayed slightly. If you are using a USB audio interface through a USB hub, try connecting the interface directly to the computer's USB connection, bypassing the hub. You may also get better performance by removing any other USB devices from your computer (leaving only the mouse, for example, or using the trackpad on a PowerBook and removing even the mouse). Some audio interfaces provide direct-input monitoring, which lets you hear your performance without any delay. If you are still getting some delay and you are adding a performance to a project that has other tracks, you may have to shift the performance track in time to compensate for the delay. This is due to the delayed output through GarageBand, and it may cause you to play a bit behind the other tracks (even though it doesn't sound that way while performing). You can use the Track Editor, described in Chapter 9, to shift a track in time.

loop — very useful when you choose a drum kit, because you can overlay different parts of the drum kit, playing them all yourself. As the cycle region plays over and over, you can hear all the performances and tracks you added previously as you add more performances, so you can build up a complex loop very quickly.

- With a Real Instrument track, you can record into a cycle region, *replacing* what you performed before. This is useful for correcting parts of performances — in studio lingo, replacing a region of a performance is called "punching in" and the start and stop points of the region are called "punch in" and "punch out" points. Just like the superstars of the 1970s that overdubbed corrected parts on their supposedly "live" albums, you can correct pieces of recorded performances to your heart's content by rerecording over them. The cycle region makes this easy by restricting the recording to the specific time segment defined as the cycle region in the selected track. When the cycle region plays back, you hear the performance you just recorded.

You can record a performance into a cycle region into a track of the same type (Real Instrument recording into a Real Instrument track, or Software Instrument recording into a Software Instrument track), overwriting any region already there. In effect, you're splitting and shortening regions to make the new cycle region fit, as if you had dragged the new cycle region over the existing regions.

To create a cycle region, follow these steps:

1. **Click the Cycle button.**

   The Cycle button, with the revolving arrows, is in the row of transport control buttons. This button opens the cycle ruler, which is a tiny second ruler that appears below the beat ruler. A yellow bar appears in the cycle ruler, and the mouse pointer changes to a double-headed horizontal arrow.

2. **Drag the edges of the cycle ruler's yellow bar to define a cycle region in the timeline, as shown in Figure 8-4.**

   You can drag the beginning and end of the yellow bar to set it accurately in the timeline. You can also drag in an empty part of the cycle region ruler to set the cycle region to a new position.

▼ Tip

To make it easier to start your performance and play exactly on the beat, set the cycle region to start a full measure or two before the actual "punch in" point, so that you can hear the music play for a measure or two before starting. You may also want to extend the cycle region past the "punch out" point in case your last note extends past that point, particularly if you have Echo turned on for the track.

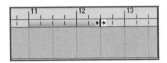

Figure 8-4
Defining a cycle region by dragging in the opened cycle ruler

3. **Select a track and record a performance.**

   With the cycle region defined, you record directly into the cycle region of that track. As you record, a new

region appears in the track, as shown in Figure 8-5, shortening any region that lies underneath the new region, and splitting a region into two if necessary, in order to fit the new region.

In Real Instrument tracks, the cycle region records only one performance of an instrument (or vocal). When the cycle region repeats, you hear only that one performance.

However, in Software Instrument tracks, you can record while the cycle repeats, overlaying one recording over another, and you can keep doing it to create a multilayered loop — each cycle is merged with the region created the first time through. You can use this feature to create incredibly textured and multilayered loops.

▼ Cross-Reference

You can also use a cycle region to export just a portion of a track from GarageBand, effectively creating your own loops. See Chapter 11 to learn how to export a cycle region.

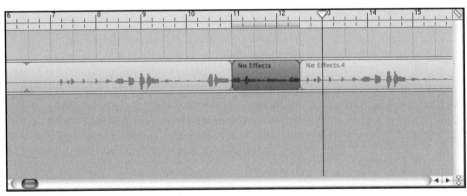

Figure 8-5
After recording into a cycle region

JIMMY SANCHEZ: MAKING 21ST CENTURY LOOPS

Jimmy Sanchez, a drummer for 10 years with producer and slide guitarist Roy Rogers (who also recorded or performed with a wide range of artists including Boz Scaggs, Bonnie Raitt, Dr. John, Bob Weir, J. J. Cale, Steve Miller, and Tom Waits), uses GarageBand to create drum loops. "Long before home multitracking recording systems, I used to record a drum part on tape and then play the tape through a speaker with a microphone to record it while I played another drum part on top of the first part. I would put that on tape and play that through a speaker and record along with it yet another drum part, or some percussion. Each time I did this I would lose quality in the recording, but the result would be an ensemble sound of multiple drums and percussion instruments. Now, in the 21st century, I can do all this in GarageBand without losing any quality — just set a cycle region and record into it, overlapping whatever else has been recorded in that region. I can record several performances into the same region, creating a large sound with no loss in quality."

Recording vocals

Some vocalists chew gum before singing. Others drink honey-lemon tea to soothe the throat before singing. One thing I *don't* recommend is eating salty potato chips or corn chips before singing. Try to keep your mouth moist.

The most common mistake is holding the microphone either too close or too far from your mouth. To understand how to sing into a microphone, remember that a microphone's diaphragm reacts with varying sensitivity to your vocal performance — it helps to adjust your body according to the dynamics of the delivery. If you're going to deliver a quiet, intimate vocal from start to finish, you can afford to position the microphone just a few inches from

your mouth. If you need to deliver a full-volume vocal throughout the song, you should probably stand a few feet away from the microphone. Quite often, though, a song is dynamic enough to require different amounts of air to be pushed at different times — and you should move your body closer to or farther away from the mike depending on your singing volume. Ideally, your mouth should be as close to the mike as possible without overloading it. Don't be afraid to move your head back a couple of inches for just a phrase or even a syllable — you can also aim your mouth slightly above or to the side of the diaphragm of the microphone for particularly loud moments.

Certain consonants create sounds that, when electrically amplified, become abrasive or detract from the intended effect. *B* and *P* sounds can be overexaggerated, causing a popping sound, and the natural sibilance of the letters *C, S,* and *Z* can produce a hissing sound. You can avoid these problems by using correct diction and appropriate microphone placement. Most microphones are extremely sensitive and capable of picking up sound from any direction, so moving the microphone farther from your mouth, angling it to one side, or lowering it and angling it more toward the ceiling will lessen the sensitivity by just enough to prevent the pops and hisses. You can also get a microphone pop filter for about $25 (such as the Music People Microphone Pop Filter) to place in front of the mike — it has a steel clamp to attach the filter to any microphone stand, and a gooseneck that lets you place the filter properly at about 6 inches in front of the mike.

One reason why vocalists overdub their voices and blend them together is that the vocals sound more confident, and one reason for that is the vocalist can hear the first performance while overdubbing the second. While you can't do this in a single Real Instrument track using a cycle region, you *can* use multiple tracks for each vocal performance, and, if necessary, align the vocal tracks on the beat by editing the tracks in the Track Editor as described in Chapter 9.

PERFORMING WITH GARAGEBAND EFFECTS

When you connect a real instrument or microphone to your Mac and create a Real Instrument track, as described in Chapter 7, you can play your instrument or pick up sound through the microphone and hear it without actually recording it and using disk space. You can use your Mac as a "super-pedal" for your instrument when performing live, choosing effects and amplifier settings on the fly.

All you need to do is connect your real amplifier or mixing console to your Mac's audio output (the headphones or line-out connections). I use this method to route my harmonica sound from my handheld microphone to my standard Fender amplifier — the sound goes through GarageBand so that I can change the effects while playing.

To route the sound from your instrument or microphone through GarageBand and back out to your headphones or to an amplifier, turn on the track's monitor in the New Track dialog box when creating the track, or turn it on in the Track Info window as shown in Figure 8-6.

▼ Caution

You may get feedback if you place a microphone in such a way that it picks up the sound from your amplifier's speaker or a stage monitor speaker. Try placing the microphone so that it points away from the speaker.

Figure 8-6

Turning on the monitor for a track to perform with a real instrument

BILL PAYNE: CREATE A ROAD MAP FOR YOUR SOLO

It is important to be confident while playing on stage, especially when performing a solo. "The way to build confidence is to give yourself an advantage," wrote Bill Payne of Little Feat in *Player Magazine*. "Try to visualize the solo in your head, where you want to take the solo musically: the beginning, the middle, and the end. There is no danger in taking away the spontaneity of performance by creating a road map. If anything, it should free you up even more, as it is just a device to get you started. It can be a long way from where you start a solo to where you take it in the middle and then from that point to your resolution. The freedom is in between."

Using the simulated amplifier and effects

The best reason for using GarageBand as your instrument "pedal" when performing live is to use GarageBand's simulated amplifier settings and effects with the sound before routing the sound to your real amplifier. If effect, you are using GarageBand as a preamp.

To set the effects and simulated amplifier settings for a Real Instrument track before performing, create a Real Instrument track, as described in Chapter 7, and then follow these steps:

1. **Open the Track Info window.**

   Double-click the Real Instrument track's header (or click the track, and then click the *i* button or choose Track ➡ Show Track Info) to open the Track Info window.

2. **Click the Details triangle to reveal the settings for effects.**

The Track Info window provides a more detailed view of settings for each Real Instrument — click the Details triangle to reveal these settings, as shown in Figure 8-7.

3. **To set the simulated amplifier settings, choose Amp Simulation from the first or second pop-up menu on the left side.**

   In the Track Info window's detailed section, the instrument effects (such as a noise gate, a compressor, an equalizer, echo, reverb, and so on) are on the left side, and the settings for the effects are in pop-up menus on the right side. The effects are applied from top to bottom, which means that the compressor is applied before the equalizer, and so forth. The two pop-up menus on the left let you choose various effects. You can choose Amp Simulation in either menu, depending on whether you want to use another effect first.

4. **Choose an Amp Simulation preset in the corresponding pop-up menu on the right side.**

   Preset settings for the Amplifier effect are provided in the pop-up menu on the right side, as shown in Figure 8-8. These include American Clean, American Crunch, British Clean, and so on. You can choose a preset, or you can create your own preset by choosing Manual (as described later in this section). For a complete description of track effects, see Chapter 10.

5. **Play your instrument or sing into your microphone as you adjust settings.**

   As you change the effects in the Track Info window, you can hear the difference in sound in real time by playing the tracks while you adjust the settings. This makes it possible for you to adjust settings while performing live.

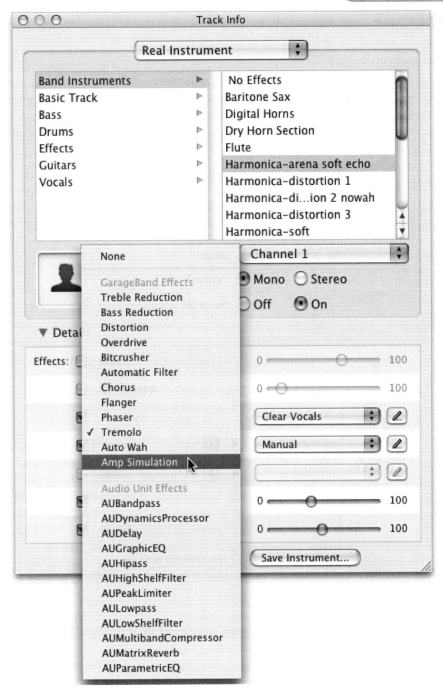

Figure 8-7
Choosing Amp Simulation for a track to change its settings before performing with a real instrument

Figure 8-8
Choosing a preset for the simulated amplifier before performing with a real instrument

6. **Close the Track Info window after performing, or click Save Instrument to save a custom Real Instrument.**

The changes to settings are automatically saved with the Real Instrument's track in the song even though you didn't record anything — you can use the song project just to store your settings, and you can create multiple tracks for different settings. You can also save a single track's settings as a custom Real Instrument, as described in Chapter 7.

To create your own custom preset for Amp Simulation (or other effects that offer presets), click the pencil button to the right of the effect's pop-up menu of presets. When you click the pencil button, a new window appears, as shown in Figure 8-9, with many options you can use to modify an effect preset.

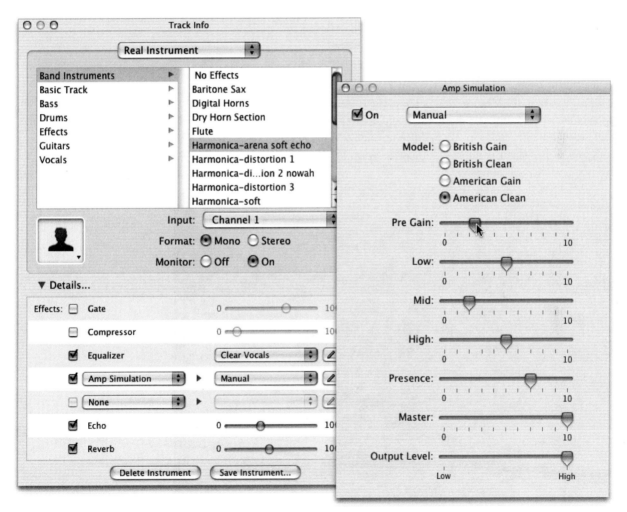

Figure 8-9

Modifying a preset for the simulated amplifier before performing with a real instrument

After changing settings, click the Close button to close the window. A dialog box appears that asks, "Do you want to save the file before switching to a new one?" Click Save to save the settings as your own custom preset (and give the preset a name), or click Don't Save to discard the settings.

You can create multiple Real Instrument tracks, each with different settings, so that when you are performing live, you can switch settings simply by clicking a different track. For example, to perform with a harmonica (as I do), you could set up several tracks, each with a different type of harmonica sound, as shown in Figure 8-10.

Because the effects settings (especially Amp Simulation) affect the overall volume of the sound, you can set the volume for each track in the Mixer section of the track, as described in Chapter 4. In Figure 8-10, for example, I set the different harmonica effects' tracks to different volume settings so that the volume is automatically correct when I switch tracks while performing live.

Looping live

You can use a cycle region to overlay new Software Instrument recordings as the previous ones repeat, and perform the cycle region *live*, adding a new performance with each loop — and building up layers of sound within the cycle region. As described in "Recording into a cycle region" in this chapter, you can record a Software Instrument while the cycle repeats, overlaying one recording over another, and you can keep doing it to create a multilayered loop — each cycle is merged with the region created the first time through.

To set up a cycle region for looping live, create a Software Instrument track (as described in Chapter 6) and define a cycle region as described in "Recording into a cycle region" in this chapter. Figure 8-11 shows a cycle region defined for eight measures. Because I'm performing live and not recording anything further than the cycle region, I defined

Figure 8-10
A song project with several tracks set up for switching sound effects while performing live

I. HENRY SARMIENTO II: SIMPLIFY YOUR SETUP

"You can simplify performance with a laptop and an audio interface," says L. Henry Sarmiento II, a sound technician and producer at Herbie Herbert's Sy Klopps Studio in San Francisco. "Let's say your instrument is connected to a PowerBook using an audio interface for input and output, with quarter-inch cable going to a direct box on the stage for the sound engineer to use for the house sound, which the audience hears, and the monitor system, which you as the performer hear on the stage through a monitor speaker or in-ear monitor. Not only can you dispense with an amplifier, cleaning up the stage, but you can also perform with your own playback loops or even an entire rhythm track for a song. GarageBand is not as professional as, say, having an engineer under the stage with a Pro Tools system set up with the entire show, and multiple outputs for house and monitor, as Madonna might do, but you can get great sounds with it."

the cycle region at the beginning of the timeline out to the start of the ninth measure.

Using MidiKeys (as shown in Figure 8-11), I can record a different performance with the same drum kit repeatedly, adding a new layer with each performance, and doing it

live using my laptop's keyboard. Starting with a single layer of simple percussion, I can build with improvisational performances on each individual part of a drum kit. You can do this live on a stage with any Software Instrument, turning yourself into a one-person band.

Figure 8-11
Using a cycle region to perform a loop live, adding new performances with each loop

PART III

In Search of the Lost Chord

Editing Tracks

In This Chapter

Editing Real Instrument performances • Editing and transposing Real Instrument loops • Editing Software Instrument loops and performances • Editing Software Instrument notes and fixing the timing • Transposing Software Instrument regions • Editing Software Instrument controller information

Do you know why you never hear a bum note in today's recordings? Mistakes and bum notes (also known as "clams" in the music industry) can be removed almost as easily as deleting typos from a text document.

Editing music wasn't always as easy as digital technology now makes it. The days of using a sharp knife to cut sections from a tape and then splicing the segments back together again are long gone. But the mindset is still prevalent: GarageBand offers the ability to split and join regions, as well as cut, copy, and paste segments of recorded music (as described in Chapter 3).

In this chapter, I describe how you can use cut, copy, and paste to change the notes you played. With the Track Editor, you can view the music in a region as if through a microscope, viewing either the actual notes in a Software Instrument track (displayed as dots and dashes on a timeline grid, similar to a player piano roll), or the waveform of a Real Instrument track.

OPENING THE TRACK EDITOR

To open the Track Editor, select the track you want to edit and click the Track Editor button (the one with the scissors). The Track Editor appears below the transport buttons, and has its own zoom slider. You can also open the Track Editor by double-clicking the track in the timeline.

Depending on the type of track, you see either a note-by-note representation of a Software Instrument, as shown in Figure 9-1, or the waveform of a Real Instrument, as shown in Figure 9-2.

With both kinds of tracks, you can move the region forward (to the right) or backward (to the left) in the timeline. You can zoom in to see larger notes or a more detailed waveform by dragging the Track Editor's zoom slider, located in the lower-left corner.

▼ Tip

When you move the playhead in the Track Editor (either by dragging it or by playing the song), the timeline in the main GarageBand window scrolls with the movement, and vice versa: moving the playhead in the Timeline window also scrolls the Track Editor window. You can unlock the playheads in the Timeline and the Track Editor so that only one window scrolls with the playback head, and you can see a different part of the song in the Track Editor than in the Timeline. To unlock the playheads, click the playhead lock button (refer to Figure 9-2) so that the two playhead pointers are not lined up. Click it again to line up the playhead pointers and resynchronize the Track Editor and the Timeline window.

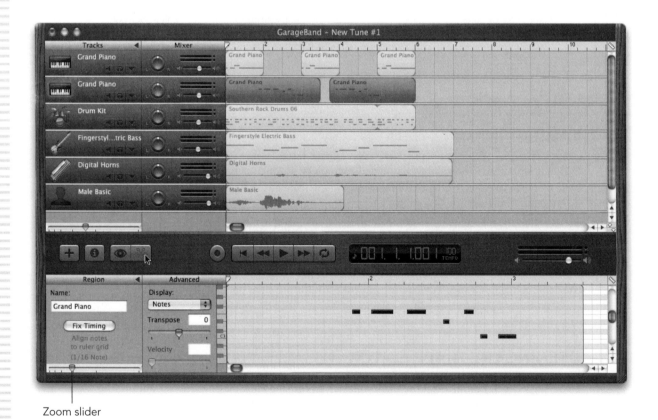

Zoom slider

Figure 9-1
The Track Editor (bottom portion of window) shows a region from the selected Software Instrument track

Playhead lock button

Figure 9-2
The Track Editor shows a region from the selected Real Instrument track

EDITING REAL INSTRUMENT TRACKS

You can edit Real Instrument tracks by cutting or copying any portion of the waveform in the region, or move the region to a different place in the timeline. For example, you can do the following:

- **Line up a recording to match the beat.** You can drag a region in the Track Editor to precisely adjust its location in the song.

- **Delete sections of the recording.** Don't like a small part of the region you recorded? You can simply delete it without disturbing the rest of the region.

- **Copy sections of the recording to other parts of the song.** You can cut or copy parts of a region and paste them in other regions of the same track, or in other Real Instrument tracks. For example, you can copy a guitar part you recorded and paste it into another track that is set up to sound like a sax, so that the guitar part sounds sax-like. You can even paste a region on top of another part of the same region, shortening the latter part.

Rather than deleting an entire region from a track, you can delete a portion of a region that has bad notes, leaving the rest of the region intact and still synchronized to the timeline.

Copying and pasting regions

To copy and paste sections of a Real Instrument region, follow these steps:

1. **Select a Real Instrument region.**

   Click on a region in a Real Instrument track, or click on the track itself to select the entire track.

2. **Open the Track Editor by clicking the Track Editor button (or double-click the selected region).**

   The selected region (or regions, if you selected an entire track) appears in the Track Editor.

3. **Select a section of a Real Instrument region in the Track Editor.**

   Select a section by dragging a selection rectangle with the crosshairs pointer, as shown in Figure 9-3.

4. **Choose Edit ➔ Copy to copy the section, choose Edit ➔ Cut to cut it, or choose Edit ➔ Delete to delete it.**

   If you cut or delete a section, it disappears, leaving the rest of the track locked in the same position in the timeline, as shown in Figure 9-4; by doing this you can delete small sections without disturbing the rest of the performance.

5. **To paste a copied or cut section, move the playhead to the new location in the Track Editor and choose Edit ➔ Paste.**

   You can zoom out first to see more of the track if you need to.

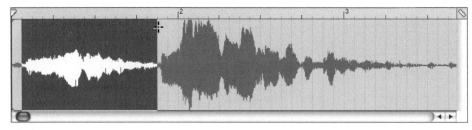

Figure 9-3
Selecting a portion of a Real Instrument region

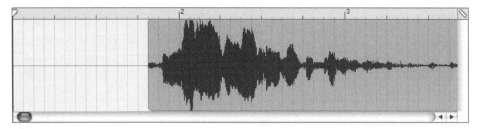

Figure 9-4
After cutting or deleting the selected portion, the rest of the region is still locked in the timeline.

A CUT AND PASTE IN THE LIFE

Perhaps the most famous "cut" and "paste" in the history of pop music is "A Day in the Life" (Lennon/McCartney) by the Beatles. At the stage of recording the take that would be used on the album *Sgt. Pepper*, the Beatles still had no idea what they would do for the song's middle section of 24 measures. "To mark out the place where the item would go," writes Beatles recording historian Mark Lewisohn in *The Complete Beatles Chronicles* (Harmony Books, New York, NY; 1992), "they had Mal Evans count out the bars, one to 24, his voice plastered with tape echo and backed by a tinkling piano, and to flag the end of this section an alarm clock was sounded." (You can hear this version on the *Anthology Vol. 2* CD.) Nearly a month later the Beatles and Sir George Martin brought together a 40-piece orchestra. An orchestral build-up, proposed by Paul McCartney, was recorded in Abbey Road's Studio One by Geoff Emerick while Paul and Sir George Martin conducted the orchestra. This part was then "pasted" over (actually spliced into) the 24 bars, leaving only the sound of the alarm clock from the backing-track recording (which, by happy coincidence, appears before the line "Woke up, fell out of bed").

Transposing Real Instrument loops

The Track Editor also lets you transpose any Real Instrument loop region to a different key without changing the rest of the song. This works only with Real Instrument *loops*, not your own recordings. You may want to create dissonance or tension in a song by using a loop in a different key to offset the music in the original key. The results may not be as good as choosing a Real Instrument loop that's in the appropriate key, but it's worth a try if you don't mind experimenting.

To transpose a Real Instrument loop region, follow these steps:

1. **Select the Real Instrument loop.**

   Click on a region in a Real Instrument track, or click on the track itself to select the entire track.

2. **Open the Track Editor by clicking the Track Editor button (or double-click the selected region).**

   The selected region (or regions, if you selected an entire track) appears in the Track Editor.

3. **Click the triangle to the left of the Track Editor's beat ruler to open the Advanced section.**

   The Advanced section, which appears to the left of the timeline in the Track Editor, as shown in Figure 9-5, offers the Transpose slider.

4. **Drag the Transpose slider in the Track Editor to transpose the region up or down in pitch.**

   If you prefer, you can type the number of semitones in the Transpose field above the slider (a semitone is the smallest measure of difference between two pitches, either a half step up or down in a scale).

▼ Note

Changes you make in the Track Editor window do not affect original loops — just the versions you added to your song.

Shifting regions in time

You can move a Real Instrument region forward (to the right) or backward (to the left) in the timeline by simply dragging it. Drag the region in the Track Editor rather than in the timeline view for more precise results.

As you drag, your cursor turns into a double arrow pointing left and right. You can align the region more precisely in the Track Editor using the grid as a guide. GarageBand duplicates the beat ruler in the Track Editor, and the grid

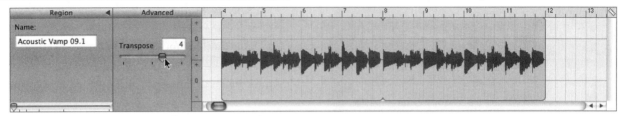

Figure 9-5
Transposing a Real Instrument loop in the Track Editor

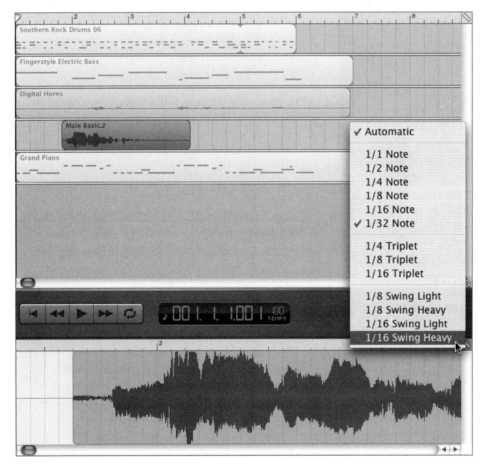

Figure 9-6
Setting the Track Editor grid to a different note value

TAKING A LOOP UP THE SCALE

Let's say you picked a Real Instrument guitar loop in the key of C, and you want to use the same loop two more times but raise the scale to D, and then E. Start by dragging the loop into a track, then copy the loop and paste it twice, so that you have three versions of the loop in a row. Double-click the second version to open the Track Editor with the selected loop, and transpose that version by 2 semitones to change it to the key of D. Click the third version so that it is selected in the Track Editor, and transpose that version by 4 semitones to the key of E. You now have a nice progression, C-D-E, using the same loop. You can create complex music from simple loops.

notes of a Software Instrument track (performance or loop), including the note's duration, pitch, velocity, and location in the timeline. You can also transpose an entire region to a different key, and fix the timing of notes automatically.

When you open a Software Instrument region in the Track Editor (refer to Figure 9-1), it looks like an old-style piano roll with holes that serve as instructions to a player piano. The notes are rectangular and very precise: the left edge of each note indicates where the note starts in the timeline, and the right edge indicates where it stops. If you use a MIDI keyboard with velocity-sensitive keys, GarageBand also shows each note's velocity, which is how hard you pressed the key. Notes played lightly (softly) are light gray, and those played more forcefully (loudly) are darker.

lines up with the beat ruler, so you can align musical regions precisely to the beat. The timeline and Track Editor both offer the ability to snap these regions into place in the grid: to turn it on, choose Control ➜ Snap to Grid. You can set the grid to different note values in the time measure, such as quarter notes, eighth notes, sixteenth notes, thirty-second notes, quarter-note triplets, eighth-note triplets, and so on. To set the grid to a different note value, click the grid button in the upper-right corner of the Track Editor's beat ruler, as shown in Figure 9-6, and then choose a grid value from the menu. In addition to the note values, you can set the grid to Automatic so that the grid becomes more detailed as you zoom in or out with the Track Editor zoom slider.

EDITING SOFTWARE INSTRUMENT TRACKS

You probably won't truly appreciate the value of playing a Software Instrument until you realize how easy it is to edit the recordings. The Track Editor lets you change the actual

Editing the notes played

The Track Editor lets you change almost everything in a Software Instrument recording or loop.

COMPOSING IN THE TRACK EDITOR

What if you want to add a guitar chord but you don't know the first thing about how to play a guitar chord (and you don't have a guitar, anyway)? You could borrow a section of a Software Instrument guitar loop that plays a chord (any chord, really), and then change the pitch of each note of the chord by dragging the notes in the Track Editor. You can also click inside the Track Editor window to create notes at different pitches. You may find it easier to "hunt and peck" in the Track Editor — clicking to make notes — rather than performing with a MIDI keyboard, because you don't have to do it in real performance time. You can adjust each note to your heart's content.

Changing the duration of a note

Drag the right edge of the note to lengthen or shorten it. If you have the Snap to Grid option turned on in the Control menu (choose Control ➜ Snap to Grid or press Command-G), the note's edges snap to the lines in the beat ruler as you drag. For example, in Figure 9-7, I drag a Grand Piano note to extend it into measure 11.

 Tip

> When you change a note in a region that has been extended as a loop (as described in Chapter 3), the notes in the repeated extensions are also changed automatically, preserving the integrity of the looping region.

Changing a note's starting point

Drag the note itself left or right, using the timeline grid as a guide, as shown in Figure 9-8. Click anywhere in the note *except* the right edge to select the note and drag it.

Changing a note's pitch

Drag the note up or down. The vertical position of the note in the grid shows the note's pitch, as it would appear on a piano (a piano keyboard is displayed along the left edge of the timeline as a guide).

Selecting and changing multiple notes at once

Drag a selection rectangle around two or more notes, as shown in Figure 9-9. The green-shaded selection rectangle turns every note it touches green, which indicates that they are selected. Any change you make to a single note is also made to the other selected notes. For example, if you drag one note up to raise its pitch, the other notes also move up in pitch by the same increment.

Changing a note's velocity

You may have to first click the triangle to the left of the Track Editor's beat ruler to open the Advanced section, which offers the Velocity slider. Then drag the Velocity slider from left to right to change from low velocity (a soft touch) to high velocity (a hard slam), and vice versa. The note becomes lighter (softer) or darker (harder) as you drag the slider. Hold down the Shift key while dragging to change the velocity by finer increments.

Fixing the timing of notes

You don't have to be good with a Software Instrument or even play all your notes in time to the music: you can fix the notes you played so that they match the beat. Professional musicians may even miss the beat when using the

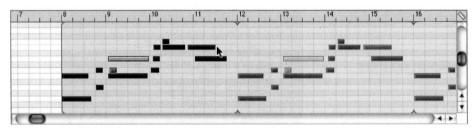

Figure 9-7

Extending the duration of a single note of a Software Instrument

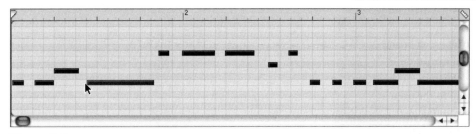

Figure 9-8
Changing the starting point of a Software Instrument note

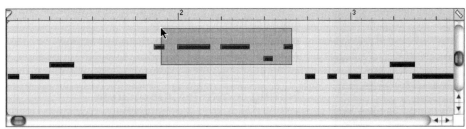

Figure 9-9
Selecting multiple Software Instrument notes at once

onscreen keyboard or MidiKeys; and of course, if you are like me and have no talent at all with a keyboard, this feature is a godsend.

To fix the timing with the Track Editor, first select the Software Instrument track and region, and then open the Track Editor. Click the Fix Timing button, which is in the Region section of the Track Editor (on the left side). After clicking the Fix Timing button, all the notes in the region are automatically moved to the nearest grid position. (If you don't like the results, you can always choose Edit ➜ Undo.) You can also drag notes manually if you want any of them to be slightly behind the beat.

Transposing to a new key

GarageBand can automatically change an entire song's Software Instrument tracks to a different key; find the

setting in the Key pop-up menu in the Master Track Info window. Click any track and choose Track Info ➜ Master Track from the pop-up menu to reach the Master Track Info window.

But what if you just want to change one Software Instrument region to a different key? With the Track Editor, you can transpose any Software Instrument region to a different key without changing the rest of the song.

Another reason for transposing only certain regions is to change tracks to a new key based on a Real Instrument recording of a different key. You can't change a Real Instrument recording, but you *can* transpose the Software Instrument tracks to match the key of the Real Instrument recording.

SWINGING OR GROOVING TO THE BEAT

Nothing is more unnerving to a bass player than to hear that the bass notes are not "behind" the beat or "in front of" the beat. It means that the bass notes are too dead-on the beat and, as a result, the bass part doesn't "swing" or "groove" or something. Funny thing is, if you want the bass notes to be "behind" the beat, you actually want them to be slightly *ahead* (forward, or to the right) in the timeline — you want the beat to sound first, then the bass note slightly afterwards, so that the bass is late for the party, not early. So if you are like me and can't play bass to save your life, you may have added bass notes using some other instrument or a bass loop. If you used a Real Instrument track or loop, you can shift the entire region in time slightly by dragging in the Track Editor, and lo and behold: your bass notes might just fall in the right position after such a tweak.

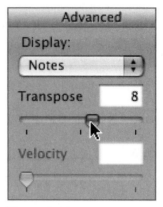

Figure 9-10
Transposing a Software Instrument region

To transpose a Software Instrument region in the Track Editor, drag the Transpose slider as shown in Figure 9-10. (You may have to first click the triangle to the left of the Track Editor's beat ruler to open the Advanced section, which offers the Transpose slider.)

As you drag the slider, the region is transposed up or down in pitch. If you prefer, type the number of semitones in the Transpose field. A *semitone* is the smallest measure of difference between two pitches — the tonal difference between a black and white piano key.

 Tip

To transpose a region up an octave, type **12** for the number of semitones (or drag the slider until it says 12). To transpose a region down an octave, type **–12** (or drag the slider until it says –12). This is similar to counting 12 piano keys (black and white) to move up or down an octave on a piano.

Editing controller information

If you use a USB MIDI keyboard with a pitch bend wheel (a control that bends notes up and down), a modulation wheel that changes the Software Instrument sound, or a sustain pedal that sustains the sound, you can edit the controller information in the Track Editor — which you may want to do if you overdid the pitch bend or sustained a note too long. The *controller information* is the set of MIDI instructions related to specific types of controllers (such as pitch bend, sustain, and modulation) that is applied to the sound.

Select the Software Instrument region and open the Track Editor. You may have to click the triangle to the left of the Track Editor's beat ruler to open the Advanced section, which offers the Display pop-up menu.

Choose the type of controller information from the Display pop-up menu, as shown in Figure 9-11. Any movements recorded for the control appear in the timeline view of the Track Editor. The movements are shown as lines connected by control points, similar to a volume curve in the timeline's Master Volume track, as shown in Figure 9-12.

OF TELEPHONES AND SYNTHESIZERS

The pitch bend wheel, or something similar that could change the pitch (a.k.a. tone) of a note, was part of the very first electronic musical instrument, invented by Elisha Gray in 1876 as a by-product of his telephone technology. In fact, Bell Telephone might have been called Gray Telephone if Gray had gone one hour earlier to the patent office, where Alexander Graham Bell was applying for his patent. But electronic music might have been delayed for another decade or two. Gray's Musical Telegraph used a self-vibrating electromagnetic circuit to create a basic single-note oscillator with steel reeds whose oscillations were transmitted over a telephone line by electromagnets. Gray also built a simple loudspeaker consisting of a vibrating diaphragm in a magnetic field to make the oscillator audible. His earliest version contained enough single-tone oscillators to play two octaves, and later models were equipped with a simple tone wheel control that is the forerunner of today's pitch bend wheel. The next step in the evolution of electronic instruments wouldn't occur until physicist William Du Bois Duddell invented the Singing Arc in 1899, which linked a carbon arc lamp to a keyboard that varied the voltage and created controllable audible frequencies. To learn more about the history of electronic instruments, see "120 Years of Electronic Music," an ongoing project by Simon Crab (`http://www.obsolete.com/120_years/intro.html`).

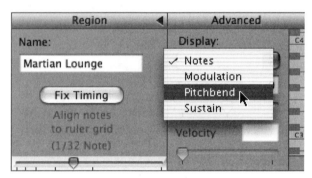

Figure 9-11
Choosing the pitch bend controller from the Display pop-up menu

The curve created by the pitch bend wheel is actually composed of points and lines in a typically stepped formation (as shown in Figure 9-12). You can smooth it out by dragging the control points in the Track Editor's timeline. You can move points up or down to change their value, or move them left and right to change the time in the song in which they occur.

Add a new control point to a line by Command-clicking a segment that has no point, or draw a new line by Command-clicking an empty area. (When you Command-click, a pencil icon appears for pointing and clicking.)

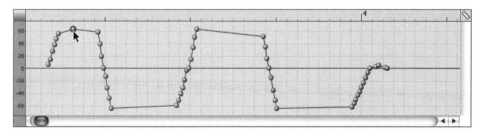

Figure 9-12
Editing the control points for a performance that used the pitch bend wheel

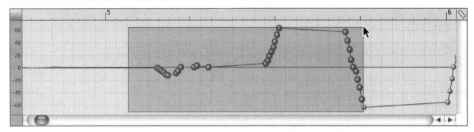

Figure 9-13
Selecting a set of pitch bend control points to move or delete all at once

To delete a control point, select the point and press the Delete key; the line adjusts automatically.

Select a range of points by dragging a selection rectangle around them, as shown in Figure 9-13, and then delete or move the points all at once.

The effect of your changes depends on the controller. For example, removing selected points of a pitch bend control

(as shown in Figure 9-13) smoothed the performance's transition from one semitone to the next as it changed in pitch.

Wow, you're modifying the curve produced by a MIDI pitch bend wheel just like a professional electronic music expert. The world of digital audio effects is at your fingertips, and the information is just a chapter away.

10

All About Effects

In This Chapter

Setting effects for individual tracks and the master track • Modifying characteristics of the
Software Instrument sound generator • Simulating the sound of different amplifiers with
Real and Software Instruments • Using standard and special audio effects,
including AU effects • Saving and deleting custom effect presets

Understanding audio effects (as opposed to *sound effects* such as horses galloping, doors closing, and
fists punching) is a process of learning a new language. Studio talk presents a cornucopia of strange
terms (such as reverb, flanger, phaser, mixer, equalizer, and overdrive) not unlike the terms we use
to describe computing — words borrowed from elsewhere, such as physics or mathematics, or
made up on the spot as the effect was invented.

This chapter helps you learn this new lingo of audio effects and describes what they do, so that you
can use them wisely to sweeten your sounds. GarageBand offers a set of standard effects and lets
you use compatible plug-in effects from other effects vendors.

SIR GEORGE MARTIN: ON THE ORIGINS OF THE WORD *FLANGE*

One word for an effect, invented at the spur of the moment, is *flange*. In his autobiography, *All You Need is Ears* (St. Martin's Press, New York, NY; 1979), Beatles producer Sir George Martin once replied to John Lennon's query about how his voice was altered by a technique that had no name (and is now called artificial double tracking, or ADT), "Well John, it's a double-bifurcated sploshing flange." Lennon, guessing correctly that Martin was putting him on by speaking in gobbledygook, began using the term regularly, telling engineers in his deadpan Liverpool accent to "just flange it" whenever he needed the effect. Thus, "flanging" entered the lexicon to describe a variation of ADT, in which the tape speed is slightly changed over time to make the copied sound slightly out of tune. It is similar to *phasing*, in which the sound is played out of phase with the original to create a "whooshing" sound (and which came first, the phaser in the studio or the phaser in *Star Trek*?). Today a *flanger* effect is similar to a *chorus*, in which copies of the sound are played back a bit out of tune from the original, offering an effect similar to what Lennon was asking for.

▼ Tip

GarageBand Jam Pack, available separately from Apple (`www.apple.com/ilife/garageband/accessories.html`) for $99 as of this writing, provides over 100 extra presets for built-in effects, including Amp Simulation presets for different amplifier sounds. If you are serious about using effects in GarageBand, this pack is essential. As I describe effects in this chapter, I also include information about presets available in this pack.

SETTING EFFECTS FOR TRACKS

The familiar blues song "You Don't Love Me" (by Willie Cobb) seems to take off in the hands of Al Kooper and Stephen Stills on the classic album *Super Session*, not just because it is set to a rock beat. It's the creative use of the *phaser* effect on all the tracks that makes the song sound like a rocket taking off.

Vocalists have recorded in bathrooms and churches to get the right echoing sound. John Lennon wanted his lead vocal on the Beatles song "Tomorrow Never Knows" to sound like it came from the top of a windswept mountain, so the producer had to record Lennon's vocals by running the microphone cable into a Hammond organ and recording with another microphone through the organ's special Leslie loudspeaker that produces a swirling effect.

You don't have to resort to buying a Hammond organ with a Leslie loudspeaker, bending the rules of physics, or moving your equipment into the bathroom or even out to a cathedral to get that lofty church sound. You can use effects on any track or set effects for all the tracks by using the master track. When you save your song, all the effects you set in individual tracks and in the master track are

"WAH-WAH, YOU MADE ME SUCH A BIG STAR" (GEORGE HARRISON)

If you think that audio effects are for cliché-ridden groups like the Strawberry Alarm Clock, think again. Innovative musicians have gone to great lengths to get the sounds they want. Jimi Hendrix employed all kinds of studio tricks and guitar effects; Eric Clapton mastered the *wah-wah* pedal during his highly successful stint with Cream, and used it to great effect on "While My Guitar Gently Weeps" for the Beatles.

saved with it. When you save a Real Instrument or Software Instrument as a custom instrument, the effects you set for the track used for that instrument are saved with the instrument so that you can instantly re-create the same track effects and instrument sound in another song.

Setting effects for a single track

Setting effects on a track-by-track basis gives you control over how effects are used with the instrument sound. You might, for example, want to add reverb to a piano track but not to a guitar track. You might also want to define a set of effects and an instrument sound as a custom instrument to use in multiple songs. To do this, you need to assign the effects to a track first, then save the instrument and track effects as a custom instrument.

To assign effects to a track, click the track header and click the *i* button for Track Info (or choose Track → Show Track Info), and then click the triangle next to Detail to reveal the effects and their settings. Each effect has a slider or pop-up menu in the detail section, as shown in Figure 10-1.

The two pop-up menus on the left side set by default to "None" let you pick two different effects from a wide variety of effects that include amp simulation, bass and treble reduction, and chorus, as well as an entire set of Audio Unit (AU) effects (in Figure 10-1, I picked Automatic Filter and AUMultibandCompressor as the effects for these pop-up menus). Audio Units are special audio plug-ins described in "Audio Unit effects" in this chapter.

All of these settings are available for both Real Instruments and Software Instruments, with the exception of Gate, which is used only with Real Instruments. Of course, setting a drum to play with an amp simulator might produce a weird result, but you can certainly try it.

The echo and reverb effects for individual tracks are based on the echo and reverb settings for the master track — see the next section about setting effects for all tracks. If you turn off echo or reverb in the master track, the effects are not available for individual tracks.

The pop-up menus on the right side of the Track Info window provide presets for the effects and also let you control the settings manually and make your own presets. After choosing an effect on the left side, you can choose a preset (or Manual to manually change the settings) from the pop-up menu on the right side. You can modify a preset's settings or change the effects settings manually by clicking the pencil icon to the right of the preset pop-up menu (see Figure 10-1); a window appears with settings for the effect, as shown in Figure 10-2 (the Equalizer window), and the preset changes to Manual. When you finish making changes, close the settings window.

▼ **Caution**

After choosing a different preset or making changes to a preset (or to Manual), a warning dialog box appears that asks, "Do you want to save the file before switching to a new one?" Click Save to save the previous settings as a preset, as described later in this chapter. This is a precaution in case you change settings that you really didn't mean to change. You can click Cancel to cancel the changes, or Save to save and provide a name for the previous settings (to recall them later) so that you can use the new settings. You can click Don't Save to throw out the previous settings.

Although your track effects settings are saved with the song automatically, you can save your effects settings as custom instruments to use with other songs, as described later in this chapter.

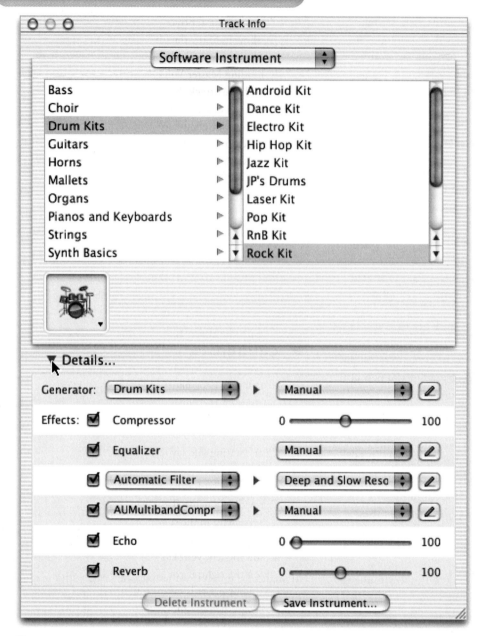

Figure 10-1
Setting effects for a Software Instrument track in the Detail section of the Track Info window

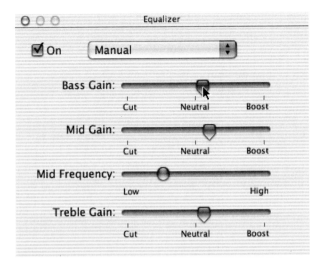

Figure 10-2
Changing the settings manually for the Equalizer effect

Setting effects for all tracks

You may want to set an effect that works on all the tracks, without setting it explicitly for each track. You can also control the uppermost limit for effects used on individual tracks, in case you discover late in the process that you have used too many effects at once and you need to reduce the intensity of the combined effects.

The master track decides the uppermost volume of all the tracks, and turns on the Echo and Reverb effects for all the tracks. It also lets you apply other effects to all the tracks, and offers presets for different kinds of music and simulated environments. For example, you can choose a Stadium Rock preset such as Large Arena or Stadium Empty, or a Jazz preset such as Jazz Club or Lounge.

Every song has a master track, usually hidden until you explicitly show it. Show the Master Track by choosing Track ➡ Show Master Track. The master track appears with the heading Master Volume at the bottom on the timeline as the last track. You can then double-click the Master Volume header, or click the Track Info button (with the *i* icon), or choose Track ➡ Show Track Info, to open the Track Info window for the master track. You can choose a preset, and either modify that preset or create your own by clicking the triangle next to Details to reveal the detailed section, as shown in Figure 10-3.

▼ **Caution**

The standard Echo and Reverb effects should be turned on in the master track. If you turn them *off* in the master track, they do not work in the individual tracks, either.

You can apply the effects across all tracks or turn off certain effects for all tracks. As shown in Figure 10-3, I chose the Hip Hop preset Deep Thump for all the tracks, which not only turns on Echo and Reverb but also provides overriding settings for the Equalizer and Compressor (overriding any settings made in the individual tracks).

Master track settings are saved with the song automatically, but you can also save your master track settings as a custom preset (to use with other songs) by clicking Save Master and providing a name. The preset appears in the Master Track presets menu in the submenu of the category you already selected. For example, if you had already selected Hip Hop on the left, your custom preset is saved in that submenu on the right; if you had selected Stadium Rock on the left, your preset is saved in the Stadium Rock submenu. You can then use the preset for any song.

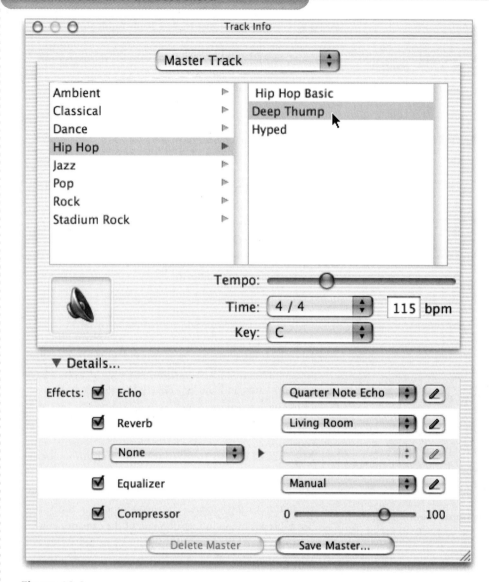

Figure 10-3
Setting effects in the master track that affect all tracks

GENERATING THE SOUND

Software Instruments use MIDI instructions to generate the digital sound wave that produces the sound you hear. MIDI information is *performance* information. Each note you play is converted to an instruction, which, like the holes on a piano roll for a player piano, tells the software what note to play. Each MIDI instruction includes information such as what type of sound to use, the note's pitch and duration, its velocity (how hard the note was struck), whether a pitch bend wheel was used to bend the note, and so on. To control the type of sound for a Software Instrument, you can adjust the Generator effect. You can change *any* playback aspect of a Software Instrument, right down to adjusting the notes in the Track Editor.

Real Instruments are recordings stored as digital sound waves (there is no performance information). The effects that work on Real Instruments modify the sound wave itself. A Real Instrument "sound" is really a set of effects settings applied to a waveform. The Real Instrument choice you make when you create a Real Instrument track is actually a set of digital effects and settings saved with a name for easy selection. You can record without any effects or sound treatment, and then add effects and change the characteristics of the sound later.

GarageBand lists the effects in the Details section of the Track Info window in the order in which they work. For a Software Instrument, the Generator creates the initial sound, and then the Compressor performs its thing, and after that the Equalizer, and so forth. Effects are applied to Real Instruments the same way. The order in which effects are applied can affect the resulting sound. GarageBand gives you some flexibility by providing two open pop-up menus (usually set to None) so that you can apply one effect, and then another on top of that one. For example, if you turn on Bass Reduction in the first open pop-up menu, and then turn on Distortion in the second open pop-up menu, the bass is reduced *before* the sound is distorted.

Software Instrument Generator

MIDI allows you to assign an instrument sound, which in MIDI parlance is a *program* or a *patch,* and then play with that sound. GarageBand is a software *multitimbral* synthesizer, which means it can play multiple instrument sounds at the same time. In GarageBand, the sound generators are available in the Generator pop-up menu in the Details section of the Track Info window, as shown in Figure 10-4.

The settings you have for your sound generator depend on which generator you choose. The pop-up menu to the right of the Generator pop-up lets you choose any presets associated with the Generator, and you can change the settings manually. For example, if you choose Piano as your generator, you can adjust the volume, cutoff, and release settings. If you choose a more complex generator, such as Digital Basic (a basic digital synthesizer), you can adjust a range of settings from volume, mix, and tuning to timbre, attack, decay, and harmonics, as shown in Figure 10-5.

 Tip

You can also add professional-quality software synthesizers and instrument generators from other sources, such as Native Instruments (`www.native-instruments.com/`) or macmusic.org (`http://macmusic.org/softs/softcat.php/lang/EN/id/7037/`) that use the Audio Unit (AU) format — see the section "Audio Unit effects" in this chapter.

Amplifier Simulation

While your guitar gently weeps, you can simulate the tone of various amplifiers using your Mac and GarageBand without having to spend a penny or pound on a special-effects pedal.

The sound of the amplifier is an important part of the overall electric guitar tone. The Amp Simulation effect lets

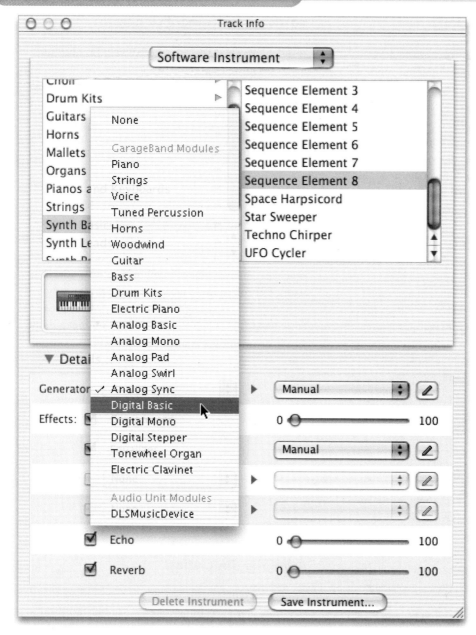

Figure 10-4
Choosing a sound generator for a Software Instrument

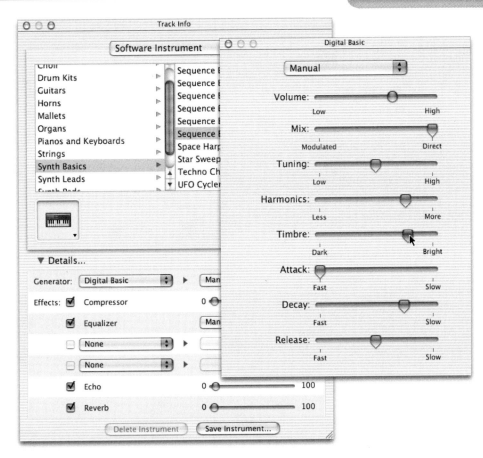

Figure 10-5
Manually adjusting the preset for the Digital Basic sound generator

you change the sound of either Real Instrument or Software Instrument tracks based on the known characteristics of typical guitar amplifiers. Many of the Real Instrument settings in the Guitars category already include amplifier simulation. To see if a track uses it, click the track header and click the *i* button for Track Info (or choose Track → Show Track Info). Click the Details triangle to see the

effects settings. If included, Amp Simulation will appear in one of the two pop-up menus for additional effect.

You can add the Amp Simulation effect by choosing it from one of the two open pop-up menus in the Details section of the Track Info window, and choosing a preset from the pop-up menu to the right, as shown in Figure 10-6.

Figure 10-6
Choosing a preset for the Amp Simulation effect for a Real Instrument guitar sound

To adjust the Amp Simulation preset, follow these steps:

1. **Click the pencil button next to the effect preset pop-up menu to open the Amp Simulation window.**

2. **Choose an option for Model — the type of amplifier sounds, which are loosely defined as British Gain, British Clean, American Gain, or American Clean.**

   The difference between "clean" and "gain" (or "crunch") is related to the number of *gain stages*. Each gain stage is like a pump, or miniature amplifier; the more pumps, the greater the potential amount of distortion. "Clean" means very few gain stages with very little (if any) distortion. "Crunch" means more gain stages and more distortion. The American types are loosely based on Fender amps, while the British types are loosely based on Marshall amps. The Fender and Marshall circuits are tailored differently. Fender amps are geared toward providing clean and chunky tones at clean and early-overdrive levels (*overdrive* is a circuit that boosts the signal and/or adds distortion). Marshall amps are best at low-to-middle and crunchy rock tones, played at medium- to high-overdrive levels. (This is overgeneralizing, of course, as both amplifier manufacturers offer multiple models spanning a wide range of frequency-response characteristics.)

3. **Adjust the settings manually by clicking and dragging the sliders.**

   Drag the sliders to adjust the preset settings for Pre Gain, Low, Mid, and High tone controls, Presence, Master, and Output Level, as shown in Figure 10-7. Pre Gain pumps up the volume overall, while Low, Mid, and High boost the low (bass), mid-range, and high (treble) frequencies.

If you are playing your guitar connected to GarageBand, you can hear the changes to the effect settings immediately.

This is the preferred method, as you can never really know what it's going to sound like until you plug it in and try it.

▼ **Tip**

You may want to record without any amplifier simulation so that you can then try different amp simulation settings on the same recording. To get a clean, unaffected recording of your instrument (or voice), at the top of the Track Info window, choose Basic Track in the left column and choose No Effects in the right column. You can click the Details triangle to open the Details pane and verify that no other effects are applied, and that Echo and Reverb are set to 0 (zero). This setting is also useful if you are using an external amp simulator or synthesizer and recording the sound coming through that device, or sending GarageBand's output (for monitoring) through an external amp and preamp with its own settings.

STANDARD EFFECTS

The Beach Boys were right when they sang "Good Vibrations" because that's what music is — the sensation of hearing audible vibrations conveyed to the ear by a medium such as air. The *frequency* of vibrations per second is how we measure pitch. The waves can fluctuate slowly and produce low-pitched sounds, or they can fluctuate rapidly and produce high-pitched sounds. The *amplitude* is a measurement of the amount of fluctuation in air pressure. Therefore, amplitude is perceived as loudness.

As these frequencies at different amplitudes travel through GarageBand (metaphorically speaking, of course), the effects that work with frequencies and amplitudes are applied sequentially — GarageBand lists the effects in the Details section of the Track Info window in the order in which they work. The order in which effects are applied can affect the resulting sound.

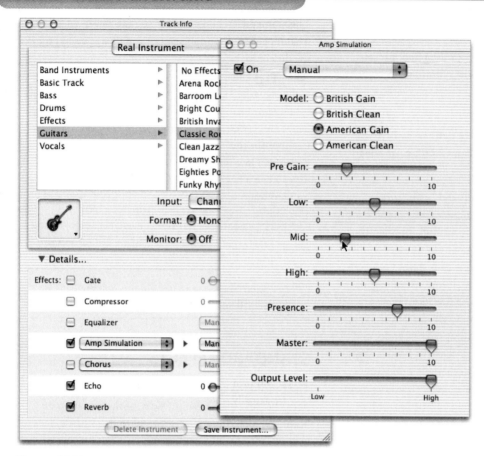

Figure 10-7
Manually adjusting the settings for the Amp Simulation effect

For a Software Instrument, the Generator creates the initial sound, and then the Compressor compresses the sound before the Equalizer boosts certain frequencies, and so on. Effects are applied to Real Instruments the same way. First a Gate (noise gate) limits the sound, then the Compressor compresses it, followed by the Equalizer, and so on. The best way to test effects and to see how they work together is to play your instrument while connected to Garage-Band, so that you can hear the changes immediately.

Gate and Compressor

The Gate and Compressor effects shape the music according to amplitude levels. The Gate limits the sound by passing only amplitude levels that are above a certain threshold, usually set to just above background noise to filter it out. Only Real Instrument tracks offer the Gate effect. The Gate can be set to close at a level that is just above the noise "floor" so that as soon as the main signal stops (the instrument stops playing or the singer stops singing), the Gate closes the input, reducing noise.

Where does the noise come from? Unwanted noise can be caused by air conditioners, fans, noisy computers, and other human factors in the environment, and the noise can make its way into your recording possibly without your knowledge — such as the rustling of paper and a chair squeaking as the Beatles recorded the piano chord at the very end of "A Day in the Life" (Lennon/McCartney). Mark Lewisohn, Beatles recording historian and author of *The Beatles Recording Sessions* (Harmony Books, New York, NY; 1988), mentions this and engineer Geoff Emerick's response years later, in 1987: "Actually the sound could have gone on a bit longer but in those days the speakers weren't able to reproduce it. So we thought there wasn't any more sound but there was — the compact disc proves it." Today, with CDs, you have to be more careful about noise from the recording environment, as you can hear everything. You also have to be aware of noise that can be generated by, or in, the recording/processing circuitry or storage medium. This problem is magnified with multitrack recording because the noise on each track accumulates and gets louder when you play all the tracks. This means that the volume of the noise can go well past audible and into the really annoying region. If you hear noise in a track, try using the Gate to eliminate it.

The slider (from 0 to 100) for the Gate corresponds approximately to the loudness of the noise level you are removing from the sound, but doesn't strictly match amplitude levels, so you have to listen as you adjust the Gate slider to see how much background noise is being filtered out. If the Gate is set too high, soft vocals and whispers may not pass through, so you want to set the Gate low enough to capture everything but also limit background noise.

The Compressor adds punch to a song to make it play better on speakers with a narrow dynamic range by decreasing the difference between the loudest and softest parts of the song. The Compressor reduces the dynamic range of an audio signal so that both the low and high amplitude sound waves are closer to a particular ideal level somewhere in-between. The slider (from 0 to 100) for the Compressor roughly corresponds to the amount of compression; a low amount reduces the dynamic range only a little, while a high amount reduces the dynamic range a lot. Pop songs were routinely compressed in the early 1960s to make them sound better on AM radios. Reducing the dynamic range also means that recording levels could be set higher, therefore improving the signal-to-noise performance. On the other hand, classical and jazz music, and a lot of acoustic music, are usually not compressed, at least not nearly as much as pop and rock music.

Equalizer

When you turn up the bass or treble on a stereo system, you are actually increasing the volume — or intensity — of certain frequencies while the music is playing. The Equalizer lets you fine-tune the sound spectrum frequencies in a more precise way than with Bass and Treble controls. It increases or decreases specific frequencies of the sound to raise or lower highs, lows, and midrange tones in the sound. The Equalizer does this with several band-pass filters all centered at different frequencies, and each filter offers controllable gain (the ability to boost the volume).

The Equalizer effect offers a pop-up menu with lots of presets from Add Bass Clarity to Vocal Presence. Each preset offers a different balance of frequencies designed to enhance the sound in certain ways. You can see how each preset controls the frequencies, or adjust the Equalizer effect settings manually by clicking the pencil icon next to the presets pop-up menu. The Equalizer offers four controls as shown in Figure 10-8:

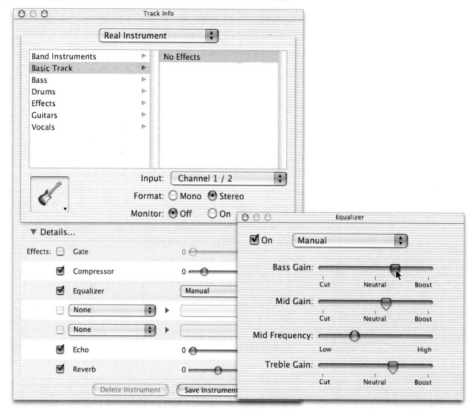

Figure 10-8
Manually adjusting the settings for the Equalizer effect

- **Bass Gain:** Using the slider, you can cut or boost the volume for the lowest frequencies or leave them neutral.

- **Mid Gain:** The slider lets you cut or boost the middle frequencies or leave them neutral. Most sounds that are audible to human hearing lie in this frequency range.

- **Mid Frequency:** This slider lets you shape the curve between high and low frequencies so that the middle frequencies are higher or lower in volume.

- **Treble Gain:** This slider lets you cut or boost the high frequencies or leave them neutral.

Echo and reverb

Hear that ringing tone after playing a note? Want to know why you can play the guitar just like ringing a bell (just like Johnny B. Goode)? What you are likely hearing is reverberation, or *reverb*. Hear the note again? That's *echo*.

Reverb re-creates the sound of an acoustic space by playing back many copies of the original signal at slightly varied times and volume levels. Reverberation is the result of the many reflections of a sound that occur in a room. Echo, on the other hand, plays back the original sound later in time and lower in volume (enough to be heard distinctly from the original). While it may seem that the two are similar, they are not, but they are often used together. With reverb, each delayed sound wave arrives in such a short period of time that we do not perceive each reflection as a copy of the original sound.

We hear reverb in large rooms and concert halls, so why do we need to add it to recorded music? Because many listening environments offer no reverb, such as headphones and car speakers, and a lack of reverb can sound dry and unnatural. You could record your guitar (or in my case, harmonica) through a miked amplifier in a concert hall or church, or simply add reverb. It is the most popular effect for guitars and other electric instruments; I routinely use a little reverb for harmonica tracks and playing harmonica live.

With Echo and Reverb, the slider (from 0 to 100) roughly corresponds to the amount of echo or reverb. As you slide the Echo slider higher, the echo itself is louder and more distinct. As you slide the Reverb slider higher, the reverberations are louder to the point where they seem to sustain the note itself.

SPECIAL EFFECTS

GarageBand offers a lot of cool special audio effects and even lets you add more. You can get a lot of interesting sounds using just the built-in effects and the professional Audio Unit (AU) effects. You can assign two effects in sequence using the open pop-up menus, and adjust the settings of those two effects using presets or manual adjustments in the pop-up menus to the right of the two open menus.

Built-in effects

Built-in effects include Amp Simulation (covered earlier in this chapter) and the following:

- **Treble Reduction:** Reduces the high (treble) frequencies and offers presets for Hard, Medium, Soft, and Ultra (soft).

- **Bass Reduction:** Reduces the low (bass) frequencies and offers presets for Hi Pass (reduces the emphasis of lower-frequency sounds, allowing higher-frequency sounds to pass through), Remove Bass, and Remove Deep Bass.

- **Distortion:** Lets you increase the Drive and Output Level to distort the sound waveform itself. You can also color the distortion's Tone from Dark to Bright, as shown in Figure 10-9.

- **Overdrive:** Lets you increase the Drive and Output Level to simulate tube amplifier distortion, while also coloring the Tone from Dark to Bright. Generally, Overdrive is better than Distortion for getting a great loud rock guitar sound.

- **Bitcrusher:** Lets you down-sample music for various listening environments or just to get that grungy, low-fi effect. Bitcrusher offers presets including AM Radio, Classic 8 Bit, Meet Atari, and Sample Rate Crusher. You can adjust Bitcrusher manually to raise or lower the bit resolution, which is number of bits for the sound (usually 16 for high quality), and the sample rate, which is the number of times per second the sound waveform is captured digitally (or *sampled*). CD-quality sound is sampled at a 44.100 kHz rate. Lower sample rates yield lower-quality sound.

- **Automatic Filter:** Lets you combine four different kinds of filters for widely varying effects. The presets range from Club Next Door and Deep and Slow Filter, to Fast Pulse, Resonance Filter, Soft Auto Wah, and Triple Offset Filter. You gotta hear these to understand how they work; physics descriptions would just get you more confused. You can manually adjust the Frequency and Resonance filters from low to high, the Intensity from Down to Off or Up & Down, and the Speed from slow to fast.

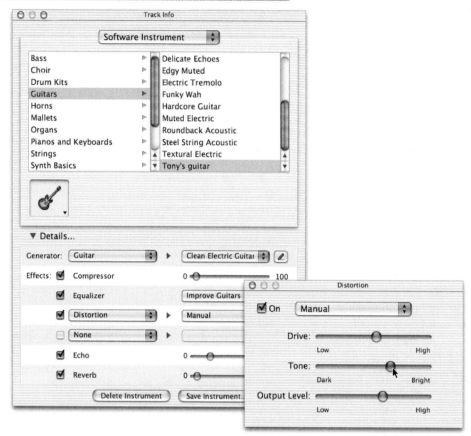

Figure 10-9
Manually adjusting the settings for the Distortion effect

○ **Chorus:** Makes the recording of a vocal track sound like two or more people singing in chorus or two instruments playing in unison. Two vocalists or instruments are not always playing in precise synchronization — there is some delay between the sounds they produce. In addition, the pitch of the two instruments or vocalists can deviate somewhat, despite careful tuning. Chorus adds a single delayed signal (echo) to the original input but varies the delay continuously between a minimum delay and maximum delay at a certain rate in order to reproduce the effect

of a chorus, which adds some thickness to the sound (often described as "lush" or "rich"). You can manually adjust the Intensity of the echo effect from low to high and the Speed of the delayed signal from slow to fast.

○ **Flanger:** Copies and plays back the sound slightly out of tune from the original signal, which is useful for double-tracking a vocal part to make one singer sound like two. Flanging has a very characteristic sound that many people refer to as a "whooshing" sound, similar to the sound of a jet plane flying overhead. The

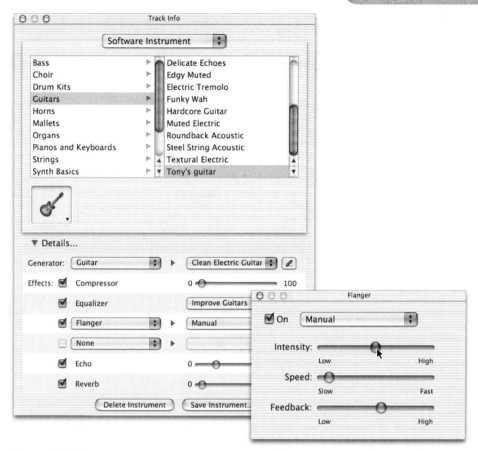

Figure 10-10
Manually adjusting the settings for the Flanger effect

Flanger comes with a wide variety of presets, from Dolphin Flange and Intergalactic Police (don't ask), to Laser Fire, Slow Sweep, Soft Flange, Stadium Flange, and Super Flange. You can also manually adjust the Intensity of flanging from low to high, the Speed of the delayed signal from slow to fast, and the Feedback effect from low to high, as shown in Figure 10-10.

- **Phaser:** Copies and plays back the sound slightly out of phase and filtered. Phasing is very similar to flanging in the way it combines the signal with its copy.

Phase shifting produces partial cancellations (where the signals cancel each other out) and partial enhancements, and can also cause something similar to a "whooshing" sound like a flanger. The Phaser offers presets ranging from Circle Phases and Funk Phase to Harmonic Filter, Rock Phaser, Singing Phase, Vocoder Phase, and Wild Phase (something I went through in my youth). You can manually adjust the Intensity of phase shifting from low to high, the Speed of the delayed signal from slow to fast, and the Feedback effect from low to high.

Tremolo: Repeats a single tone or alternates two tones rapidly to produce a tremulous, shaking sound. You can also turn on the Auto Panning to pan this effect so that it seems to revolve around the sound in space. This is where you find a preset for the Leslie Rotor speaker sound, as well as Fast Mono Tremolo, Deep Slow Pan, Soft Tremolo, and Ultra Pan. You can manually adjust the Intensity of the Tremolo effect from low to high, and the Speed of the alternating tones from slow to fast.

Auto Wah: Creates a "talking guitar" sound similar to a wah-wah pedal (put to great effect by Jimi Hendrix and many other guitar gods — to hear an example,

listen to Hendrix's "Still Raining Still Dreaming" or "Voodoo Chile," or Cream's "White Room"). This effect is simulated using a single band-pass filter with a center frequency that can be controlled and varied anywhere in the audio frequency spectrum as with parametric equalization (see the section "Audio Unit effects" in this chapter). The Auto Wah effect has presets ranging from Bass Snap and Crunch Wah, to Cry Baby, Filter Ducks, Hi Pass Autofilter, Static Peak, Strong Gate, and Wow. You can manually adjust the Auto Wah effect as shown in Figure 10-11, setting the Mode (Thick, Thin, Peak, or Classic 1 to 3), Sound

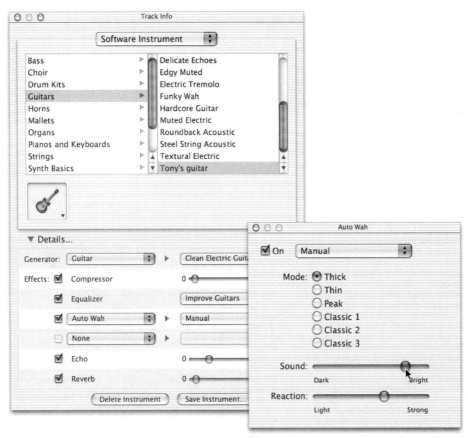

Figure 10-11
Manually adjusting the settings for the Auto Wah effect

(from dark to bright tones), and Reaction (from light to strong). For example, the Crunch Wah preset uses Thick Mode, a Bright Sound, and a medium-Strong Reaction, while the Cry Baby uses Classic 1 Mode, a medium-Dark Sound, and a medium Reaction.

Audio Unit effects

The two open pop-up menus in the Details section of the Track Info window offer not only GarageBand effects but also some professional effects inherited from a generation of professional audio applications on the Mac. All of the items listed under the grayed-out Audio Unit Effects text in the pop-up menus are effects that work with Audio Unit plug-ins that come with GarageBand, and you can add AU plug-ins from other sources. *Audio Units* are special audio plug-ins that conform to an Apple-defined specification and work with GarageBand, and are also supported by other professional audio applications on the Mac.

Tip

You can add professional-quality software synthesizers, instruments, and effects from other sources, such as Native Instruments (www.native-instruments.com/) or macmusic.org (http://macmusic.org/softs/softcat.php/lang/EN/id/7037/) that use the AU format. To add an AU plug-in, install the AU plug-in component file in the Macintosh HD/Library/Audio/Plug-Ins/Components/ directory. Start GarageBand, and when you use the Generator pop-up menu with a Software Instrument track, the AU plug-in instrument appears in the menu.

GarageBand offers a set of AU plug-ins for various effects, including the following popular ones:

- **AUBandPass:** Allows frequencies within a certain range to be heard, while filtering out (or at least de-emphasizing) all frequencies above or below that range. With a band-pass filter you can accentuate different frequencies, controlling the bandwidth (the range of frequencies to emphasize) and the center frequency (the center point's position in the range of frequencies).

WISDOM OF IHNATKO: BEYOND THE BOX

Apple really did intend GarageBand to be a credible contender as a music-recording tool. So just as I realized that I hardly knew everything about music recording and thus left the previous chapter mostly to Tony, Apple understood that it couldn't possibly come up with every possible effect and feature. So they devised the Audio Unit (AU) architecture. AUs are software plug-ins that enhance GarageBand by adding extra instruments, effects, filters, and enhanced functionality to the software. Many of GarageBand's built-in effects are actually implemented through AUs. If you look at the Info box for a track and click the effects popup, you'll see that AUs get their own little section.

To see what sort of AUs are out there and what they can do for your GarageBand projects, go to www.audio-units.com.

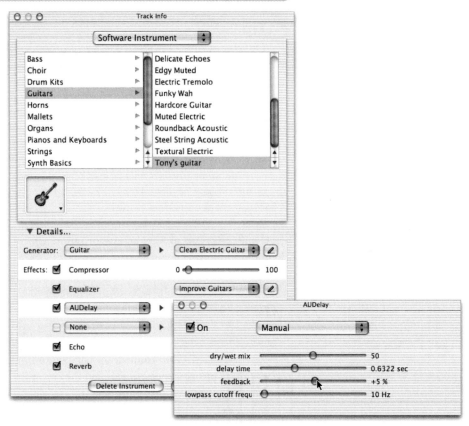

Figure 10-12

Manually adjusting the settings for the AUDelay effect

○ **AUDelay:** Replays the sound repeatedly to create an echo effect. AUDelay offers more control over echoing than the basic Echo effect, as shown in Figure 10-12. The dry/wet mix slider controls how the repeating sounds are mixed, with a higher value (wetter) producing a more crowded sound of many repetitions at the same time. You can control the delay time from 0 to 2.0000 seconds, and control the feedback by raising or lowering the number of repetitions played (with the middle point, 0, as neutral). You can also define which frequencies to remove using the lowpass cutoff slider (from 10 Hz to 22050 Hz).

○ **AUGraphicEQ:** Displays a graphical equalizer, as shown in Figure 10-13, that gives you control over boosting (up 20.0 decibels) or reducing (down 20.0 decibels) frequencies. It provides an interface similar to a mixing board, with sliders for frequency ranges that start at 20 Hz and go up to 20 kHz. You can also flatten the equalization curve by clicking the Flatten EQ button.

○ **AUHiPass:** Filters (reduces the emphasis on) low-frequency sounds so that higher-frequency sounds pass through. You might use this effect to filter out low rumbling noises from interference or machines.

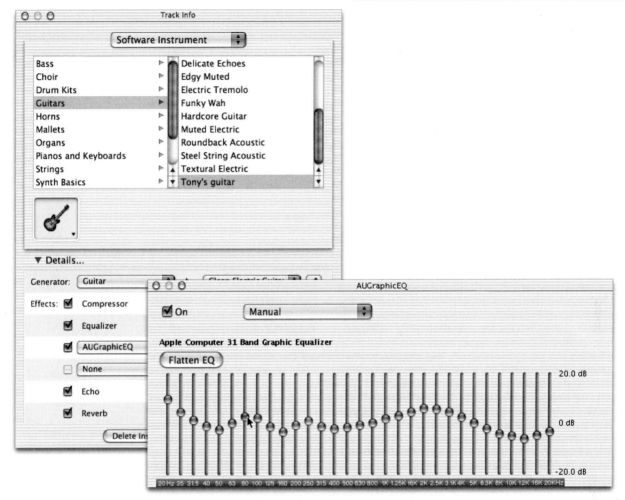

Figure 10-13
Manually adjusting the graphic equalizer displayed by the AUGraphicEQ effect

AUHiPass lets you set the cutoff frequency for the filter and the amount of resonance in decibels.

- **AUPeakLimiter:** Lowers the amplitude of the particular frequency of sound when the amplitude is high relative to the rest of the sound (such as loud spikes). You might use this effect to filter out the loudness of certain instruments, and certainly to remove spikes. It offers the ability to set the attack and release time at

units of ten-thousandths of a second, which determines how quickly the filter goes into effect (the attack) and how quickly it stops (the release). You can also set the limiting amount, as shown in Figure 10-14, which is the amount the amplitude is decreased when a peak occurs. This effect is useful for accommodating spikes after boosting the volume of the track, such as a microphone recording where the volume jumps up and down.

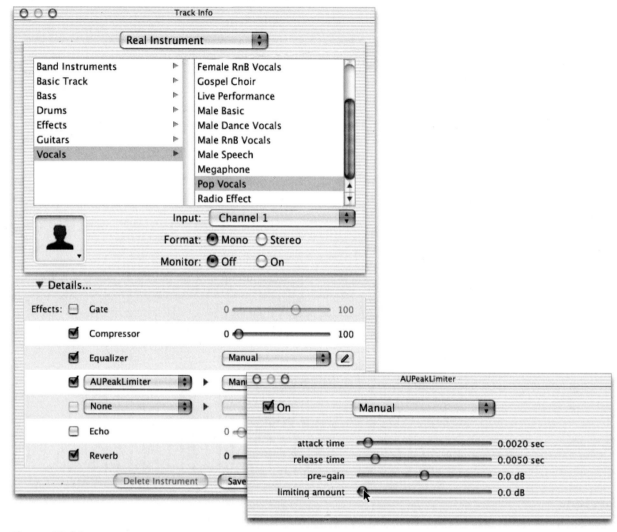

Figure 10-14
Manually adjusting the AUPeakLimiter effect to deal with spikes in a microphone recording

- **AULowpass:** Filters (reduces emphasis on) high-level frequency sounds so that lower-frequency sounds pass through (the opposite of AUHiPass). You might use this effect to filter out high-pitched whines, hisses, or machine noise. AULowpass lets you set the cutoff frequency for the filter and the amount of resonance in decibels.

- **AUMultibandCompressor:** Lets you select the compression settings for multiple bands of frequencies, rather than just one, as shown in Figure 10-15. AUMultibandCompressor offers factory presets such as Fast and Smooth, Analog, and Gentle, but you can manipulate the controls and make your own presets. You can set the attack (how quickly it takes effect) and release (how quickly it stops the effect), the threshold to reach before the effect turns on, and the amount of compression. One way to obtain a radio-friendly mix — one that is tightly compressed for small radio speakers — is to apply multiband compression on the master track rather than on individual tracks. Multiband compression blends the tracks together and makes it easier to get a good mix (to be used in addition to master-track mixing, described in Chapter 11). You may have to increase the master volume to get the levels back to normal after applying multiband compression.

- **AUParametricEQ:** Lets you boost or decrease the amplitude of a signal within a certain frequency range. While GarageBand offers a standard Equalizer effect, this effect is useful for removing a very specific frequency and is easier to use for that purpose than the graphic equalizer in AUGraphicEQ. For example, if you have a track with a tone at 150 Hz that you don't want, you can specify a low Q (width of the frequency to change), a negative gain (dB setting), and a center frequency of 150 Hz to remove the tone.

 Tip

If you use the AUParametricEQ or AUGraphicEQ equalizer and Amp Simulation or Distortion, you get better results using the equalizer *before* using Amp Simulation or Distortion. Use the first open pop-up menu for the equalizer and the second pop-up menu underneath it for the Amp Simulation or Distortion effect. It is usually better to do equalization before turning on any kind of distortion effect.

SAVING AND DELETING EFFECT PRESETS

After spending some time adjusting an effect and getting it to sound just right, you might want to save the settings for that effect as a preset so that you can choose it quickly and easily from the preset pop-up menu.

Saving effects presets

To save a new preset after adjusting the settings for an effect, choose Make Preset from the pop-up menu in the effect's settings window, as shown in Figure 10-16 (click the pencil icon to open the effect's window), type a name for the new preset, and click Save.

You can also save settings as a preset whenever you make changes to an effect's settings window. When finished making changes to a preset, click the Close button to close the window. A warning dialog appears that asks, "Do you want to save the file before switching to a new one?" Click Save to save the settings; in the subsequent dialog box, type a preset name and click OK.

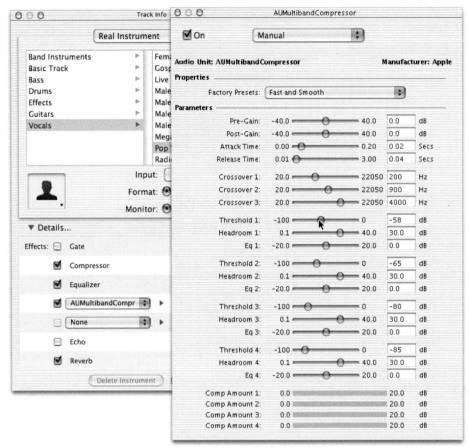

Figure 10-15
Using AUMultibandCompressor to manually adjust compression settings for multiple bands of frequencies

Deleting effects presets

To delete one of your custom presets, select the preset first. Delete Preset appears in the pop-up menu so that you can delete it, as shown in Figure 10-17.

▼ **Note**

The Delete Preset option appears only for your custom presets. You can't delete the built-in presets this way.

Although settings for effects and your instrument choices are saved with the song, with custom presets you can use the exact same settings with other instruments in the same song and with instruments in other songs. While you can also save the track settings along with the choice of instrument sound by saving a custom instrument, saving a preset lets you use the settings with other instrument sounds. To save track settings as a custom Software Instrument, see Chapter 6; to save track settings as a custom Real Instrument sound, see Chapter 7.

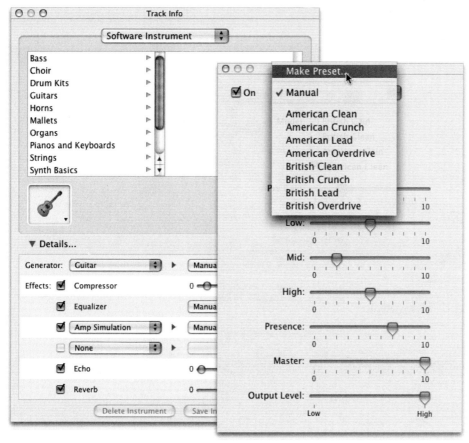

Figure 10-16
Saving the Amp Simulation settings as a custom preset

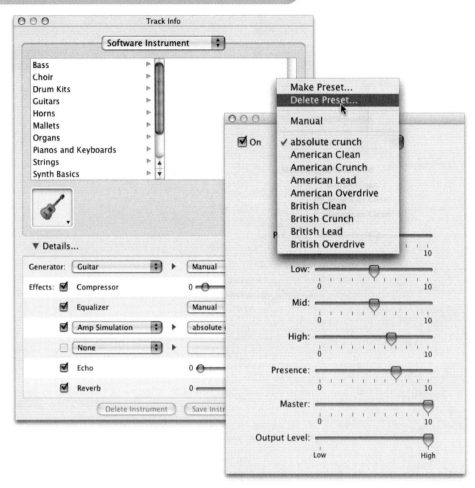

Figure 10-17
Deleting a custom preset

Mixing and Shaping the Sound

In This Chapter

Muting a track to hear or export other tracks • Soloing a track to hear or export only that track
• Setting the track pan position and volume • Fine-tuning both track and master volume curves
• Exporting loops, songs, mixdown tracks, or separate tracks

"For me, making a record is like painting a picture in sound." This is how Sir George Martin, producer of The Beatles and arguably one of the most influential music producers of his time, opens his chapter on multi-track recording titled "Layering the Cake" for his autobiography, *All You Need is Ears* (St. Martin's Press, New York, NY; 1979).

The goal is to mix all the tracks into two tracks for stereo sound. Stereo was designed to give the listener a broader auditory experience; sounds coming from both the left and right speakers add a spatial dimension. That picture Sir George Martin was talking about is more like a *panorama*. Consequently, you have in GarageBand the ability to "place" the sound in this panorama, as well as control the volume of each track so it doesn't drown out other tracks. A common studio technique, used extensively by Pink Floyd, Jimi Hendrix, the Moody Blues, and other bands, was to pan the sound across this dimension so that the sound seemed to travel from left to right (or vice versa). In this chapter, you learn all about mixing and shaping the sound to create an excellent stereo result.

LISTENING TO TRACKS

Simply put, to get a good mix of your song, you need to hear everything. At first you may want to hear only certain tracks at a time, before listening to all the tracks at once. GarageBand offers easy controls for doing just that. You can mute some tracks to hear others distinctly, or silence all of the tracks in order to hear just one.

Muting a track

Turning off one or more tracks while listening to other tracks is often necessary, especially if the track is loud but you don't want to adjust its volume yet. Muting some tracks while recording a performance into another track is particularly useful — you want to mute any tracks that may distract you or compete with the performance you are recording.

Each track has a header that shows the instrument icon and name. You can click a track and then click the Mute button (with the speaker icon) to mute the track, as shown in Figure 11-1 (the mute button turns blue when turned on). Notice that the top three tracks — Rock Kit, Muted Electric Bass, and Cymbal Swells — are muted.

▼ **Tip**

You can also mute a track by selecting the track and then pressing M on your keyboard.

A MUTE POINT

Producers or engineers sometimes mute a track because the performance in the track is weak, in their opinion, and detracts from the music in the other tracks. But producers don't always know what's right. Producer Tom Wilson thought the organ track on Bob Dylan's "Like a Rolling Stone" was weak (as played by Al Kooper, who admittedly had little keyboard experience and had not expected to play organ at the session), but Dylan simply responded, "Turn it up." The rest is music history — that organ part is widely imitated even today.

Regions in muted tracks lose their color and appear gray, while the Mute button itself is highlighted blue. As the song plays, the muted regions are silent until you click the Mute button again.

Figure 11-1
Muting the top three tracks so that they are silent during playback

▼ **Note**

You can't tell from Figure 11-1 that the Mute button turns blue when activated, but take my word for it — it does.

Soloing a track

Sometimes you want to hear just one or more tracks quickly, without having to mute all the other tracks manually. This is especially true when you want to define the volume curve for a track (as I describe in the section

"Fine-tuning the track volume curve" later in this chapter). You want to hear everything a certain track has to offer without other tracks adding to the sound.

Next to the Mute button is the Solo button (with the headphones icon). Click the Solo button in the track header to play a track solo, as shown in Figure 11-2, in which the Electric Piano track is set to play solo.

 Tip
You can also select a track and press S on your keyboard to solo it.

Figure 11-2
Setting the Electric Piano track to play solo

After clicking the Solo button for a track, the other tracks are automatically muted. The muted tracks lose their background color in the timeline (the background appears white), while the Solo button itself lights up blue. As the

song plays, the muted tracks are silent until you click the Solo button again. You can turn on Solo for more than one track and play them together while the rest are muted.

 Note
Again, even though you can't see the button colors in Figure 11-2, take my word for it that the Solo button turns blue when activated.

SETTING THE TRACK PAN POSITION AND VOLUME

If your goal is to mix a song for stereo, you have to take into consideration the *stereo field* of sound in which instruments and vocals are placed in the left and right channels. You can make a song sound like it was recorded live with instruments in different places on a stage, with you as the listener in the first row, front and center.

Each track has its own pan (short for panorama) wheel and volume control in the Track Mixer. The Mixer section of each track appears between the section with the track name and the timeline; if it is not visible, click the triangle next to the word "Tracks" at the top of the window, or choose Track → Show Track Mixer.

When you create a track in GarageBand, the volume of the track is typically set to three-quarters full and the pan wheel is set to the center of the stereo field. If you leave it that way, all your tracks will probably sound too loud and compressed, and not ideal for adjusting the volume. I therefore recommend that you set the pan position of each track before adjusting the volume.

Tip

By separating the sound into pan positions first, you can hear the tracks in their appropriate positions in stereo, and adjust the volume for each track accordingly.

Adjusting pan positions

The pan position of the track defines the location of the track's sound in the stereo field. You can use the pan wheel in the Mixer section of a track to set the position anywhere in the field, from left to middle to right. Click inside the pan wheel to set the position, as shown in Figure 11-3; drag down to pan left or up to pan right. The white dot on the pan wheel indicates the position. You can also drag the white dot itself to move the pan wheel.

Tip

Option+clicking on the pan wheel returns it to the center position.

Figure 11-3
Setting the pan position for the Classic Rock Organ track

Conventional wisdom has it that you should put the drum and bass tracks in the middle (balanced between left and right stereo fields), and place the vocals, lead instruments,

and supporting instruments in either channel, but you can do whatever you want. In Figure 11-3, I have two drum tracks, so I place each one left and right, with Electric Bass at center, both Acoustic Guitar tracks far to the left, and the Classic Rock Organ track on the right.

Adjusting the track volume level

Each track has a Volume control in the Mixer section that sets the volume level for the entire track (relative to the master volume, which controls the entire song's volume). Adjust each track's overall volume first before fine-tuning it in specific places with the track volume curve (see the next section, "Fine-tuning the track volume curve").

To adjust the volume of a track, drag the track's volume slider to the left to lower the track's volume, or to the right to raise it, as shown in Figure 11-4.

You can adjust the volume while the song plays; watch the track level meters to monitor the volume and the amount of clipping or distortion. The track level meters are the two narrow grooves, one for each channel of stereo sound input, immediately above the track volume slider (Real Instrument tracks that use only one channel of input show volume in only one of these channels). The meters show green, then orange, and then red as the volume gets louder (just like the master volume slider, only smaller). If the red dots to the far right of the meters appear, the volume for the track is way too high — these are called *clipping indicators*, and they stay on to remind you that clipping occurred in the track. In fact, the red clipping indicators stay on even after the song quits playing, and even after you click Rewind to move back to the beginning. The indicators stay on until you click the Play button again, or until you reset the indicators by clicking them. If clipping occurred, lower the track's volume until no clipping occurs on playback.

Figure 11-4
Adjusting the Guitar track volume while playing the song

Fine-tuning the track volume curve

Controlling the volume of the entire track is fine, but what if the track has extreme highs you want to adjust, or extreme lows that you want to punch up to be louder? Although you can add effects to tracks, including an equalizer to adjust the gain on certain frequencies, you can also (and more easily) use the volume curve to adjust the volume of specific sections of the track.

Note that adjustments made to the track volume curve are relative to the master track volume curve, as described in "Fine-tuning the master volume curve" in this chapter.

To precisely adjust the volume curve of a track over the duration of the song, follow these steps:

1. **Open the Track Volume row for the track.**

   Click the down-arrow button in the Track header section to open the Track Volume row. This row appears underneath the track, as shown in Figure 11-5.

2. **Click the check box to turn on the Track Volume option.**

   Turn on the Track Volume option in the header of the Track Volume row, so that a dark horizontal volume line appears in the row underneath the track.

3. **Click on the volume line to create a point, or drag a point to define a curve, as shown in Figure 11-6.**

   The volume changes evenly between points on the volume curve, providing smoother volume control for the track.

▼ Tip

When dragging a point on the curve, you can align it with a beat or measure on the beat ruler by turning on the Snap to Grid option. Choose Control ➜ Snap to Grid.

Songs often have a fade-in at the beginning and a fade-out at the end, and you can set the volume curve to define these. The volume curve gives you ultimate control over the volume of any track at any point in a song; you can set it so that a portion of the track is higher or lower than the rest. For example, an easy way to remove unwanted notes from a performance without editing the track is to reduce the volume for that section of the track. Add control points to define a dip in the volume, as shown in Figure 11-7.

Figure 11-5
Opening the Track Volume row for the Digital Horns track

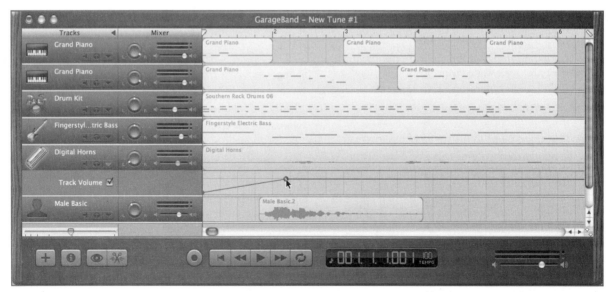

Figure 11-6
Defining a volume curve that fades up the Digital Horns track

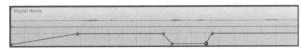

Figure 11-7
Defining a curve that reduces the volume of a section of the track

▼ **Tip**

To delete a point in a track volume curve, select the point and press the Delete key. You can straighten a curve that runs between three points by deleting the middle point.

The track now plays without the unwanted notes because their volume is too low to hear them. The volume curve fades down and then up smoothly on the track so that you don't notice the difference.

SETTING THE MASTER VOLUME

GarageBand offers both a Master Volume control (for controlling the volume of the entire song), and a master track that enables you to fine-tune the volume of all the tracks in a song (good for setting fade-ins and fade-outs). Precise adjustments of the volume level are possible with the curve; however, the Master Volume control defines the uppermost volume level for the entire song, affecting not only all tracks but the master volume curve as well.

Adjusting the master volume level

You can change the master volume whenever you want, for playback or for monitoring the recording of performances. However, when you are ready to export the song to iTunes, you should set the master volume of the song to its final setting. GarageBand uses that setting when exporting the song to iTunes.

The Master Volume slider is below the lower-right corner of the timeline. To adjust the master volume and set the upper limit for all tracks, drag the slider to the right to raise it, or to the left to lower it, as shown in Figure 11-8.

▼ **Cross-Reference**

See "Exporting the entire song" in this chapter to export a GarageBand recording to iTunes.

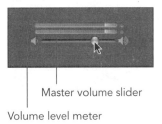

Master volume slider

Volume level meter

Figure 11-8
Adjusting the master volume for the song

▼ **Tip**

You should add effects to tracks first *before* setting the master volume, and then adjust the master volume while playing the song. See Chapter 10 for information about effects.

Set the volume level high enough to eliminate background noise, but not high enough to cause *clipping,* a sharp, crackling sound caused by volume overload. As the song plays, watch the level meters (two narrow grooves, one for each channel of stereo sound) immediately above the master volume slider.

The level meters show green, then orange, and then red as the volume gets louder. The red part at the far right appears only when the volume is at its highest. If the red dots on the right side of the meters appear (refer to Figure 11-8), the volume is way too high. These red dots are called *clipping indicators,* and they stay on to remind you

THE SOUND OF THICK AIR

Pioneering young rock musicians in 1967 wanted to try things that would cause the button-down producers and engineers at record labels to throw up their hands and sometimes give up altogether, as when the producer for the Grateful Dead's album *Anthem of the Sun* walked out in the middle of production. Bob Weir of the Dead has asked what it would be like to record with "thick air," according to Dennis McNally in his book about the Dead, *A Long Strange Trip* (Broadway Books, New York, NY; 2002). "Years later [Weir] would understand exactly what he meant and how to produce it — namely, the feel of a hot, humid summer night, created with an audio compressor, which literally thickened the sound." Too bad Bobby didn't have GarageBand back then. You can use the master track to put an effect on the entire song, such as a compressor setting, as described in Chapter 10.

THE ANALOG MIXER ANALOGY

Analog mixer freaks — you know who you are, and you probably look down your nose at primitive mixers like GarageBand's — can use these controls just like the ones they are used to. Track volumes are like trim knobs that control the sound of each track. The master volume curve is like a level fader that lets you raise or lower the volume for all the tracks at different points in the song. The master volume slider is the ultimate volume control, the master fader.

that clipping occurred in the song (so that you can go back and change the volume). You can reset these indicators by clicking them. Before exporting a song, you should make sure that clipping has not occurred.

You can reduce or eliminate clipping by lowering a specific track's volume, or by lowering the level of an effect that may be causing the distortion. Otherwise, the best way to handle clipping, other than lowering the master volume slider, is to fine-tune the master volume curve, adding control points and lowering the volume at the moment in the song when the distortion occurs.

Fine-tuning the master volume curve

The master volume curve overrides the track volume curve to establish an upper limit for the volume. Your settings in each of the tracks still controls the volume at levels lower than the limit set by the master volume curve,

but volume can't increase above the master limit. With the master volume curve, you can even define points for curves to fade all the tracks up and down at different places in the song.

To fine-tune the overall volume of the song, show the Master Track by choosing Track ➜ Show Master Track. The Master Track appears at the bottom of the timeline as the last track (with the heading Master Volume). Turn on the Master Volume by clicking the checkbox, as shown in Figure 11-9.

Figure 11-9
Turning on the Master Volume in the master track

Click on the horizontal line to establish a point, and then drag the point to define a curve, as shown in Figure 11-10. In the figure, the curve is set to fade the volume down for all the tracks at the same time.

 Tip

To delete a point in the master volume curve, select the point and then press the Delete key.

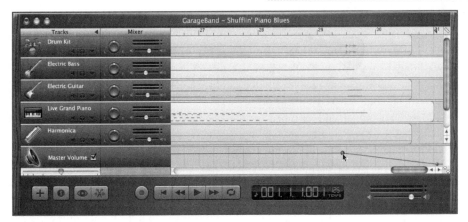

Figure 11-10
Adjusting the master volume curve in the master track

▼ **Tip**

If you use effects such as echo, reverb, or any other similar effects that "trail off" at the end of a song, you may want to fine-tune the master volume curve to fade-out the song at the end. You can extend the volume curve past the last region to make sure it controls the volume of any reverberations or echoes.

To summarize, you might mix a song by using the following controls in the following order:

1. Set the volume for your Mac and speakers (or headphones) for optimal listening.

2. Set the Master Volume slider to full volume (all the way on).

3. Set pan positions and adjust track volume sliders and volume curves relative to each other.

4. On playback, check the master volume levels to see if clipping occurs; if it does, ease up on the Master Volume slider to lower the volume of the entire song.

5. Use the master volume curve to make adjustments such as fading the entire song in or out.

CREATING THE FINAL MIX

You can stop trying to contact Ed Cherney, Bob Clearmountain, Tom Dowd, Geoff Emerick, Brian Eno, Glyn Johns, Daniel Lanois, Steve Lillywhite, Alan Parsons, or any other mixing geniuses you can't afford. GarageBand can automatically mix your song into stereo. You can play the song back in iTunes or burn the song onto an audio CD — but these are not your only choices. You can also use GarageBand to export individual tracks to separate files, which you can then bring into a professional studio program such as Digidesign Pro Tools for further mixing and effects.

If you want to create a different type of mix, you should save a copy of the song under a different name, thereby creating two versions — one version for mixing into stereo, and another for other types of mixes. Choose File → Save As, and give the song project the name of the final song. Use the "final song" project when exporting to iTunes, leaving the other version of the project ready for other kinds of mixing.

Before doing any exporting of any kind, sit back and listen to the song through speakers or headphones. When listening, you can emphasize a particular track by boosting its volume relative to the others (using the track volume slider). Listen for details and flaws, such as noises and musical mistakes, and fix them either by fine-tuning the volume curve for that track, or editing the track in the Track Editor.

Once you have set the track volume, fine-tuned the track volume curves, set the Master Volume slider, fine-tuned the master volume curves, and fixed any mistakes discovered in the final run-through, listen to the song again several times, focusing on rhythm, the sound, particular instrument performances, or vocals. This process is a bit like intense proofreading: many people have made what they thought was a great final mix, only to find flaws with it on a later hearing.

BILL PAYNE: SOUND WORKS LIKE A PYRAMID

Mixing tracks is an art, and in many ways the mixing of tracks recorded in GarageBand is similar to mixing a live performance in a club or concert hall. Performers on stage require a mix of the entire sound in their onstage monitor speaker in order to hear what's going on; at the same time, they need to hear their own instrument in the monitor mix. Performers often try to fix volume-balancing problems by turning their instruments *up* in volume rather than down, and this is the wrong thing to do. Instead, the way to bring an instrument up is to lower the volume of the other tracks. "Sound works like a pyramid," wrote Bill Payne, vocalist, keyboardist, and founder of Little Feat, in *Player Magazine*. "One person has it too loud in the monitors, starting a chain reaction of 'more of me.' It's not long before the volume level permeates everything — especially the vocal mics. Vocals are sometimes the toughest to get above the fray. I have rarely seen people ask for less volume in order to hear, when in fact that is exactly what they should be doing."

Exporting the entire song

Before exporting your song as a stereo music file, type the name of an iTunes playlist as well as the artist or composer in the Export pane of the GarageBand Preferences window, as described in Chapter 5. Choose GarageBand ➔ Preferences, click the Export tab, and type the playlist name in the iTunes Playlist field.

To export your song as a stereo file from GarageBand, choose File ➔ Export to iTunes. GarageBand automatically mixes the tracks down to two stereo channels, and exports the song to iTunes in the uncompressed AIFF format. Although the AIFF format occupies a lot of hard drive space (and way too much space and power in an iPod), it is the ideal format to burn to CD, or to use for a mixdown that you intend to use again in GarageBand. A *mixdown track* is a track that contains multiple finished tracks pre-mixed into one track, as described in "Exporting and using a mixdown track" later in this chapter.

▼ Cross-References

After you export your song to iTunes, you can convert it to a compressed format as described in Chapter 5. To learn more about playing and organizing songs in iTunes, see Chapter 12; to put your song on your iPod, see Chapter 13, and to burn your song onto a CD, see Chapter 14.

Setting and exporting a cycle region

You can define a *cycle region* to export only a piece of a song, such as a sample or a loop. When you export to iTunes, GarageBand exports the song from the very first measure to the end of the last region in the song, or exports just a cycle region if the Cycle button is turned on.

To set a cycle region, click the Cycle button, which is on the far right in the set of transport buttons.

To create a cycle region and export a song to be used as a loop, follow these steps:

1. **Click the Cycle button.**

   The Cycle button, with the revolving arrows, is located in the row of transport control buttons. This button opens the cycle ruler, which is a tiny second ruler that appears below the beat ruler. A yellow bar appears in the cycle ruler, designating a cycle region.

2. **Drag the edges of the cycle ruler's yellow bar to define the cycle region in the timeline, as shown in Figure 11-11.**

   You can drag the beginning or end of the yellow bar to set it accurately in the timeline. You can also drag the entire cycle region in the ruler, as shown in Figure 11-11, to set the cycle region to a new position. If the musical sequence is designed to repeat as a loop, click the Play button to make sure the cycle region loops properly.

3. **Choose File → Export to iTunes.**

   GarageBand automatically mixes down the sections of the tracks defined in the cycle region, and exports the song to iTunes using the project name and playlist defined in GarageBand's export preferences.

With the loop saved in iTunes, you can drag it from iTunes and into a GarageBand project. Open a new or existing project in GarageBand, and then open iTunes and locate the loop (which is stored as an AIFF file in iTunes). Drag the loop directly to the GarageBand window, as shown in Figure 11-12. GarageBand automatically creates a Real Instrument track for the loop.

A cycle region can also be useful for extending a song past the last region, so that GarageBand exports the silence at the end. This is useful if you used any effects that cause reverberations, echoes, or remnants that trail off at the end of a song. Normally, the trailing end would be cut off, because GarageBand stops exporting at the end of the last region. But if you set the cycle region to start at the very beginning of the song and end at some point past the last region, as shown in Figure 11-13, the exported song should include any sound trailing off at the end.

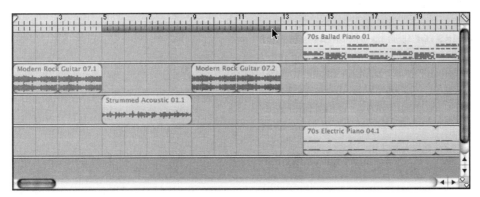

Figure 11-11
Defining a cycle region to export a portion of a track as a loop

Figure 11-12
Dragging the exported loop from iTunes back into a GarageBand project

Exporting tracks for use in other programs

You can export specific tracks of a GarageBand project rather than exporting the entire project. This technique is useful if you intend to import the individual tracks into another program, such as Digidesign Pro Tools. Here's how:

- To export one track, select the track and click the Solo button (or press S). This sets the track to solo, so only that track plays and the rest are muted. Then export the project, as described in " Exporting the entire song," and the song consists of just the solo track.

- To export several tracks mixed down, either click the Solo button (or press S) for each track, or click the Mute button (or press M) for the other tracks that are not to be included. Then export the project, and the song consists of a mixdown of the solo tracks (or un-muted tracks).

The track or mixed-down tracks are exported as a song in the AIFF format, and the song is automatically saved in your iTunes library. From there, you can either drag the song from your iTunes folder, as described in Chapter 12, or drag the song from the iTunes window into a professional editing program as an AIFF track.

Figure 11-13
Setting a cycle region past the ending of a song to include any reverberations at the end

Exporting and using a mixdown track

A song with many tracks can become too complicated for your Mac's processor, causing GarageBand to issue a system overload message. One way to reduce tracks is to *mix down* multiple finished tracks into one track, and then use the mixdown track along with other tracks to finish the song. The mixdown track requires far less processing power to play than the multiple tracks that created it.

You don't lose quality by creating a mixdown track, but you *do* lose the ability to balance the sounds within the mixdown track, or separate it back into multiple tracks. For that reason you should save your project with Save As to preserve a version that still contains the original multiple tracks.

STACY PARRISH: USING BOTH GARAGEBAND AND PRO TOOLS

"I can create the music bed in GarageBand with short loops, perhaps two or three parts, and then move them into Pro Tools," says producer and engineer Stacy Parrish. "After importing them into Pro Tools, I set up a tempo map, and then use loops I've created myself or from other musicians that are more original, or use loops from professional libraries. The ones in GarageBand are fine to use, but if you want something that's a little more cutting-edge, then you have to make them yourself. GarageBand makes it really easy to come up with ideas. Sometimes I'll use both — loops from GarageBand and others I made or found that have a more professional sound."

Assuming you have several tracks that are completely finished in terms of track volume, pan settings, and effects, and no longer need to do any editing in those tracks, you can use this process to reduce performance problems in two ways:

- **Create a new project with the mixdown track and add more tracks.** You can export the tracks as an AIFF file (as an iTunes song), then drag the iTunes song back into a *new* GarageBand project. Make sure the new project uses the same tempo, key, and time signature settings, and turn off any echo or reverb for the newly added mixdown track (because it is already finished and you don't want to add more effects). You can then add more tracks to the new project and mix them with the mixdown track. When finished, export the new project as your final song.

- **Re-import the mixdown track to your project.** You can export the tracks to an AIFF file (as an iTunes song), then mute the exported tracks in the Garage-Band project. Drag the iTunes song back into *the same* GarageBand project that has the original tracks muted. You can then continue editing and improving the other tracks in the GarageBand project, using the mixdown track as a guide. When you are ready to do a final mixdown, delete the mixdown track, and un-mute the

original tracks that you used to create the mixdown track. Then export the project as your final song.

L. HENRY S ARMIENTO II: DOING MIXDOWNS FOR PRO TOOLS

"If you use echo, reverb, or other effects that might be better done with professional software like Pro Tools, or you want to use professional versions of effects not available in GarageBand, I'd advise turning off the GarageBand effects first, then doing a mixdown," says sound technician and producer L. Henry Sarmiento II. "The exported tracks can then be worked on in another program. You can still use the effects on tracks in GarageBand as a reference."

Adds Henry, "It is not as easy to export drum tracks — in a professional environment, each part of a drum kit is miked separately to create multiple tracks for a kit. You could use separate tracks for separate parts of a drum kit and record it that way in GarageBand. However, loops you might use are not separated and are therefore not as good as professionally recorded multi-track drum loops."

PART IV

Sympathy for the Demo

Managing Your Music

In This Chapter

Browsing songs in your iTunes library and understanding song indicators
• Editing iTunes song information for one song or multiple songs at once • Using iTunes to organize songs into playlists and creating smart playlists • Copying music files and playlists from your iTunes library • Backing up or copying your entire iTunes library • Backing up your GarageBand song projects

Your song is finished. You've exported it to iTunes after mixing it down as described in Chapter 11, or perhaps you exported a loop or just a few tracks. Either way, your new song is now stored in your iTunes library. It's a *demo* — a demonstration version of the song, by commercial production standards — but the wonderful thing about iTunes is that your song appears in a list with all the other songs in your library, right next to your favorite albums. Songs are songs, whether they are by highly successful commercial artists or anyone else. Give your songs enough *song information* so that you can list them by album in iTunes. Give your songs *ratings* so that they sort to the top when you select the best music in your collection. This chapter shows you how to manage your demo songs just like all the other songs in your library.

The potential of your iTunes library is awesome, even by jukebox standards: it can hold up to 32,000 songs (depending on how much space you have on your hard drive). Finding a particular song would be a challenge if iTunes didn't offer the ability to add information to each song.

Whether you are a professional musician or just a music lover with a large collection, you'll want to organize your iTunes library to make finding songs easier. In this chapter, I show you how to organize your music so that you can find any song in seconds, and how to display songs sorted by artist, album, genre of music, or other attributes.

This chapter also explains how to create *playlists,* which are lists of songs to be played, transferred to an iPod, or burned to a CD. iTunes even offers *smart playlists* — playlists that generate their own lists, without your help, based on the song information (which is another good reason to edit the song information). You also find out how to back up songs in your iTunes library, and how to back up your GarageBand song projects.

BROWSING SONGS IN ITUNES

iTunes offers two views of your library: a song list view and Browse view. The Browse view is useful as long as you add song information, such as the album name, for the songs. You aren't overwhelmed by a long list of songs — when you select an album, Browse view displays only the songs for that album. It's similar to the way I browse for music in stores or in my CD collection — I look for artist names (in alphabetical order), and pull out albums to scan their contents.

To select the Browse view, click the Browse button in the upper-right corner. iTunes organizes your music library by artist and album, which makes finding just the right songs easier. Click the Browse button again to return to the song list view: the Browse button toggles between the two views.

The Browse view sorts the songs by genre, artist, and album. If you click a genre such as Blues, all the artists included in that genre appear in the Artist column. If you click All in the Genre column, all the artists of every genre appear. If you click a specific artist, the album titles for that artist appear in the Album column on the right, as shown in Figure 12-1.

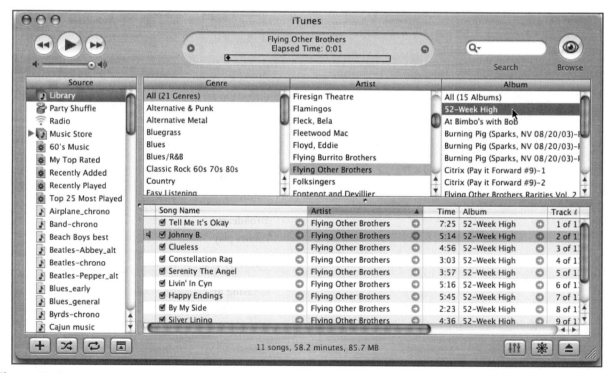

Figure 12-1
Browsing by genre, artist, and album in iTunes

As you click different albums in the Album column, the Song Name list displays the songs from those albums. The songs are listed in proper track order as on the original album, just as the artist intended them.

This is great for selecting songs from specific albums, but what if you want to look at all the songs by an artist in the library at once? Simple: Select the All option in the Artist column, and all the songs available in the iTunes library from a specific artist appear in the Song Name list.

 Note

iTunes considers "Flying Other Brothers" and "The Flying Other Brothers" to be different groups. I edit the artist name and other information whenever necessary, as described in "Editing Song Information in iTunes" later in this chapter.

CHANGING YOUR VIEW OF ITUNES

Don't let the rigorously organized iTunes display fool you — you can customize the iTunes song list to display more or less information, or different information; you can also display columns in a different order from left to right, or with wider or narrower column widths. You can also change the order of columns from left to right by clicking a column heading and dragging the entire column to the left or right. In addition, you can Control-click (press Control and click) any of the column headings to display a shortcut menu offering the Auto Size Column option, the Auto Size All Columns option, and the ability to add or remove columns. You can pick columns that don't usually appear — such as Size (for file size), Date and Year (for the date the album was released, or any other date you choose for each song), Bit Rate, Sample Rate, Track Number, and Comment. You can also add or delete columns by choosing Edit ➜ View Options.

To play the song you've found, just click the Play button in the upper-left corner of the iTunes window.

 Tip

Whether you're in Browse view or viewing the song list in its entirety, the column headings double as sorting options. For example, clicking the Time heading reorders the songs by their duration in ascending order (from shortest to longest). If you click the Time header again, the sort is reversed, starting with the longest song. This can be useful if you are looking for songs of a certain length — for example, looking for a song to match the length of a slideshow or a movie clip.

Song indicators

To show you what it's doing, iTunes displays an action indicator next to each song as you perform operations. Here's a list of indicators and what they mean:

- **Moving zigzag:** iTunes is importing the song.

- **Green check mark:** iTunes has finished importing the song.

- **Exclamation point:** iTunes can't find the song. You may have moved or deleted the song accidentally. Drag the song from the Finder to the iTunes window.

- **Broadcast icon:** The song is on the Internet, and iTunes plays it as a music stream.

- **Speaker:** The song is currently playing.

- **Chasing arrows:** iTunes is copying the song from another location, or downloading the song from the Internet.

SIMPLE DJ TRICKS

Want to annoy the neighbors or repel invaders? Repeat your playlist or album over and over at a loud volume. You can repeat an entire song list by clicking the Repeat button at the bottom of the Source pane on the left side of the iTunes window (or by choosing Controls ➤ Repeat All). The Repeat button icon changes to show blue highlighting. Click the Repeat button again to repeat the current song (or choose Controls ➤ Repeat One) — the icon changes to include a blue-highlighted numeral 1. Click it once more to return to normal playback (or choose Controls ➤ Repeat Off).

How about showing off the diversity of your music collection by shuffling through songs at random? The Shuffle button, to the left of the Repeat button, plays the songs in the list in a random order, presumably with no bias. (iTunes won't reject those cute songs from when you were five years old.) You can then press the arrow keys on your keyboard or click the Back and Forward buttons to jump around in random order.

▼ Tip

In addition, songs that have a black check mark (in the checkbox to the right of the song indicator) are marked for the next operation, such as importing from an audio CD or playing an album or playlist. To skip tracks in a playlist or album, click the box next to the song name to remove the check mark. To remove check marks from a list simultaneously, hold down the Command key while clicking a check mark. Click an empty check mark box while pressing the Command key to add check marks to the entire list.

Searching for songs

As your music library grows, you may find that browsing and scrolling to locate a particular song is too time consuming.

You can use the Search field — the oval field in the top-right corner, to the left of the Browse button — to search for songs. Follow these steps:

1. **Click in the Search field.**

   You can search for a song title, an artist, or an album title.

2. **Type the first characters of your search term.**

   The search operation works immediately, searching for matches in the Song Name, Artist, and Album columns. The results appear as you type. Typing very few characters results in a long list of possible songs, as shown in Figure 12-2, but the search narrows down as you type more characters. The Search features ignore case; for example, when I search for "miles," iTunes finds "Eight Miles High," "She Smiles Like a River," and everything by Miles Davis.

PUT ON YOUR OWN LIGHT SHOW

iTunes iCandy and the Electronic Lava Lamp Multimedia is just a click away. The visual effects in iTunes can turn your display into a light show synchronized to the music in your library. You can watch a cool visual display of eye candy while the music plays — or leave it on like a lava lamp.

Click the Visual Effects button on the bottom right side of the iTunes window to display visual effects. The visual animation appears in the iTunes window and synchronizes with the music. In addition to the animation replacing the iTunes song list, an Options button replaces the Import button in the upper-right corner of the iTunes window. You can click the Options button to open the Visualizer Options dialog box, which provides options that affect the animation (but not the performance of iTunes when it's playing music), such as displaying the song information and the frame rate of the animation. Sorry folks, no figures, because black-and-white book figures don't do justice to the display — you have to try this to see it for yourself.

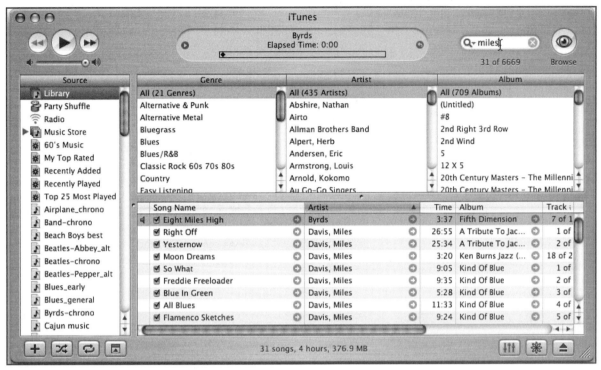

Figure 12-2
Using the Search field to search for a song or artist in iTunes

If you have a particular artist and album selected in Browse view, you can't search for anything else. Use browsing with searching, as described in Step 3, to further narrow your search.

3. **Scroll through the search results and click a song to select it.**

If you want to search the entire library, before using the Search field select All at the top of the Artist column to browse the entire library. Or, if you prefer, turn off the Browse view by clicking the Browse button again, and then use the Search field with the library's song list. To back out of a search so that the full list appears again, you can either click the circled X in the Search field, or delete the characters you typed in the Search field.

EDITING SONG INFORMATION IN ITUNES

Song and album titles, composer credits, and ratings for songs may seem trivial. But you can use the song information to search for songs or sort song lists, and the information is absolutely necessary for making smart playlists.

At some time or another you may want to edit the artist information you set for your GarageBand songs, songs you get from the Internet when you rip CDs, or music you buy from the iTunes store. For example, for solo artists, I like to list the artist by last name rather than first name. I routinely change the name of the artist for songs I buy from the iTunes store, because I'd rather have songs by Miles Davis be listed as "Davis, Miles" in my iTunes library.

Also, I routinely remove "The" from the names of bands such as The Who, The Band, the Beatles, and The Flying Other Brothers, even though it is cosmetic and doesn't affect sorting by alphabetical order.

You can edit a song's information in either Browse view or song list view. The fast and dirty way to edit a song's name or album name is to click directly in the field, and click again so that the mouse pointer turns into an editing cursor. You can then select the text and type over it, or press Command+C (copy), Command+X (cut), or Command+V (paste) to move bits of text around within the field. As you can see in Figure 12-3, I changed the Artist field for a song to be "Bove, Tony."

You can edit the Song Name (for some reason Apple doesn't like the more grammatically correct "song title"), Artist,

Album, Genre, and My Ratings fields right in the song list, or edit a group of songs at once. Editing in the song list is fine if you're editing the information for one song, but typically you need to change the artist name in *all* the tracks of an audio CD, and you need to do it in a hurry. To change a group of songs at once, go ahead and plunge right in:

1. **Select a group of songs by clicking the first song, and then holding down the Shift key as you click the last song.**

   All the songs between the first and last are highlighted and selected. You can add to a selection by Shift-clicking other songs, and you can remove songs from the selection by Command-clicking.

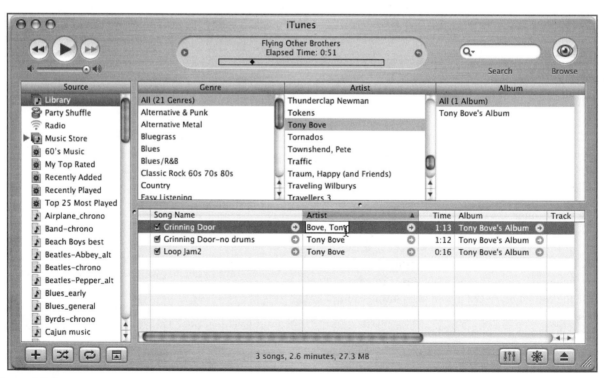

Figure 12-3
Editing the artist information for a song

2. **Choose File → Get Info, or press Command+I.**

A warning message displays "Are you sure you want to edit information for multiple items?" as shown in Figure 12-4. This type of editing can be destructive, so be careful. If, for example, you change the composer name, *the entire selection* then has that composer name, not just one song. I recommend leaving the "Do not ask me again" warning option deselected, so that the warning appears whenever you try to edit information for multiple songs at once.

Figure 12-4
A warning before editing information for multiple songs at once

3. **Click Yes.**

The Multiple Song Information dialog box appears, as shown in Figure 12-5.

YOUR OWN TOP 40

Ratings are particularly important for creating smart playlists. For example, the My Top Rated playlist in the Source pane is a smart playlist that updates itself when ratings are changed. My Top Rated plays only the top-rated songs in the library. The cool thing about ratings is that they're *yours*. You can use them to mean anything you want. For example, you may rate songs based on how much you like them, or whether your mother would listen to them, or how they blend into a work environment. Then you can use the My Top Rated playlist to automatically play the top-rated songs in the library.

YOUR FIRST ALBUM COVER

Songs you buy from the iTunes Music Store typically include an image of the album cover art or a photo of the artist. You can see the artwork in the lower-left corner of the iTunes window by clicking the Show/Hide Artwork button. However, your GarageBand songs don't have album art yet. What to do? Get out your digital camera, take some pictures and unload them into iPhoto (see Chapter 15 for information). To add the photo to a song, select the song in your iTunes library, and drag the song from the iPhoto library into the artwork viewing area in the bottom left corner of the iTunes window. To add the same image as artwork for an entire album of songs, rather than just individual songs, select the album in Browse view first (or select all the songs in the album in song list view), then drag the image file into the artwork viewing area.

To remove the artwork from a song, to view the artwork in a larger window, or to resize the artwork, choose File → Get Info and click the Artwork tab. You can add a different image or delete the image with the Add or Delete buttons, and resize the image with the size slider.

4. **Edit the fields you want to change (typically the Artist field) for multiple songs.**

When you edit a field, a check mark appears automatically in the box next to the field. iTunes assumes you want that field changed in all the selected songs. For example, in Figure 12-5, we've changed the Artist field (by typing a name), the Genre field (by selecting a genre from a pop-up menu), and the My Rating field (by dragging inside the field to add rating stars). Make sure that no other checkbox is selected except for the fields you want changed.

5. **Click OK to make the change.**

iTunes changes the fields for the entire selection of songs.

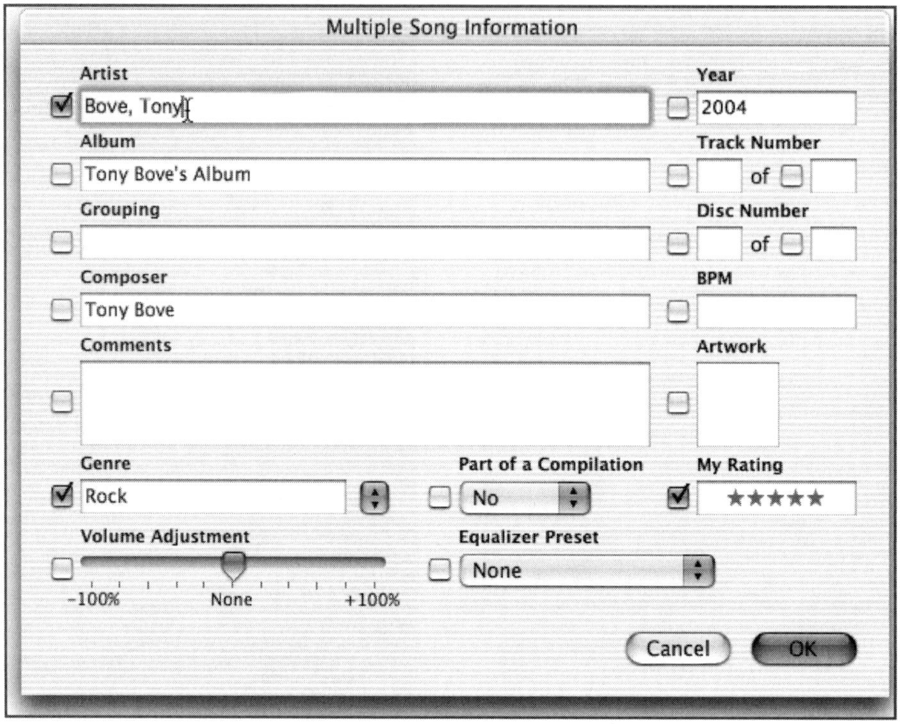

Multiple Song Information

Artist		**Year**
☑ Bove, Tony		☐ 2004
Album		**Track Number**
☐ Tony Bove's Album		☐ ☐ of ☐ ☐
Grouping		**Disc Number**
☐		☐ ☐ of ☐ ☐
Composer		**BPM**
☐ Tony Bove		☐
Comments		**Artwork**
☐		☐

Genre	**Part of a Compilation**	**My Rating**
☑ Rock ⬍	☐ No ⬍	☑ ★★★★★

Volume Adjustment   **Equalizer Preset**

☐ –100%   None   +100%   ☐ None ⬍

[Cancel]   (**OK**)

Figure 12-5
Editing song information for multiple songs at once

You may think you provided enough song information in GarageBand's export preferences (see Chapter 5), but don't be lulled into complacency — you should add ratings to make creating playlists easier (as described later in this chapter). Another piece of information you should add is the composer credit — composer information is important for iPod users, because the iPod allows you to scroll music by composer as well as by artist, album, and song. Adding composer credits, ratings, and other information is usually worth your while because you can then search, sort, and create playlists based on this information.

To add information to a single song, select the song and choose File ➜ Get Info (or press Command+I). You see

the Song Information dialog box, as shown in Figure 12-6. The Song Information dialog box offers the following tabs:

- **Summary:** The Summary tab offers useful information about the music file's format and location on your hard drive, its file size, and the digital compression method (bit rate, sample rate, and so on). You can read more about compression methods in Chapter 5.

- **Info:** The Info tab allows you to change the song name, artist, composer, album, genre, and year, as well as add comments.

- **Options:** The Options tab offers a volume adjustment option, a choice of equalizer presets, ratings, and start

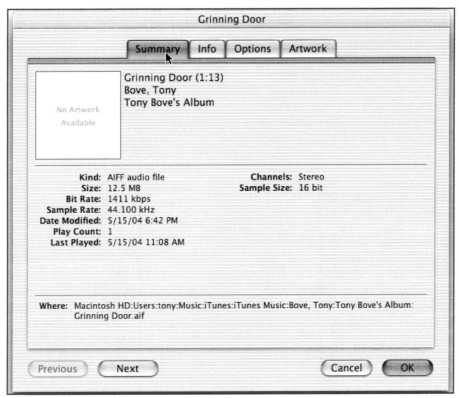

Figure 12-6
Viewing and editing information for a single song

and stop times for each song. You can assign up to five stars to a song (your own rating system — five stars means best).

- **Artwork:** The Artwork tab allows you to add or delete artwork for the song. The iTunes Music Store supplies artwork with most songs.

ORGANIZING PLAYLISTS IN ITUNES

To organize your music for different operations in iTunes, such as copying to an iPod or burning onto a CD, you make a list of the songs called a *playlist*. Make a playlist from a set of exported tracks to be used for your band's

next album. Compile a playlist of demo songs for a trip to a music industry confab. I routinely create playlists specifically for use with an iPod on road trips, and other playlists that combine songs from different albums based on common themes or similarities.

You can create as many playlists of songs, in any order, as you want. The song files don't change, nor are they copied anywhere. The music files stay right where they are; only their names are stored in the playlists. You can even create a smart playlist that automatically includes songs based on the criteria you set up, or removes songs that don't match the criteria.

You can drag individual songs or entire albums into a playlist and rearrange the songs quickly and easily. To create a playlist, dance along to these steps:

1. **Click the + button or choose File ➔ New Playlist.**

   Clicking the + button, in the bottom-left corner of the iTunes window under the Source pane, creates a new playlist called "untitled playlist," as shown in Figure 12-7.

Figure 12-7

Creating a new playlist and editing its name in iTunes

2. **Type a descriptive name for the playlist.**

   After you type a new name, such as "A1 studio takes," iTunes automatically sorts the playlist into alphabetical order in the Source pane, underneath the preset

smart playlists and other sources, as shown in Figure 12-8. Sorting alphabetically and quickly: that's what computers are for.

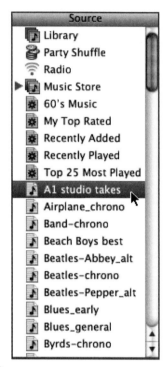

Figure 12-8

The new playlist (empty) is sorted by name in the Source pane

3. **Select Library in the Source pane, and then drag songs from the library to the playlist.**

   Drag the song directly over the name of the playlist, as shown in Figure 12-9 (don't worry, you won't hurt it). The order of songs in the playlist is based on the order in which you drag them to the list. You can drag a group of songs to a playlist at once by selecting the entire group (either by clicking the first song and Shift-clicking the last song in a range of songs, or by Command-clicking any songs you like to add them to the group).

4. Select the playlist in the Source pane, and then drag songs to rearrange the contents.

To move a song up the list and scroll at the same time, drag it over the up-arrow in the first column (the song number) as shown in Figure 12-10; to move a song down the list and scroll, drag it to the bottom of the list. You can move a group of songs at once by selecting the entire group (either by clicking the first song and Shift-clicking the last song, or by Command-clicking songs to select a noncontiguous group).

You can drag songs from one playlist to another; only links are copied, not the actual files. Besides dragging songs, you can also rearrange a playlist by sorting it: click the Song Name, Time, and Artist column headings to sort by those headings. And when you double-click a playlist, it opens in its own window, displaying only the songs in that list.

▼ **Tip**

To create a playlist quickly, select the group of songs that you want to make into a playlist (Shift-click or Command-click to select the group), and then choose File ➜ New Playlist from Selection. A new playlist appears in the Source pane, and you can then type a name for it.

Figure 12-9
Dragging songs from the library to the playlist

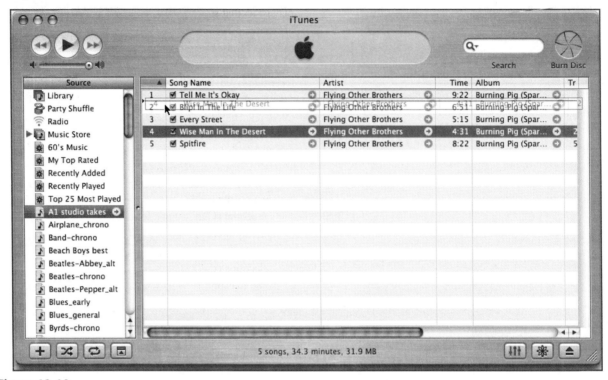

Figure 12-10
Rearranging songs inside a playlist

Creating playlists of albums

You may want to play entire albums of songs without having to select each album as you play them. To create a playlist of entire albums in a particular order, follow these steps:

1. **Create a new playlist.**

   Create a playlist by clicking the + sign under the Source pane, or choosing File ➜ New Playlist. Type a descriptive name for the new playlist.

2. **Select Library in the Source pane, and then click the Browse button to find the artist.**

   The Album list appears in the right panel.

3. **Drag the album name over the playlist name.**

4. **Select and drag each subsequent album over the playlist name.**

   Each time you drag an album, iTunes automatically lists the songs in the proper track sequence.

Note

You can rename a playlist at any time by clicking its name and typing a new one, just like you would rename any file name in the Finder.

Creating smart playlists

Smart playlists add songs to themselves based on pre-arranged criteria. The smart playlists, listed at the top of the Source pane under the Music Store option, are indicated by a gear icon. Several smart playlists, such as the My Top Rated and Recently Added, are provided with iTunes to show you how to make your own. For example, as you rate your songs, the My Top Rated playlist changes to reflect your new ratings. You don't have to set anything up: My Top Rated is already defined for you.

To view and edit a smart playlist, select the playlist and choose File ➜ Edit Smart Playlist. The Smart Playlist dialog box appears. You may want to modify the smart

playlist so that songs with a higher rating are picked: simply add another star or two to the My Rating criteria. You can also choose to limit the playlist to a certain number of songs, selected by various methods such as random, most recently played, and so on.

To create a new smart playlist, choose File ➜ New Smart Playlist. The Smart Playlist dialog appears, as shown in Figure 12-11, giving you the following choices for setting criteria:

- **Match the Following Condition:** Select any of the categories used for song information from the first pop-up menu, and select an operator, such as greater than or less than, from the second pop-up menu. The selections you make in these two pop-up menus combine to express a condition, such as Year is greater than 1966. You can also add multiple conditions by clicking the + button (refer to Figure 12-12); when you do, you also have to decide whether to match *all* or just any one of these conditions.

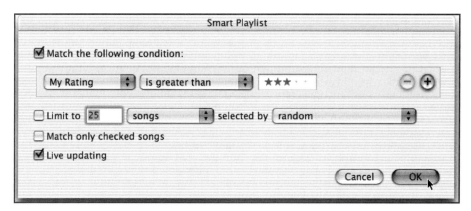

Figure 12-11
Creating a smart playlist with a single match criteria for choosing songs

- **Limit To:** You can make the smart playlist a specific duration, measured by the number of songs, total time, or size in megabytes or gigabytes. Limiting a smart playlist to what can fit on a CD — or to the duration of a drive or a jog with an iPod — is useful. You can select the songs by various methods such as random, most recently played, and so on.

- **Match Only Checked Songs:** This selects only songs that have a black check mark beside them, along with the rest of the criteria. You can fine-tune your selections for a smart playlist by adding check marks to (or removing check marks from) specific songs.

- **Live Updating:** This allows iTunes to automatically update the playlist continually as you add or remove songs from the library.

After setting up the criteria, click OK to create the smart playlist. iTunes labels the playlist with a gear icon and the name "untitled playlist." You can then click in the playlist and type a new name for it.

Setting up multiple criteria gives you the opportunity to create playlists that are way smarter than the ones supplied with iTunes. For example, I created a smart playlist with the criteria shown in Figure 12-12 that does the following:

- Adds any song added to the library in the past week that also has a rating greater than three stars.

- Limits the playlist to 72 minutes of music to fit on an audio CD, and refines the selection to the most recently added if the entire selection becomes greater than 72 minutes.

- Matches only checked songs and performs live updating.

COPYING ITUNES SONGS AND PLAYLISTS

The need to copy songs is a necessary fact of life. They're *your* songs, after all, and you need backup copies in case your hard drive fails. Even songs you purchase online can be freely copied to make backups — there are restrictions on playing them on different computers, but otherwise you are free to copy the song files. I talk more about sharing music files with others in Chapter 14; this chapter assumes you want to make copies for yourself.

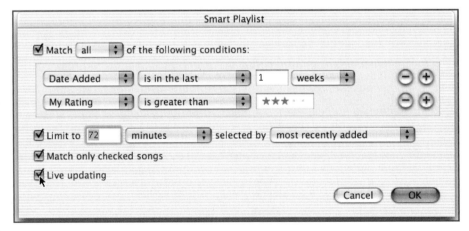

Figure 12-12

Creating a smart playlist with multiple criteria for choosing songs

WISDOM OF IHNATKO: RATE 'EM ALL, LET IPOD SORT 'EM OUT

It seems like the one way to make sure you hate every song in your library is to methodically go through all four (dozen, hundred, thousand, -ty thousand) of them and rate them individually. It's like when your Dad forced you to smoke a whole carton of cigarettes as a kid to ensure that you lost all interest in tobacco forever (my Dad never did this to me, but I saw it in a sitcom once and it seemed to work).

Instead, I've added a final qualifier to all of the Smart Playlists that I've synced to my iPod: Only add music that has no rating. During the course of the day I've got my earphones in and at the start of each track I reach down and use my iPod's scroll wheel to set a rating...if I happen to think of it. When iTunes resyncs my iPod, it replaces that track with one that needs a rating. Eventually, I'll get to all 11,000 of them, but to be honest, when I'm down to just the Paula Abdul greatest hits dance-remixes, I'll probably just remove that option from my Smart Playlists and consider the job complete.

By default (that is, if you don't change your storage preference), iTunes stores your music library inside your home folder; the path to this folder is typically your home folder/Music/iTunes/. Inside this folder is an iTunes Music folder, where all songs you export from GarageBand are stored. Even music files you drag to the iTunes window are stored here: iTunes makes a copy and stores the copy in the iTunes Music folder.

Tip

You can change where iTunes stores your music library by choosing iTunes ➜ Preferences, clicking Advanced, and then clicking the Change button, which lets you select another location.

You can find the location of any song by selecting the song and choosing File ➜ Get Info, and then clicking the Summary tab in the Song Information dialog. Look in the Where section for the pathname to the file and the song's file name.

Using the Finder, you can copy song files — and artist folders containing song files — freely from your iTunes Music folder to other folders, or to hard drives on other computers. The files are organized in folders by artist name and by album within the iTunes Music folder. Copying an

entire album is easy: simply drag the album folder to another hard drive.

To copy all the music files in your iTunes library to another hard drive, locate the iTunes folder using the Finder, drag this entire folder to another hard drive or backup device, and you're all set. The copy operation may take some time if the library is large.

Note

Copying the contents of your iTunes library copies the music itself, not your playlists. You still have to export your playlists separately.

Exporting playlists

You can export a playlist from one computer and import it into a different computer. Select the playlist, choose File ➜ Export Song List, choose the XML option from the Format pop-up menu in the Save: iTunes dialog, and then click Save.

When you export a playlist, you get a list of songs in the XML (Extensible Markup Language) format, but not the songs themselves — you still need to copy the actual song files to the other computer as described in the previous section. You can then import the playlist into iTunes on the other computer by choosing File ➜ Import, selecting the XML file, and clicking Choose.

You can export all the playlists in your library at the same time by choosing File ➜ Export Library, and then import them into iTunes on the other computer by choosing File ➜ Import and selecting the exported XML file.

Backing up your library

You can make a backup copy of your entire iTunes library, or move your library to another computer.

▼ Tip

If you have songs in different locations — on different hard drives connected to the same Mac, or shared over a network — you can have iTunes consolidate your music library by copying everything into the iTunes Music Library folder. By consolidating your library first, you make sure that your backup is complete. To consolidate your music library, choose Advanced ➜ Consolidate Library. The original songs remain where they are, but copies are made in your music folder.

To copy your entire music library to another Mac, follow these steps:

COPYING SONGS PURCHASED ONLINE

When Apple announced the iTunes Music Store, Apple chairman Steve Jobs remarked that other online services put forward by the music industry tend to treat consumers like criminals. Steve had a point. Many of these services cost more and add a level of copy protection that prevents consumers from burning CDs or using the music they bought on other computers or portable MP3 players. Record labels had been dragging their feet for years, experimenting with online sales and taking legal action against online sites such as Napster that were allowing free downloads and music copying. While the free music attracted millions of listeners, the free services were under legal attack in several countries and the digital music distributed was not of the highest quality (not to mention widespread and sometimes intentional misspellings in the song information and artist names). Consumers grew even warier when the Record Industry Association of America (RIAA), a legal organization looking out for the interests of record companies, drove prosecutors to arrest for illegal copyright infringement people who were downloading free music.

No one should go to jail for being a music junkie. Consumers and the industry both needed a solution, so Apple did the research on how to make a service that worked better and was easier to use, and it forged ahead with the iTunes Music Store. By all accounts, Apple has succeeded in offering the easiest, fastest, and most cost-effective service for buying music inexpensively online for your computer and your iPod.

The computer you use to set up your account is automatically authorized by Apple to play the songs you buy. Fortunately, the songs aren't locked to that computer — you can copy them to another computer and play them using iTunes on the other computer. When you first *play* the songs on the other computer, iTunes asks for your Music Store account ID and password in order to authorize that computer. You can authorize up to five computers at any one time. If you want to add a sixth computer, you can remove the authorization from a computer by choosing Advanced ➜ Deauthorize Account on that computer. For more about burning CDs and sharing purchased music, see Chapter 14.

1. **Locate your iTunes Music folder in the Finder of your old Mac.**

   Locate your iTunes folder, which is usually within the Music folder in your home folder. Inside the iTunes folder is the iTunes Music folder, which contains your music library.

2. **If the new Mac has a music library, move the files inside the iTunes Music folder to another folder, or copy them to another hard drive and delete the original files.**

   If the music library is empty, you can skip this step.

3. **Copy the iTunes Music folder from the old Mac to the iTunes folder of the new Mac.**

   The iTunes Music folder contains all the music files.

4. **On the old Mac, choose File → Export Library, browse to a location on your hard drive or network, and click Save.**

   When you export your entire library, iTunes creates an XML file that contains all the playlist information and links to the music files.

5. **Start iTunes on the new Mac.**

6. Choose File → Import, select the Library.xml file, and click Choose.

   The music library is now available on the new computer.

BACKING UP SONG PROJECTS

Your GarageBand songs don't exist anywhere else in the universe; the original tracks are precious, especially if you want to try new mixes with them someday. You should therefore routinely copy your GarageBand song projects to another hard drive or removable storage device, burn a CD or DVD, or even use the iDisk on the Internet provided by the .Mac service.

To copy a song project to another disk, use the Finder to locate the GarageBand music folder. The folder is usually located within the Music folder in your User folder. The GarageBand folder contains the project files with file names you should recognize (they are the names of your songs).

 Tip

You can see what's inside a project file by holding down the Control key while clicking on it to bring up a pop-up menu. Choose Show Package Contents from the pop-up menu, and the Finder displays a separate window with the project's contents: a Media folder and the projectData file. Do not rename or move these items. You can open the Media folder to see the AIFF files containing recorded Real Instrument tracks, but do not rename or move either the Media folder or the projectData file.

WISDOM OF IHNATKO: BUY NOW, PAY LATER

Your other big motivation for backing up your iTunes library is that if your Mac's hard drive crashes or gets too close to the barbecue grill or if your Uncle Salty swipes it to help bankroll his next theatrical production, Apple won't replace any of the songs you purchased from the iTunes Music Store. I still have my 600 original CDs tucked away in storage, and if my main iTunes drive did the big firework, I could always just rip 'em again. But unless I had backup files stored somewhere, my iTMS songs would be gone for good.

Drag one or more project files, or the entire GarageBand folder, to another hard drive or backup device, and you're all set.

If you subscribe to the Apple .Mac service, you can use its hassle-free Backup 2 software to copy specific folders and files (such as your GarageBand projects). Backup 2 allows you to save the latest versions of your files regularly and automatically, so you never have to worry about losing photos or any other important documents. With Backup 2, which comes free with a .Mac membership or which can be purchased directly from Apple, you can quickly and easily store important files on your iDisk (a portion of an Internet hard drive hosted by .Mac), or on CD or DVD as data files (not as CD songs — see Chapter 14 to burn an audio or MP3 CD).

The iDisk method is perhaps the least convenient, even though you get free space with a .Mac membership: It offers up to 100 MB, which is barely enough for one song project, and copying to the iDisk is slow with a modem connection. I use iDisk to transfer large files, and to back up very important documents. But you are better off using CD or DVD as a backup medium for your song projects, as well as audio CD for your finished songs (as described in Chapter 14).

 Tip

If you don't have Backup, you can still burn data files onto DVD using iDVD, which is part of the iLife package. See "Putting Song Projects on DVD" in Chapter 16.

If you want to obtain Backup 2, follow these steps to download and install it:

1. **Download the Backup 2 installation package.**

   Go to the .Mac main page (www.mac.com), click the Backup button, and then click the Download Backup link. The software may also be available in the download section of the main Apple site (www.apple.com). (You need to stay connected to the Internet to complete the next steps.)

2. **Read the instructions.**

   Instructions are available on how to download and install Backup 2. These instructions have probably changed since I wrote this; the helpful people at .Mac always try to make things easier for you.

3. **Double-click the installation package to install it.**

   When the installation completes, the Backup application is placed in the Applications folder on your hard drive.

To use Backup 2 to copy folders to your iDisk, a recordable CD, or a disk drive, follow these steps:

1. **Double-click the Backup icon.**

   The Backup 2 software displays a list of items to back up and a checkbox next to each item.

2. **Select the folders for backup.**

   You can add any folder you like to the backup list by clicking the + (plus sign) button and choosing your library in the Open File dialog box.

3. **Choose a backup destination in the Backup to iDisk pop-up menu.**

   You can choose another disk drive or destination device rather than iDisk for your backup. If you have an Apple-supported CD-RW or DVD-R drive (such as the Apple SuperDrive), you can choose CD or DVD to store your project files.

4. **Click Backup Now, or schedule a backup to happen later.**

   The Backup Now button saves your files to the backup destination immediately. You can schedule automatic backups by clicking the calendar button, and the backup occurs at the time and date you specify.

5. **Quit Backup.**

That's it. Your song project is now safe and secure because it is stored in two different places.

13

Putting Songs on an iPod

In This Chapter

Connecting an iPod • Setting up an iPod in iTunes • Automatically
copying the entire iTunes library to an iPod • Updating an iPod automatically
by playlist or by selected songs • Copying and deleting songs manually
Using an iPod as a portable hard disk

After you've exported your GarageBand songs to your iTunes library, you can copy all your songs to an iPod in one step, and then take the iPod with you everywhere.

If you've been living under a rock for the last two years, you should know that the iPod is the king of music players. That explains why posters and billboards advertise it everywhere. People are buying these things. And you call yourself a music lover? The iPod was built for music lovers.

Music has changed so much in the transformation to digital that the music industry hardly recognizes it. The Apple iPod music player is the catalyst that has changed the music industry. It holds so much music that, no matter how large your music collection, you will seriously consider putting all your music into digital format on your computer, transferring portions of it to the iPod, and playing music from both your computer and from your iPod from now on. You may never stop buying CDs, but you won't have to buy all your music that way. And the music you own will never need to be replaced again.

COMPARING IPOD MODELS

Introduced way back in the Stone Age of digital music (2001), the iPod family has grown by three generations and spawned at least one private-label version (the H-Pod from Hewlett-Packard). Even from the beginning, iPod models were truly innovative for their times. With the MP3 music players of 2001 you could carry about 20 typical songs (or a single Phish jam) with you, but the first iPod could hold more than 1,000 typical songs (or an all-night Phish concert).

Today's iPod works with iTunes on either Windows computers or Macs. But that wasn't always the case. The first generation iPods work only with Macs. In 2002, Apple introduced the second generation — one version for Windows and another for the Mac, using the same design for both. By the third generation (2003), Apple had changed the design once again.

Third-generation models, still available in stores as of this writing, work with either Windows or Mac and come in a variety of hard-drive sizes. Some would argue that the Mini iPod, introduced in early 2004, is a fourth generation, but in many ways it is more like a spin-off of the third generation, and works with either Mac or Windows.

All iPods are designed for holding in your hand while you thumb the scroll wheel (our generic term for scroll wheel, touch wheel, or click wheel). The LCD screen in full-size models offers backlighting so that you can see it in the dark. For a nifty chart that shows the differences between iPod models, see the specifications page on the Apple iPod site (`www.apple.com/ipod/specs.html`).

The iPod is essentially a hard drive and a digital music player in one device. The 40GB iPod model can hold around 10,000 songs. That's more than 21 *days* of nonstop music. Even the 40GB model (the largest capacity iPod as of this writing) weighs less than two CDs, and iPod mini is smaller than a cell phone and weighs just 3.6 ounces.

This chapter shows you how to get your iPod connected, synchronized with iTunes, and ready to play the music you created in GarageBand. You also gain a working knowledge of how to use the iPod to store files temporarily, such as your GarageBand projects. You can even use an iPod like a portable hard drive to transfer projects from one computer to another.

The iPod supports the most popular digital audio formats, including MP3 (including Variable Bit Rate), AIFF, WAV, and the new AAC format, which features CD-quality audio in smaller file sizes than MP3. The iPod also supports the Audible AA spoken word file format. To learn more about the file formats used by iPod and iTunes, see Chapter 5.

▼ Caution

Your GarageBand songs are exported to iTunes as AIFF files, but these files are too large to use with an iPod, use too much power, and cause problems on playback such as skipping. Before copying music to your iPod, you should convert your songs to AAC or MP3, as described in Chapter 5.

CONNECTING AND SETTING UP AN IPOD

Got power? The current model iPod includes a built-in rechargeable lithium polymer battery that provides up to 12 hours of continuous music playtime on four hours of charge. You can also fast-charge the battery to 80 percent capacity in only one hour. The iPod battery recharges automatically when you connect the iPod to a power source. That power source can be either the power adapter supplied with the iPod, or a Mac connected by FireWire cable.

Note

Playback battery time varies, however, with the type of encoder you use for the music files in iTunes.

Older iPod models offer a Mac-like FireWire connection on the top of the iPod, but current models use a dock that connects to the iPod and offers FireWire and USB connections to various devices. The dock can also connect to your home stereo through a line-out connection. The dock includes a cable with a dock connector on one end and a FireWire (or optional USB) connector on the other. You can connect the FireWire end of the cable to either the Mac (to synchronize with iTunes and play iPod music in iTunes), or to the power adapter to charge the iPod battery. The FireWire connection to the Mac provides power to the iPod as long as the Mac is not in sleep mode.

FireWire has been a part of every Mac since at least 2000, and it is much faster than the USB connections typical on Macs. Current models offer a dock-style connection and a special cable with a flat dock connector to connect the dock, or the iPod itself, to the Mac's FireWire connection. The dock includes a cable with a flat dock connector on one end and a FireWire (or optional USB) connector on the other, as shown in Figure 13-1.

You can connect the FireWire end of the cable to either the computer (to synchronize with iTunes and play iPod music in iTunes), or to the power adapter. Third-generation full-size iPods don't support USB 2.0 on the Mac, but the iPod mini and fourth-generation iPods support it if your Mac offers USB 2.0, and a USB cable is provided. First-generation and second-generation models offer only a six-pin FireWire connection, so you can use a six-pin Mac-style FireWire cable to connect the iPod to the Mac's FireWire connection. Plug one end of the FireWire cable into the iPod, and plug the other end into the FireWire port on your Mac.

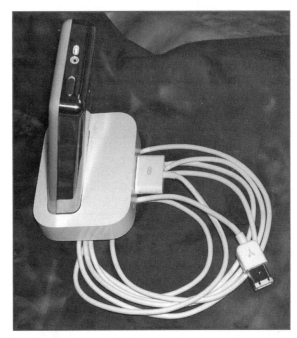

Figure 13-1
Third-generation iPod with dock and FireWire cable

BATTERY CARE AND FEEDING

The iPod's built-in rechargeable lithium ion battery is, essentially, a life-or-death proposition. Once dead, it is costly to replace. Fortunately the battery is easy to maintain. You can calibrate the battery once — running it all the way down (a full discharge), then charging it all the way up for four hours. Although this doesn't actually change battery performance, it does improve the battery gauge so that the iPod displays a more accurate indicator. It also gives you something useful to do — and a sense of being in control.

Unlike batteries that require you to fully discharge and then recharge in order to get a fuller capacity, the iPod lithium ion battery prefers a partial rather than a full discharge. The literature on the subject says that "frequent full discharges should be avoided after the initial calibration"— which means, don't run it down often. Lithium ion batteries typically last three years or more but are vulnerable to high temperatures, which decrease their life spans considerably — don't keep your iPod in a hot place, such as a sunny car dashboard. For an excellent technical description of how to maintain rechargeable lithium ion batteries, see the BatteryUniversity.com site (`www.batteryuniversity.com/parttwo-34.htm`).

Even when not in use, your iPod drinks the juice. If your iPod is inactive for 14 days, you must recharge its battery.

If you already use the cable to charge up the iPod, you can disconnect the cable from the power adapter and connect that same end to the Mac. In fact, you can also leave your dock connected to a powered-on Mac in this fashion, and use the Mac to charge up the iPod battery (as long as your Mac does not go to sleep).

 Caution

If you leave the iPod in a dock connected to a Mac, and the Mac goes to sleep, you could drain the battery.

When you first connect the iPod to the Mac that is powered up, the iTunes Setup Assistant starts up, as shown in Figure 13-2. In this dialog box, you can name your iPod, which is a good idea if you plan on sharing several iPods among several computers.

In the Setup Assistant, you can also turn on or off the option to automatically update your iPod.

▼ **Caution**

If this is your first time using an iPod, you probably want to fill it up right away, so leave this automatic update option checked — *unless* you have unconverted AIFF songs in your iTunes library that were exported from GarageBand and not deleted. If you do have AIFF files in your library (which you should not copy to your iPod), or you want to copy only a portion of your library to the iPod, uncheck this option and read "Copying songs manually" later in this chapter.

The Setup Assistant allows you to register your iPod with Apple to take advantage of Apple support. When you reach the last dialog box of the Setup Assistant, click Done.

After you click Done in the Setup Assistant, the iPod name appears in the iTunes Source pane under the Music Store. If you selected the automatic update feature in the

Figure 13-2
Setting up the iPod for use with a Mac

iTunes Setup Assistant, the iPod name appears grayed out in the Source pane. If you have the automatic update feature turned off (or if you turn it off as described in "Copying songs manually" later in this chapter), the iPod name appears just like any other source in the Source pane.

Also after finishing setup, the iPod icon appears on the desktop; if you leave your iPod connected to the Mac and start up iTunes, the iPod appears as a choice in the Source list.

▼ Tip

To see how much free space is left on the iPod, click the iPod in the Source pane of iTunes — the used and free amounts are displayed at the bottom of the window. You can also click the iPod icon on the Finder desktop and choose File ➜ Get Info. The Finder displays the Get Info window with information about capacity, amount used, and available space. You can also use the About command in the iPod Settings menu: choose Settings ➜ About from the main menu. The iPod information screen appears showing capacity and available space.

CONSERVING IPOD POWER

Your iPod is a hard drive, and whatever causes the hard drive to spin also causes a drain on power. Your iPod also has a *cache* — a memory chip holding in advance the next section of music to play. The iPod uses the cache not only to eliminate skipping when the hard drive is jostled, but also to conserve power, because the drive does not have to spin as much.

Playing songs continuously without using iPod controls saves power. Power drains faster when you use controls — such as selecting songs and using Previous/Rewind and Next/Fast-Forward. Not only that, but the hard disk has to spin more often when searching for songs, using more power than during continuous playback. Don't use the AIFF versions of your GarageBand songs with your iPod — convert the music first, as described in Chapter 5. The AIFF format takes up way too much space on the iPod hard drive and fills up the iPod cache too quickly, causing skips when you play them back and using too much battery power because the drive spins more often. Remember to pause playback when you're not listening, and use the iPod backlight sparingly. Press and hold the Menu button to turn off the backlight, or select Backlight from the iPod main menu to turn it on or off.

ADDING SONGS FROM ITUNES

Got space on your iPod? Fill it up with your iTunes music library. If your library is smaller than the iPod's capacity, you can keep the iPod filled and automatically updated every time you connect it to your Mac. The iPod updates itself automatically from your iTunes music library: with the automatic update feature, any changes, additions, or deletions you make to your iTunes library reflect in your iPod.

For musicians working in GarageBand, updating the iPod with their entire library causes one problem: When you export to iTunes, you end up with high-quality AIFF music files in your library that are suitable for burning on CD, but because of file size are unsuitable for the iPod. You have to convert them to the AAC or MP3 format, as described in Chapter 5. That means you have to choose your iPod update option wisely: you can update your iPod *automatically* if you remove the AIFF versions of your

songs, or you can update your iPod *manually* if you keep your AIFF versions around for burning onto CD (as described in "Copying songs manually" later in this chapter). Other iPod options include updating by playlist (as described in "Updating by playlist"), or updating by selected songs (as described in "Updating by selected songs").

Updating automatically

The default setting for a new iPod is to update itself automatically, synchronizing to your iTunes library; the iPod matches your library exactly, song for song, playlist for playlist. After making changes in iTunes (such as adding more music), those changes are automatically copied to the iPod the next time you connect it to your Mac. If you added or deleted songs in your library, those songs are added or deleted in the iPod automatically. Nice.

Tip

I'm often too busy to copy specific songs to an iPod, and since my entire iTunes music library (*sans* the AIFF versions of songs) is still less than 40GB, the entire library fits on the 40GB iPod model. So I burn my exported GarageBand songs, which are in AIFF format, onto a CD (as described in Chapter 14), and convert those songs to AAC or MP3 versions (as described in Chapter 5) before deleting the AIFF versions. I then have a clean iTunes library that updates the iPod automatically. You can use this method too, until your iTunes library gets too large for one iPod; and it makes sense, because copying your library is just as fast as copying individual songs, if not faster, and you don't have to do anything except connect the iPod to the Mac.

If your iTunes music library is too large to fit on your iPod, you can still have the iPod update automatically by keeping it synchronized to a subset of your library; add any new material to just that subset. Or you can let iTunes select the music automatically according to your ratings; you can create a smart playlist that does it for you, as described in "Updating by playlist" later in this chapter.

The iPod automatically updates itself by default. It takes maybe a few seconds to update the iPod with an hour of songs. Just follow these simple steps to set the updating process in motion:

1. **Connect the iPod to your Mac.**

   When you first connect your iPod to the Mac either through the dock or directly, the iPod automatically synchronizes with your iTunes music library (unless you turn off the automatic update option in the Setup

Assistant, or hold down the Command and Option keys while connecting the iPod).

2. **Click the iPod eject button, which appears at the bottom-right corner of the iTunes window when the iPod is connected.**

   If you checked the Enable disk use option in iPod options to use your iPod as a hard drive, you can eject the iPod by dragging the iPod icon on the desktop to the Trash. In OS X 10.3, you can click the eject icon next to the iPod icon in the Finder Sidebar. After taking a few seconds to start up, the iPod displays its main menu. Wait for the iPod to display the main menu before disconnecting the iPod from its dock, or before disconnecting the dock from the computer.

▼ Caution

Don't disconnect your iPod while the updating is in progress, or even right after clicking the iPod eject button or dragging the iPod icon to the trash; wait until the main menu appears on the iPod's display. The iPod displays a "Do not disconnect" warning until it is safe to disconnect. Like any hard drive, the iPod needs to close down properly in order to save any critical data.

If you change your iPod preferences to update manually or automatically by playlist, as described later in this chapter, you can change the setting back to automatic update at any time. After changing the setting to automatic update, updating occurs automatically until you change the setting back to manual, or unless you hold down Command+Option while connecting the iPod to your Mac (either through the dock or directly).

Change your iPod preferences to automatic update by following these steps:

1. **Connect the iPod to your Mac.**

    If this is your first time using an iPod, iTunes starts automatically. You can change this in the iPod preferences.

2. **Select the iPod name in the iTunes Source pane.**

3. **Click the iPod options button in the bottom-right corner of the iTunes window, to the left of the equalizer button, as shown in Figure 13-3.**

The iPod Preferences window appears, as shown in Figure 13-4.

4. **Select the "Automatically update all songs and playlists" option.**

    iTunes displays a confirmation message.

5. **Click OK.**

    Clicking OK confirms that you want to change to automatic update.

Figure 13-3
Click the iPod options button to set preferences

Figure 13-4
Setting the iPod's updating preference

6. **Change other iPod preferences as you wish.**

   Another preference you may want to change is "Open iTunes when attached," which launches iTunes automatically when the Mac detects your iPod being connected. (If you turn the "Open iTunes when attached" option off, you have to start iTunes by clicking its icon in the Dock, or double-clicking the application in the Applications folder.)

7. **Click OK to close iPod Preferences.**

8. **Click the iPod eject button in the bottom-right corner of the iTunes window.**

   If you checked the Enable disk use option in iPod options to use your iPod as a hard drive, you can eject

the iPod by dragging the iPod icon on the desktop to the Trash. In OS X 10.3 you can click the eject icon next to the iPod icon in the Finder Sidebar. After taking a few seconds to start up, the iPod displays its main menu. Wait for the iPod to display the main menu before disconnecting the iPod from its dock, or before disconnecting the dock from the computer.

▼ Caution

Be careful if you connect your iPod to another Mac. iTunes displays the message "This iPod is linked to another iTunes music library. Do you want to change the link to this iTunes music library and replace all existing songs and playlists on this iPod with those from this library?" If you don't want to change the iPod contents to this other music library, click No. Otherwise, iTunes updates the iPod with its library, erasing any previous contents. By clicking No, you change that computer's iTunes setting to manually update — see "Copying songs manually" later in this chapter.

If your iTunes music library is too large to fit on your iPod, you can still update automatically by keeping your iPod synchronized to a subset of your library. When you first use your iPod (which is set to automatic update by default), iTunes displays a message if your library is too large to fit:

The iPod "<your iPod's name>" does not have enough space to hold all of the songs in your music library. For your convenience, iTunes has created a new playlist named "<your iPod's name> Selection" which contains a selection of songs from your music library that will fit on this iPod. You may change the songs in this playlist at any time. Your iPod will be automatically updated with this playlist every time it is connected.

Clicking OK is your only choice. iTunes creates a new playlist specially designed for updating your iPod automatically. For example, if your iPod is named GigaMojo, you will find a new playlist named GigaMojo Selection filled with all the songs that iTunes could fit in your iPod.

On the other hand, if you have been using your iPod and already have it set to automatic update, iTunes displays this message if your iPod is full:

The iPod "<your iPod's name>" cannot be updated because there is not enough free space to hold all of the songs in the iTunes music library. Would you like iTunes to choose a selection of songs to copy to this iPod?

iTunes gives you a choice: You can click No, and iTunes updates automatically until it fills up your iPod. You can click Yes, and iTunes displays this message:

iTunes has created the playlist "<your iPod's name> Selection" using your music preferences and will update the iPod "<your iPod's name>" with this playlist every time it is connected.

Click OK (the only choice at this point). iTunes creates a new playlist specially designed for updating your iPod automatically. For example, if your iPod is named GigaMojo, you will find a new playlist named GigaMojo Selection filled with all the songs that iTunes could fit in your iPod.

iTunes decides which songs and albums to include in this playlist using the ratings you can set for each song, as described in Chapter 12. iTunes groups album tracks together and computes an average rating and play count for the album. It then fills the iPod, giving higher priority to albums with play counts and ratings greater than zero. You can therefore influence the decisions iTunes makes by adding ratings to songs — such as the songs you create in

GarageBand — or to entire albums. (As if you needed a reason to give your original GarageBand songs the highest rating!)

Tip

You can prevent the iPod from automatically updating by holding down the Command and Option keys as you connect the iPod to a Mac, and keeping them held down until the iPod name appears in the iTunes Source pane.

Updating by playlist

You can set up the iPod to automatically update only selected playlists. (If you want to copy playlists manually, see "Copying songs manually" later in this chapter.) Updating automatically by playlist is an easy way to update an iPod with an iTunes library that is larger than the iPod's capacity, or a library containing files you don't want to put on your iPod, like AIFF versions exported from GarageBand.

Tip

You can isolate your AIFF versions into playlists designed for burning to CD, as described in Chapter 14, and then simply exclude those playlists from automatically updating to your iPod.

Before using this update option, create the playlists in iTunes that you want to copy to the iPod (see Chapter 12, "Organizing Playlists"). Then follow these steps:

1. **Connect the iPod to your Mac through the Mac's FireWire connection.**

2. **Select the iPod name in the iTunes Source pane.**

3. **Click the iPod options button.**

The iPod Preferences window appears (refer to Figure 13-4).

4. **Select the "Automatically update selected playlists only" option.**

5. **In the list box, select the checkbox next to each playlist that you want to include in the update, as shown in Figure 13-5.**

Figure 13-5
Setting up the iPod to automatically update with only selected playlists

6. **Click OK.**

iTunes automatically updates the iPod by erasing its contents and copying over only the playlists you selected in Step 5.

7. **Click the iPod eject button in the bottom-right corner of the iTunes window.**

Updating by selected songs

You may want to update the iPod automatically, but only with selected songs — especially if your iTunes library is larger than the capacity of your iPod. To use this method, you must first select the songs you want to transfer to the iPod in the iTunes library, and then deselect the songs you don't want to transfer.

▼ **Tip**
You can quickly select or deselect an entire album by selecting it in Browse view and holding down the Command key.

▼ **Tip**
You can deselect your AIFF versions of songs so that they are not included in the update to your iPod.

After selecting the songs you want to transfer, follow these steps:

1. **Connect the iPod to your Mac through the Mac's FireWire connection.**

2. **Select the iPod name in the iTunes Source pane.**

3. **Click the iPod options button.**

The iPod Preferences window appears (refer to Figure 13-4).

4. **Select the "Automatically update all songs and playlists" option, and click OK when the "Are you sure you want to enable automatic updating" message appears.**

MAKING PLAYLISTS ON THE ROAD

You're on the road and you suddenly have the urge, or need, to play a certain set of songs in a certain order. These sudden impulses are quite natural for road warriors who are also music lovers — you need a certain soundtrack for the road. So what do you do if the playlists you created way back when just aren't good enough?

Create one on your iPod on the fly — a temporary On-The-Go playlist (which works in iPods using iPod software version 2.0 and newer, including the iPod mini, but not in first-generation and second-generation iPods). First locate and highlight a song, or even an entire album title on your iPod. Press and hold the Select button until the song or album title flashes. Repeat this procedure for each song or album of songs, in the order that you want them played.

To play the On-The-Go playlist, scroll the iPod main menu until Playlists is highlighted, and then press the Select button. The Playlists menu appears. Scroll to the On-The-Go item, which you can always find at the very end of the list in the Playlists menu. You can continue to add songs to the list of queued songs in the On-The-Go playlist at any time. Your iPod saves the On-The-Go playlist until you clear it.

To clear the list of queued songs, select Playlists from the iPod main menu, then select On-The-Go. The song list appears. Scroll to the very end of the song list, and select Clear Playlist. The Clear menu appears, and you can select Clear Playlist to make the songs disappear from the On-The-Go list. The songs are still in your iPod, of course.)

5. **Select the "Only update checked songs" checkbox and click OK.**

   iTunes automatically updates the iPod by erasing its contents and copying over only the songs in the iTunes library that you selected.

6. **Click the iPod eject button in the bottom-right corner of the iTunes window.**

Copying songs manually

When your iPod is set to update automatically, the iPod contents are grayed out in the iTunes window: you don't have direct access to the songs in the iPod using iTunes. If you set your iPod to update *manually*, the entire contents of the iPod are active and available in iTunes. The iPod name appears in the iTunes Source pane, and you can double-click it to display the iPod playlists. You can copy music directly to your iPod, delete songs from the iPod, and edit the iPod playlists directly.

Why would you do it any other way? Updating automatically is faster in many cases because you don't have to spend the time choosing what to copy. But copying manually is essential if you want to copy music from another computer's music library without deleting any music from your iPod.

THE DJ CONSOLE

Manual updating is also useful for providing direct access to your iPod's music library so that you can play DJ with both your iPod library and your iTunes library using iTunes. You can turn a Mac laptop or desktop into a versatile jukebox that can play music from multiple iPods and its own library. The music comes out of Mac's speakers — or you can connect your Mac to a home stereo directly (with stereo cables), or wirelessly using Apple AirPort Express.

You can set your iPod to update manually anytime you want, without disturbing the music already on the iPod. To set your iPod to update manually, follow these steps:

1. **Connect the iPod to your Mac, holding down the Command and Option keys to prevent automatic updating.**

   Continue holding them down until the iPod name appears in the iTunes Source pane.

2. **Select the iPod name in the iTunes Source pane.**

3. **Click the iPod options button.**

   The iPod Preferences window appears (refer to Figure 13-4).

4. **Check the "Manually manage songs and playlists" option.**

   iTunes displays the "Disabling automatic update requires manually unmounting the iPod before each disconnect" message.

5. **Click OK to accept the new iPod preferences.**

   The iPod contents now appear active (not grayed out) in the iTunes window.

To copy music from iTunes directly to your iPod, follow these steps:

1. **Select the iTunes music library in the iTunes Source pane.**

   The library's songs appear in List view or in Browse view, as described in Chapter 1.

2. **Drag items directly from your iTunes music library over the iPod name in the Source pane.**

   You can copy a single song, as shown in Figure 13-6, or a selected group of songs. You can also drag entire albums; when you drag an album title, all the songs in the album are copied. You can copy everything by a single artist by dragging the artist name. When you drag a playlist, all the songs associated with the playlist are copied.

3. **Click the iPod eject button in the bottom-right corner of the iTunes window.**

With manual updating, you can delete songs from the iPod directly. To delete any song in the song list (with your iPod set for manual updating), follow these steps:

1. **Select the iPod in the iTunes Source pane.**

2. **Open the iPod's contents in iTunes.**

3. **Select a song or album on the iPod and press Delete or choose Edit → Clear.**

Figure 13-6

Copying a song directly from the iTunes library to the iPod "Bobbie McGee"

iTunes displays a warning to make sure you want to do this; click OK to go ahead or Cancel to stop.

USING AN IPOD AS A HARD DRIVE

The iPod is more than just a device for listening to music. You can also use it to view calendar and contact information to help you manage your daily activities. You can even use it as a portable hard drive and transfer files from one computer to another. If you have enough space left over after copying your iTunes music library, you can use the empty space for files such as GarageBand ".band" project files you want to copy to another computer. The Garage-Band project files include Real Instrument tracks and anything else you added to the project, so you can open the project on another computer.

The iPod is smart enough to keep your files separate from your music collection so that they are not accidentally erased when you update your music. Many of the capabilities of third-party software and accessories for the iPod — such as the storing of photos, news feeds, and Web pages — depend on using the iPod mounted as a hard drive.

To use the iPod as an external hard drive, follow these steps:

1. **Connect the iPod to your Mac.**

2. **Hold down the Command and Option keys as iTunes opens (or as you open iTunes, if it doesn't launch automatically).**

   By holding down the Command and Option keys, you prevent the iPod from automatically updating itself.

3. **Select the iPod name in the iTunes Source pane.**

4. **Click the iPod Options button.**

   The iPod Preferences window opens, as shown in Figure 13-7.

5. **Select the Enable FireWire Disk Use option and click OK.**

6. **Open the iPod icon in the Finder to see its contents.**

Figure 13-7
Enabling an iPod to be used as a FireWire hard drive

The iPod opens up to show three folders: Calendars, Contacts, and Notes, as shown in Figure 13-8. You can add new folders, rename your custom folders, and generally use the iPod as a hard drive.

▼ **Caution**

Do not rename the Calendars, Contacts, or Notes folders, because they link directly to the Calendar, Contacts, and Notes functions on the iPod.

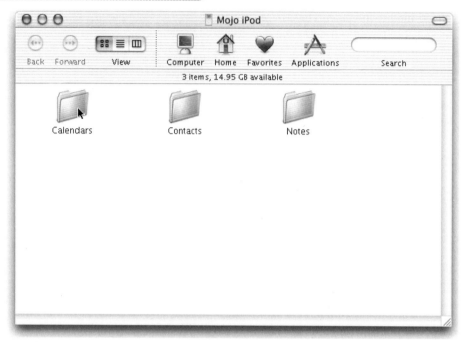

Figure 13-8
Opening the iPod as a hard drive

7. **Create new folders, and drag files and folders to the iPod.**

   To keep data organized, create new folders on the iPod, as shown in Figure 13-9, and then drag files and folders you want to back up to the newly created folders.

8. **When the system has finished copying data to the iPod, eject the iPod.**

▼ **Caution**

After ejecting the iPod, wait until its display shows the iPod main menu. You can then disconnect the iPod from the dock, or disconnect the dock from the computer. Never disconnect an iPod before ejecting it.

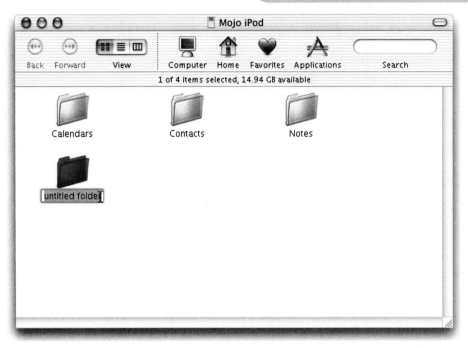

Figure 13-9
Adding a new folder to the iPod

To delete files and folders from the iPod, drag them to the Trash just as you would with an external hard drive. Use the Finder to see how much free space is left on the iPod. Select the iPod icon on the desktop, and choose File → Show Info. You can also use the About command in the iPod Settings menu: choose Settings → About from the main menu.

To learn a lot more about the iPod and iTunes, check out another book from this series, *The iLife '04 Book* (Wiley) by yours truly and Andy Ihnatko.

Burning CDs and Sharing Music

In This Chapter

Burning audio CDs and MP3 CDs • Organizing a CD playlist • Setting the recording speed and format • Adding gaps between songs • Leveling the volume of all songs on a CD • Transferring music files across networks • Sharing files with Windows PCs

Contrary to the beliefs of some record company executives, making your own CDs is not a global pastime simply because people want to steal music. As a GarageBand artist you can use CDs as your medium, whether you sell them from Web sites, record stores, or the trunk of your car, or even if you just give them away. Blank CDs are cheap and play everywhere, so they're the perfect medium for the music you create. If you are serious about your music, you will want to burn it onto CDs.

Burning a CD actually refers to the process in which the CD drive recorder's laser meets the surface of the disc and creates a new impression loaded with digital information. Nothing actually gets hot (except your music, of course) — it's not like baking a pizza. You insert a blank disc into your Mac, iTunes does its thing, and your Mac spits out a finished audio CD.

This chapter lights the fire in your CD burner — assuming that you *have* a CD burner as part of your computer system. It describes how to get your playlist ready for burning, what settings to use, and so on. You find out what you need to know to make sure that your burns are not meltdowns — the only melting will be your own music melting in your ears.

I FOUGHT THE LAW AND THE LAW WON: CDS AND PIRACY

Apple CEO Steve Jobs gave personal demonstrations of the iTunes Music Store, iTunes, and the iPod to Paul McCartney and Mick Jagger. According to Steven Levy, writing in *Newsweek* (May 12, 2003), Jobs said, "They both totally get it." The former Beatle and the Stones frontman are no slouches — both conduct music-business affairs personally and both have extensive back catalogs of music. They know all about the free music-swapping services on the Internet, but they agree with Jobs that most people are willing to pay for high-quality music rather than download free copies of questionable quality.

I agree that treating technology as the culprit with regard to violations of copyright law is wrong. Conversely, the solution to piracy is not technology, because determined pirates always circumvent it with newer technology, and only consumers are inconvenienced. In my opinion, the law already covers the type of piracy that involves counterfeiting CDs. The fact that you are not allowed to copy a commercial CD and sell the copy to someone else makes sense. You also can't sell the individual songs of a commercial CD.

Giving music away is, of course, the subject of much controversy, with services such as Napster closed by court order while others flourish in countries that don't have copyright laws as strict as the United States. Nothing in iTunes or the iPod enables the sharing of music across the Internet like the former Napster — but you *can* copy the song files or burn CDs.

As for making copies for personal use, the law is murky at best. It depends on what you mean by personal use. The iLife package allows you to use music files in creative projects. You can, for example, put together a music video to show your friends by using iMovie to combine some video footage you shot with your camcorder and the latest hit by Eminem along with your own composition created in GarageBand. But don't expect to see it on MTV or VH1 without having a license for the Eminem stuff (which you're not likely to get).

Can you legally use a pop song as a soundtrack for a high school yearbook slideshow? It sounds legal to us, given the ability to use music for educational purposes, but that is a question only a lawyer can answer. If you're interested in obtaining the rights to music to use in semi-public or public presentations, or even movies and documentaries for public distribution, you can contact the music publisher or a licensing agent. Music-publishing organizations, such as the Music Publishers' Association (`www.mpa.org`), offer information and lists of music publishers, as well as explanations of various rights and licenses. Of course, putting music in slideshows is precisely what GarageBand is good for — create your own music! Perhaps someone will hear it and want to license it from you. Remember, career opportunities are ones that never knock.

CHOOSING STANDARD AUDIO OR MP3

If you have an Apple-supported CD-R, CD-RW, or DVD-R drive (such as the Apple SuperDrive), and blank CD-Rs ("R" stands for "recordable"), you can create your own music CDs that play in most CD players. Blank CD-Rs are available in most electronics and computer stores; you can also get them online from the Apple Store. Choose iTunes ➔ Shop for iTunes Products to reach the Apple Store online.

The discs are called CD-Rs because they use a *recordable* format that uses the same amount of space as commercial

CDs (which are not recordable, of course). Audio CD-Rs play just like commercial audio CDs in most CD players. You can fit up to 74 minutes of music on a high-quality audio CD-R; some can contain as much as 80 minutes. It's easier to measure the amount of music in *minutes* (and *seconds*) for fitting onto an audio CD-R because the encoding format compresses the music information; the sound files on your hard drive may take up more than 650MB of space, but still fit within the 650MB confines of the CD-R.

You can play MP3 files burned onto a CD-R in the new consumer MP3 disc players and combination CD/MP3 players, as well as on computers that recognize MP3 CDs (including Macs with iTunes installed). If you burn music to a CD-R or CD-RW in the MP3 format, the disc can hold more than *12 hours* worth of music. Now you know why MP3 discs are so popular! To convert songs to the MP3 format, see "Converting the Song Format" in Chapter 5.

The Apple SuperDrive and ComboDrive also create CD-RWs (the "RW" stands for rewritable) that you can erase and reuse, but most CD players don't recognize CD-RWs as audio CDs. To burn a CD-RW that already has data on it, you must first erase the data by reformatting the CD using the application supplied with the drive. CD-RWs work with computers but won't work with standalone players.

If you have a DVD (Digital Versatile Disc) burner, such as the Apple SuperDrive, you can burn data files to a DVD-R to use with other computers. DVD-R is suitable for backing up copies of song projects (like those created in GarageBand), or any data files, such as movies or digital photos, as described in Chapter 12. DVD-Rs can hold about 4.7GB of music or other data files. You can only use these discs with computers that have a DVD drive; most commercial DVD players won't read data on a DVD-R or DVD-RW.

 Cross-Reference

To find out how to create DVD titles for commercial players, see iDVD in Chapter 16.

You don't need to do anything else to songs exported from GarageBand into iTunes in order to burn them onto an audio CD-R. The AIFF format used for exporting files is the standard format for uncompressed sound on a Mac, and you can't go wrong with it. You can also use the AAC music file format for burning a CD; music from the iTunes Music Store is provided in the AAC format. AAC is comparable to audio CD quality; I think AAC offers the best trade-off of space and quality.

SETTING UP A CD PLAYLIST

To burn a CD, you must first define a playlist for the CD in iTunes, as described in Chapter 12. You can include in the playlist any songs you have in your iTunes library. If you want to burn an MP3 CD, convert the AIFF versions exported from GarageBand to MP3 format as described in Chapter 5.

One reason why setting the playlist and album title in GarageBand's preferences is useful is that you can automatically organize your exported songs into a playlist, as described in Chapter 5.

▼ **Tip**

You can also assign an entire album in your iTunes library to a playlist by using Browse view and dragging the album title from the Album list (in the top-right section of the library) to the white area below the items in your Source list. iTunes automatically creates a playlist with the album name. You can then burn that playlist onto a CD.

By organizing your songs into a playlist, you can tell at a glance if you have enough songs (or too many songs) to fit on the CD. You can see the size of a playlist by selecting it; the bottom of the iTunes window shows the number of songs, the duration, and the size in megabytes (MB) for the currently selected playlist, as shown in Figure 14-1.

In Figure 14-1, the selected playlist contains 23 songs that total 1.1 hours and 724.1 MB. Although an audio CD holds only 650MB, the music is compressed and stored in a special format known as CD-DA (or Red Book). For example, you can fit a bit more than 650 MB of AIFF-encoded sound, because AIFF files are uncompressed. I can fit 1.1 hours (66 minutes) of music on a 74-minute or 80-minute CD-R disc with many minutes to spare.

You should always use the actual duration of the playlist — in hours, minutes, and seconds — to calculate how much music you can fit on an audio CD (either 74 or 80 minutes for blank CD-R discs). Leave at least one extra minute to account for the gaps between songs.

You should do the *opposite* for an MP3 CD: use the actual megabytes to calculate how many songs to fit (up to 650 MB for a blank CD-R disc). You can fit lots more music on an MP3 CD-R disc, because you use compressed MP3-encoded songs rather than uncompressed AIFF songs.

▼ Tip

If you have too many songs in the playlist to fit on a CD-R, iTunes burns as many songs in the playlist that will fit on the CD-R, and then asks you to insert another CD-R to continue burning the remaining songs in the playlist.

Figure 14-1
Checking the duration of a playlist

SETTING BURN PREFERENCES

Burning a CD is a simple process, but getting it right the first time is a good idea — when you burn a CD-R, it's done, right or wrong. You can't erase content on a CD-R as you can with a CD-RW. But because you can't play a CD-RW in most CD players, if you want to burn an audio CD, I recommend using a CD-R. Fortunately, CD-Rs are inexpensive, so you won't be out more than a few cents if you burn a "coaster" (a defective or unplayable CD-R).

Setting gaps and sound check

One professional touch you can add to an audio CD is putting appropriate gaps between songs. Follow these steps to control the gap length between the songs on your audio CD-Rs (this does not work with MP3 CD-Rs):

1. **Choose iTunes → Preferences, and then click Burning in the Preferences dialog box.**

   The Burning dialog box displays, as shown in Figure 14-2.

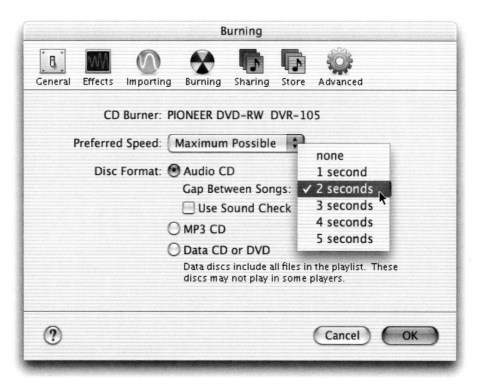

Figure 14-2
Setting the gap between songs for an audio CD

2. **Choose an amount from the Gap Between Songs pop-up menu.**

   You can choose a range from none to 5 seconds. I recommend selecting a gap of 2 seconds or less.

3. **Click OK.**

Consistent volume for all tracks also makes a CD-R sound professional. The Sound Check option in iTunes adjusts the songs in your library to play at the same volume level. To turn on the Sound Check option, choose iTunes ➜ Preferences, and click the Effects button in

the Preferences dialog box to see the Effects dialog, as shown in Figure 14-3. Click the Sound Check checkbox, which sets all the songs to the volume determined by the iTunes volume slider.

After turning on the Sound Check option, you can burn your audio CD-R so that all the songs play back at the same volume, just like they do in iTunes. Choose iTunes ➜ Preferences, and then click Burning. Click the Use Sound Check option, as shown in Figure 14-4. This option is only active if you already selected the Sound Check option in the Effects dialog box.

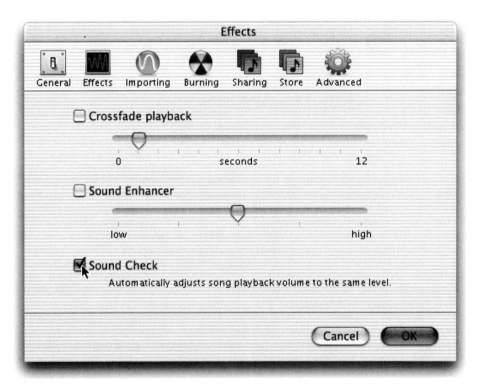

Figure 14-3
Turning on the Sound Check option for the iTunes library

Setting the format and recording speed

Before burning a CD-R, set the disc format and the recording speed by choosing iTunes ➔ Preferences, and then clicking Burning in the Preferences dialog box.

For the Disc Format setting in the Burning dialog box, select from the following three options (refer to Figure 14-4):

- **Audio CD:** Select this option to burn a normal audio CD of up to 74 or 80 minutes (depending on the

type of blank CD-R). Use any iTunes-supported music files, including songs in the AIFF format exported from GarageBand, songs in the AAC format ripped into iTunes or bought from the iTunes Music Store, and even songs in MP3 or WAV formats.

- **MP3 CD:** Select this option to burn an MP3 CD with songs encoded in the MP3 format; no other formats are supported for this option.

- **Data CD or DVD:** Select this option to burn a data CD-R, CD-RW, DVD-R, or DVD-RW with your

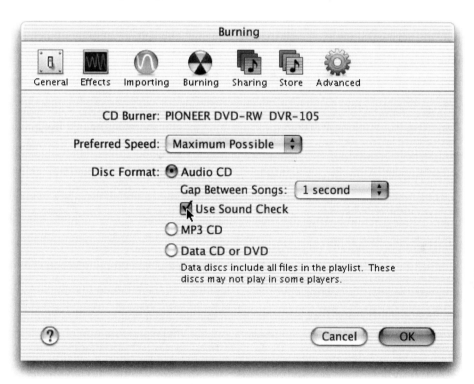

Figure 14-4
Using the Sound Check option for an audio CD

song files; however, this only stores the actual song files, not other files from your hard drive. Data discs don't play on consumer CD players: they are meant for use with computers.

▼ Tip

Data CDs or DVDs are good choices for storing your GarageBand project files, but *iTunes doesn't burn them*. The Finder can, however: Simply insert a CD-R (or DVD if you have a SuperDrive) and burn data files on the disc using the Mac Finder — a dialog box appears that lets you type a name for the disc. Drag the files and folders to copy into the open disc window and arrange the files exactly as you want them to appear when you open the disc later. Then choose File ➜ Burn Disc, select the burn speed, and click Burn. You can also use Backup 2 to store files on a Data CD (CD-R, CD-RW, DVD-R, or DVD-RW) as described in Chapter 12; you can use iDVD to store project files and other DVD elements, such as video, on a DVD-R as described in Chapter 16.

Blank CDs are rated for recording at certain speeds. Normally, iTunes detects the rating of a blank CD and adjusts the recording speed to fit. But if your blank CDs are rated for a slower speed than your burner, or you are having problems creating CDs, you can change the recording speed setting to match the CD's rating. Choose iTunes ➜ Preferences, and then click Burning in the Preferences dialog box. Choose a specific recording speed from the Preferred Speed pop-up menu in the Burning dialog, or choose the Maximum Possible option to set the recording speed to your burner's maximum speed.

WRITING A CD

You are now ready for the burn operation itself. Here are Steps 1-2-3 to burn a CD:

1. **Select the playlist designated for burning to a disc and click Burn Disc.**

   A message appears, telling you to insert a blank disc.

2. **Insert a blank disc with the label side up.**

   iTunes immediately checks the media and displays a message in the status window that the disc is ready to burn.

3. **Click Burn Disc again, as shown in Figure 14-5.**

   This time, the Burn Disc button has a radiation symbol; after clicking Burn Disc, the process begins. The Burn Disc button rotates while the burning takes place, and a progress bar appears, displaying the names of the songs as they burn to the disc.

   iTunes chimes when the CD is finished burning; the CD icon is now mounted on the Desktop.

4. **Eject the newly burned disc from your CD drive and test it out.**

Burning a CD takes several minutes. You can cancel the operation at any time by clicking the X next to the progress bar. Of course, if the burn has already started, you can't use the CD-R or DVD-R disc again.

If the playlist has more music than fits on the disc, iTunes burns as much as possible from the beginning of the playlist, and then asks you to insert another disc to burn the rest.

Figure 14-5
Clicking the Burn Disc button

The best way to test your newly burned disc is to pop it right back into your SuperDrive (or any CD-ROM drive), or try it out on an audio CD player. On most CD players, an audio CD-R plays just like any commercial audio CD. MP3 CDs play fine on MP3 CD players, and also work in computers with CD-ROM and DVD drives. If the CD works on the Mac but not on a CD player, you may have a compatibility problem with the player and CD-Rs. I have a six-year-old CD player that doesn't play CD-Rs very well. Car CD players made years ago may also have trouble playing CD-Rs.

Don't delete the playlist yet! You can print the CD liner notes and cover using any artwork you have assigned to the songs in the playlist. Select the playlist, and choose File ➜ Print to see a print dialog box with choices for CD inserts and liner notes, as shown in Figure 14-6. You can print a CD jewel case insert, a song listing, or an album listing. If you choose a CD jewel case, you have a choice of themes (Mosaic is shown in Figure 14-6, which uses the song artwork, which you can add as described in Chapter 12). If you choose a song listing, the Theme pop-up menu changes to provide options for columns in the song list.

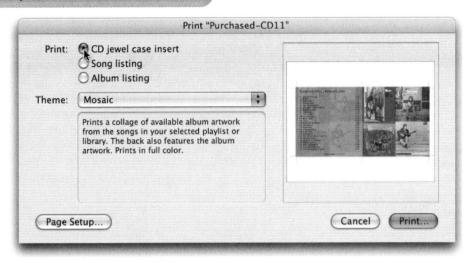

Figure 14-6
Printing a color CD jewel case insert from iTunes

ON A LAN YOU CAN SHARE FOREVER

If you live like the Jetsons — with a computer in every room, connected by wireless or wired local-area network, or LAN — iTunes is made for you. You can share the music in your library with up to five other computers in the same network. These computers can be either Macs or PCs running Windows, as long as they are all running iTunes — if they can communicate with each other over the network, iTunes can share a music library with them.

When you share songs on a network, the song is streamed from the computer that contains the songs in its library (the library computer) to your computer over the network — the song is not copied to your music library. From your computer, you can't burn the shared-library songs onto a CD, or copy the songs to your iPod. You can share radio links, MP3, AIFF, and WAV files, and

even AAC files and music purchased from the iTunes Music store.

To share your music library, turning your computer into the library computer, do these five easy pieces:

1. **Choose Preferences from the iTunes menu, and click the Sharing tab.**

   The Sharing window appears, as shown in Figure 14-7, offering options for sharing music.

2. **Select the Share My Music option.**

3. **Select either the Share Entire Library option or the Share Selected Playlists option and choose the playlists to share.**

4. **Type a name for the shared library and add a password if you want.**

Figure 14-7
Share your music library with other computers on the same network

The name you choose appears in the Source pane for other computers that share it. The password restricts access to those who know it. Use a password you don't mind letting others know, because others have to use it — don't give them an important password you use for online services or the PIN you use for ATM machines.

5. **Click OK.**

You can access the music from the other computers on the network by following these steps:

1. **Choose Preferences from the iTunes menu (or from the Edit menu in the Windows version of iTunes), and click the Sharing tab.**

   The Sharing window appears, offering options for sharing music (refer to Figure 14-7).

2. Select the Look for Shared Music option.

The shared libraries or playlists appear in the Source pane, as shown in Figure 14-8.

3. Click the shared library or playlist to select it.

Click the shared library or playlist in the Source pane (see Figure 14-8). iTunes fills the view on the right

with the artists and songs from the shared library. Click the triangle next to a shared library entry in the Source pane to see its playlists.

When you are finished sharing a music library, click the tiny Eject button that appears to the right of the shared library name in the Source pane.

Figure 14-8

Selecting the shared music library on the network using the Windows version of iTunes

▼ Caution

Before turning off sharing for your library, first notify anyone sharing the library to eject the shared library before turning off the sharing feature. Otherwise iTunes displays a warning dialog allowing you to either continue (and break off the connection to the shared library), or choose No to leave sharing turned on for the moment.

COPYING SONGS TO OTHER COMPUTERS

You can copy songs in your iTunes library freely from your iTunes Music folder to other folders, other disks, and other computers. The files are organized in folders by artist name, and by album, within the iTunes Music folder. Copying an entire album, or every song by a specific artist, is easy — just drag the folder to a folder on another hard drive.

SEARCHIN' ALL NIGHT AND DAY

You can find out the location on your hard drive of any song in iTunes by selecting the song in iTunes and choosing File ➜ Get Info. Click the Summary tab in the Get Info dialog box to see the Summary pane.

You can find the song files inside album folders in the iTunes Music folder, which is here:

Your Home folder/Music/iTunes/iTunes Music

Your playlists, including the library itself (which is in some ways a giant playlist), are stored as extensible Markup Language (XML) files in the iTunes folder along with your iTunes Music folder.

Song files are not small, and album folders filled with songs are quite large. Copying a music library from a Mac to another computer, such as a PC, is not a simple task due to the enormity of the file sizes.

Don't even think about e-mail. *If the file is over four, it won't go through the door.* (Four megabytes, that is; and the door is your Internet service provider's e-mail server.) Even though attaching a file to an e-mail message is the most popular method of transferring a file to someone, there is a limit to what you can attach and get away with. Most e-mail servers in the world — systems that process e-mail messages and either route them to other servers or route them to recipients — won't accept an attachment larger than 5MB; some won't accept larger than 4MB.

Well, heck, just about every jazz tune and Grateful Dead jam we listen to in iTunes is larger than 4MB. A song compressed in the AAC or MP3 format is typically between 2MB and 10MB, so you might get by with one pop song attached to an e-mail, but that's it.

So how do you transfer larger amounts of music, or GarageBand project files? One way would be with an external FireWire or USB hard drive formatted for a PC — the Mac should recognize it when you plug it in, and you can copy files directly to the hard drive, then take the hard drive over to your PC. You need FireWire or USB to connect an external drive (USB is much slower).

Copying files to other Macs on a LAN

If your Macs communicate over a LAN, you can share files among them, even large ones such as GarageBand project files. To copy large song files, project files, or entire album folders between two Macs on a LAN, all you need to do is allow personal file sharing on your Mac. Sounds like a liberal thing to do, inviting all sorts of mischief and voyeurism, but you can control what others can do. (The reverse is true: if someone wants to make a file or folder available to you over a LAN, all they have to do is enable personal file sharing.)

To turn on personal file sharing on a Mac, open System Preferences, and click on the Sharing icon. The Sharing preferences should appear, with the Services pane front and center, as shown in Figure 14-9. Select Personal File Sharing in the list of settings and click the Start button.

Sharing takes just a moment to set up (as your computer blushes), and when it is ready, a check mark appears next to Personal File Sharing and the Start button turns into a Stop button.

To share files with other people on other computers, first inform them that they will be able to access your folder. You have control over who can do what with your folders and files with these options:

Figure 14-9
Enabling personal file sharing in the Sharing preferences

- Public folder with Drop Box — guests can copy files, but they can't go beyond the Public folder.

After enabling personal file sharing, put the files to be shared in your Public folder. Anyone with a Mac on your LAN can access it. Using OS X 10.3, anyone can click the Network icon in the Finder Sidebar; in older versions, they can choose Go ➜ Connect to Server to log into your computer as a guest and copy files from your Public folder and to the Drop Box within your Public folder. A guest can't go anywhere else (unless he is James Bond, Agent 007, sneaking in through a window wearing a tuxedo).

- Sharing with an authorized user who can copy files and folders. For this to work, you have to first set up an account for the authorized person (or people).

Setting up an account on a Mac sounds hard, and there are quite a few steps, but the steps are easy to follow:

1. **In System Preferences, click on the Accounts icon.**

   Your accounts appear in a list (you may only have one at this time).

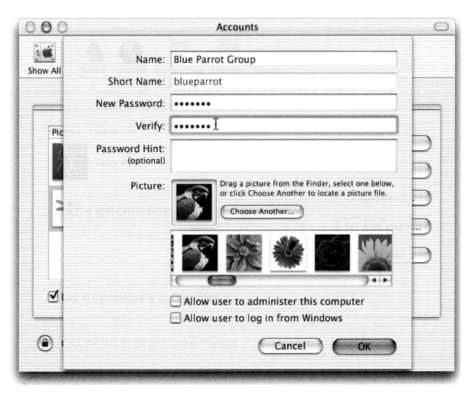

Figure 14-10
Creating a new user account on a Mac for one or more people to share files and folders

2. Create a new account.

Click the New User button to create another account. In the new account dialog box shown in Figure 14-10, type an account name, a password for the account (enter twice to verify), and a password hint (to display in case the folks forget the password). Choose a picture, and choose the option to allow other folks to log in from a Windows PC (or not — you be the judge). The system creates a new home directory for that account in the Users folder of your hard disk.

3. Tell the other folks the information they need to log on to your Mac.

Tell them the name of your Mac, the account name to use to log in, and the account password.

4. Tell them how to use the Go ➜ Connect to Server command in Mac OS X 10.2.8 and earlier versions, or the Network icon in the Finder Sidebar in OS X 10.3 and newer versions.

For people using Mac OS X 10.2.8 and earlier, give them these instructions:

a. Choose Go ➜ Connect to Server, and a list of servers and computers on the LAN appears.

b. Select the computer or server, and click the Connect button.

People using Mac OS X 10.3 and newer should follow these steps:

a. Click Network in the Finder Sidebar.

b. Click the Local icon to find any Macs on the local-area network — inside Local should be icons for other Macs.

c. After clicking an icon, log in to the computer or server with the appropriate name and password in the dialog that appears.

5. Tell them which home directory to select.

The home directory and any disk drives available on the computer appear in a list for the person to choose. Tell them to choose the appropriate disk drive or home directory, and click Connect. That's it. Now they can access that directory just like any disk drive on their Macs, using the Finder to copy files and folders.

What others can do in your folders and with your files depends entirely on how you've set up the Ownership & Permissions section of the folder's Info window. Select the folder, choose File ➜ Get Info, and click the arrow next to Ownership & Permissions to open the section. Pop-up menus provide access capabilities you can assign to others, including defined groups. "Read only" means files can be copied from the folder, but not to the folder. "Write only" provides a drop-box that people can copy to but not from. "Read & Write" provides full access.

We can share with Windows, we can copy files

Mac OS X makes it real easy to share files and folders with Windows computers. Let's say you have Winnie the Pooh whining about how he'd love to get your music files, and can't you just dump them into his Windows laptop from your Mac? Of course you can, but he has to fiddle with Windows to make that work. You can tell him to go look up file sharing on Windows, somewhere in Lesson 496 in Section 42 of his Windows tutorial book.

And while he tries to figure out Windows file sharing, you can quickly set up an account on your Mac for him to log into from Windows. Then you can interrupt his sojourn into the Windows wilderness with instructions on how to log onto your Mac from his Windows laptop. Here's what you do:

1. **On the Mac, enable Windows file sharing.**

   Open the Sharing preferences in System Preferences, and select Windows File Sharing in the list of settings. Click the Start button.

2. **Create an account for those who are logging in from Windows.**

   Click the New User button to create an account and type its name, password, and so on.

3. **In the account, enable Windows log in.**

   Turn on the option to "allow user to log in from Windows" and click OK. The account creates a new home directory for that account in the Users folder of your hard disk.

4. **Copy folders or files to share into the account's home directory.**

   Make duplicate copies of the folders or files and drag the duplicate copies into the new account's home directory (in the Users folder).

5. **Tell the person the account name and password to use to log into your computer.**

   On a Windows PC, the person can find your computer in the Windows Network Neighborhood.

On the other hand, you could access the Windows computer from a Mac, which is far more politically correct for a Mac user. All you need is a valid user ID and password for an account on the Windows computer (without one, you can still use the method outlined above). You can go right to that account's Home directory on the Windows computer, and use your Mac to copy folders and files to and from the Windows computer:

1. **Set the Windows computer to share a folder of files on a network.**

   In Windows XP, you can open My Computer and browse for the folder, then choose File ➜ Sharing and Security and turn on the options for Network sharing and security.

2. **Choose Go ➜ Connect to Server on your Mac if using OS X version 10.2.8 or earlier, or click the Network icon in the Finder Sidebar if using OS X 10.3 or newer.**

3. **Choose MSHOME (either the MSHOME folder in the Network browser, or MSHOME in the list of computers and servers).**

   The names of any Windows-based PCs on the LAN appear after selecting MSHOME.

4. **Select a Windows-based PC by name, and log in.**

   Log in with your account name and password, and then choose the shared folder on the Windows machine. The Windows folder appears just like a Mac hard drive in the Finder.

FTP FOR HIGH-OCTANE FILE TRANSFER ON THE NET

Copying very large song files over the Internet is more complex, involving use of the File Transfer Protocol (FTP). While it is easy to download an MP3 song file from a Web page or an FTP site with any browser (all you need is the Web or FTP address, and a user ID and password if the site is protected), you can't send the file to a protected site with most browsers, unless the site is set up for this function. (One easy way to share your files from a Mac is to use the .Mac service to create a Web page that accommodates anyone with the right password, even Windows-using folks, to visit and download files you put there.)

To make it easy for others to copy files to and from a Mac at their convenience, you can turn on FTP Access for the Mac. To do this, open System Preferences, click on the Sharing icon, and click the Services tab. Turn on the FTP Access option. A message appears at the bottom of the Sharing window providing the address of your FTP server on your Mac — something like "ftp://192.168.1.246/". Give this address to anyone with an account on your computer, and they can access files and folders using a Web browser, FTP client such as Fetch, or Mac OS X.

How about transferring song files to other FTP sites, such as a password-protected site that requires use of an FTP client? Here are several options:

- Use an FTP client, such as Fetch. You can find Fetch at `http://fetchsoftworks.com/` for $25 as of this writing. You can use it for several weeks before paying for it.

- Use the FTP function inside another application, such as Macromedia Dreamweaver.

- Use the free Terminal application supplied with Mac OS X, found in the Utilities folder inside your Applications folder, which offers FTP.

Fetch provides an easy drag-and-drop interface for transferring any type of file with FTP servers. Once you've established a connection with the FTP server by typing the appropriate information — the FTP server name, your ID, your password, and the directory you have access to — you can drag files to and from the FTP server window using the Finder, or you can browse folders to select files and then use the Get and Put Files buttons.

You can send an entire folder of files, such as an album of songs or an artist folder with multiple albums of songs, by stuffing the folder (or even a set of folders) into a compressed file. StuffIt Deluxe from Alladin Systems (`www.stuffit.com`) can compress the folder into one ZIP or StuffIt file ("ZIP" is a standard for Windows-based PCs). You can then transfer the ZIP file to the FTP server in one step. The compressed file is smaller and takes less time to transfer, and offers a compact way of sending an entire folder of files.

PART V

When the Music's Over

15

Making Slideshows and Videos

In This Chapter

Creating a slideshow in iPhoto and adding your music • Making a music video in iMovie and synchronizing video clips to music • Exporting slideshows and videos as QuickTime movies • Publishing QuickTime movies on the Web

When MTV started broadcasting on August 1, 1981, it opened with "Video Killed the Radio Star" by the Buggles. Sing along with us: "In my mind and in my car / we can't rewind we've gone too far." Videos dominated the music industry for more than a decade, and producing a music video is still a high priority for many bands today. At the very least, as an individual artist or as a whole band, you have to put together a press kit that includes photos to go along with the demo CD you burned in Chapter 14. You may also want to put up a Web site of photos, songs, and music videos.

As the great Yogi once said, "You can observe a lot just by watching." The public pays more attention to images than anything else, except perhaps to the music itself. But music without photos of the band or the artist is very hard to promote. Fortunately, you already have the tools at your fingertips: iPhoto for organizing photos and slideshows, and iMovie for creating video.

A SNAPSHOT OF IPHOTO

iPhoto is your digital camera's virtual darkroom that brings photos into your Mac where you can organize them and produce albums, slideshows, books, and prints. iPhoto can also improve your photos in a number of ways, such as adjusting photos that are too dark, too light, or overexposed. With one click you can zap away the dreaded *red-eye effect* — not the red eyes you have from too much late-night partying and music making, but the effect a flashbulb casts on your eyes that makes you look like a Martian. You can even crop the image — draw a smaller rectangle inside the image and cut away everything outside the rectangle. iPhoto gives you tools to remove blemishes from faces, or distracting visual elements, such as large pixels, from the image. With some skill you can even make a rock star with Keith Richards' face look better.

iPhoto is all about organizing your photos into *photo albums* — collections of photos you can name, such as

Live Gigs, In the Studio, Our Last Tour, CD Liner Notes, and so on. iPhoto makes it easy to print your own photographic prints or order them from the Internet. It even offers automatic functions for printing your own photo albums or ordering professional linen-bound books. And you can share photos and entire albums over the Internet.

As shown in Figure 15-1, the iPhoto window is divided into three major panes and offers Mode buttons to switch modes:

Source pane   Tools pane   Mode buttons   Viewer pane

Figure 15-1
iPhoto helps you organize your digital photos

○ **Tools pane:** This is the iPhoto control center, offering one-click access to iPhoto tools.

○ **Mode buttons:** When you click the mode buttons to switch the mode of operation, the tools in the Tools pane change. The four buttons are as follows:

▫ **Import:** Transfers photos from your digital camera or memory card reader. (You can also transfer images from disk drives and digital backup media by dragging the image files to the iPhoto window, or by choosing File ➜ Import.)

▫ **Organize:** Displays your photo library and lets you organize photo albums.

▫ **Edit:** Displays a single photo and lets you make improvements, such as removing red-eye and changing brightness and contrast.

▫ **Book:** Organizes photos into a layout for printing books.

○ **Source pane with album list:** This pane holds the list of albums you've created for organizing your photos, and "smart" photo albums that organize themselves based on your criteria (such as Last Roll and Last 12 Months). Buttons for creating a new album and playing a slideshow are located underneath this pane. When you first use iPhoto, the photo library appears in the Viewer pane. As you organize photos into photo albums, the names of the albums appear in the album list in the Source pane. Selecting an album's name in the Source pane shows only that album's photos in the Viewer pane. To view the entire photo library, click Photo Library at the top of the Source pane. You can fill your iPhoto library with photos taken with digital cameras, created by scanners (or sent to you by scanning services), or even copied from other computers or from the Web.

○ **Viewer pane:** In Organize mode, the viewer pane of the iPhoto window shows thumbnail images of your

photos. You can change the size of the thumbnail images — make them shrink or grow larger to see more detail — by dragging the size control slider, located in the lower-right corner beneath the viewer pane (the size control slider has an icon of a large photo on one side and a small one on the other). To look at just a single image, double-click the thumbnail of the image, or click it once (to select it) and click the Edit mode button. Either way, the image fills the viewer pane, and the tools in the toolbar change into the Edit mode tools.

Importing photos

With iPhoto, you can import pictures directly from your digital camera. All you need to do is open iPhoto, connect your digital camera to the USB port, and click Import. Your photos appear in the iPhoto viewer pane. Just follow these steps:

1. **Connect the camera to the Mac using a USB or FireWire cable.**

   USB (Universal Serial Bus) is the connection method of choice for connecting most digital cameras to a Mac; the exceptions are very high quality cameras that offer a FireWire option. Fortunately, both types of connections work the same way.

2. **Power up your digital camera by pushing the power button.**

 Tip

Connect your camera *while your camera is off*, then turn on your camera after connecting it to the Mac. The Mac may not recognize some camera models if the camera is connected while on. If the Mac doesn't recognize your camera, try turning the camera off (while connected to the Mac), and then turning it on again.

3. Click the iPhoto icon to start iPhoto (if it hasn't already started).

Depending on how you configure your Mac, iPhoto may automatically start when the computer detects the camera. If you are running iPhoto for the first time, a dialog box pops up asking if you want to always run iPhoto when you connect a camera. Click Yes. iPhoto opens, displaying the iPhoto window.

4. Click the Import mode button.

The tools pane changes to show the Import tools, as shown in Figure 15-2. iPhoto displays either a camera icon, a disk icon, or a memory card reader icon, depending on the type of camera or memory card reader you are using. Our Nikon CoolPix 4300 shows up with a disk icon.

5. Choose whether or not to delete the photos in your camera after importing them.

To empty the photos from your camera, click the Erase camera contents after transfer option in the tools pane (located at the bottom-right corner of the iPhoto window). This option lets you import pictures to iPhoto and delete them from the camera all in one step; with the photos saved in the photo library, you no longer need to keep copies in your camera or memory card, and this way you can make room for new photos quickly and easily.

6. Click Import.

While your photos are importing, the Import button changes to a Stop button that you can click at any time to cancel the photo transfer. When the process is complete, iPhoto displays a small image for each photo in the photo library. You control the size of the images in the viewing area using the zoom slider in the lower-right corner of the iPhoto window, just underneath the viewing area. These small versions of your images are called *thumbnails*.

▼ Tip

If your camera has a sleep mode, make sure that you disable it, or set it to a time increment long enough to allow your images to import into the Mac. Importing 24 photos generally takes about one minute with most digital cameras.

---

7. Disconnect the camera (eject it first if necessary).

If the camera's icon appears on the desktop, ejecting is required. Wait until all the photos transfer into iPhoto, or click Stop before disconnecting your camera. To eject the camera, click the camera's icon, keeping the mouse button held down. The Trash icon changes to the Eject icon. You can then drag the camera icon over the Eject icon to eject the camera properly.

You can also import photos that have already been scanned into a computer or supplied on CD-ROM from a service bureau; just insert the disc, or locate the photos on the computer's hard drive, and drag the photo files over the iPhoto window to add them to your library.

Figure 15-2
Importing photos from a digital camera

Creating a slideshow

You can go to a stationery store and buy photo albums that have plastic sleeves for holding prints. A *digital photo album* is similar in that it holds digital photo files instead of prints. In both cases, an album is simply a way of organizing photos and placing them in a specific sequence.

Use photo albums to organize your photos and arrange a slideshow, QuickTime movie, or a Web page of images. If your band goes on tour, organize a photo album with photos from the tour, and then add music from the tour to create a slideshow — your own rockumentary!

Make as many albums and use as many images from your photo library as you want. Go wild, like that photographer in the movie *Blow Up,* choosing photos and placing them in the right order. Because photo albums are only lists of images and don't utilize the original image files, the albums don't take up hard drive space — the actual image files remain in the photo library. You can include the same photo in several albums without making multiple copies of the photo and wasting disk space. You can also delete a photo from an album without actually removing it from your library.

To create a new photo album and add photos to it, follow these steps:

1. **Click the Organize mode button.**

    First, get organized. The photos in your library appear as thumbnails in the viewer pane (refer to Figure 15-1).

2. **Click the + button.**

    The + button is underneath the Source pane. (You can also choose File ➜ New Album or Command+N.) The New Album dialog box appears.

3. **Type a name for the album and click OK.**

The default name iPhoto assigns to the photo album appears highlighted in the New Album dialog box. Type a new name for the album (other than "Album 01" — something more descriptive).

4. **Click a photo in your library and drag it into the album.**

    You know the photo is selected when an outline appears around it. Drag the photo over the name of the album in the Source pane, as shown in Figure 15-3.

5. **Repeat Step 4 until you drag all the photos you want for this album.**

6. **Click the photo album name in the Source pane to see the photos in the album.**

    When you click an album name in the Source pane, only the photos you dragged to that album — not the entire library — appear in the viewer pane. You can switch back to the entire library by clicking Photo Library in the Source pane.

 Tip

Select multiple photos by clicking the first one and holding down the Shift key while clicking the last one — the first, last, and all the photos in between are selected automatically. You can then drag the selection over the name of an album in the Source pane. A number appears, attached to the mouse pointer, showing the number of selected photos in the range.

Tip

You can also create an album by dragging a folder of images from the Finder into the iPhoto Source pane. iPhoto creates an album with that folder's name and imports all photos contained in the folder. Using the Finder, you can add a photo to an album directly from a CD or from another location on your hard drive.

Figure 15-3
Adding a photo to a newly created photo album

Changing the photo order of your slideshow

The order in which your photos appear in the album is important, even if only to you: it defines the order of photos for a slideshow or a book layout, both of which are based on photo albums. To change the order of photos in an album, follow these steps:

1. **Click the album name in the Source pane.**

2. **Click the Organize mode button.**

iPhoto switches to Organize mode, with organization tools in the tools pane and photo thumbnails in the viewer pane.

3. **Click a photo (or multiple photos) and drag the selection to a new location.**

4. **Repeat Step 3 until all your photos are arranged in the order you want them for the slideshow or book layout.**

To remove a photo from an album, select the photo while viewing the album and press the Delete key, or choose

Photos ➜ Remove from Album. But the photo is not completely gone — it remains intact in your iPhoto main library. To delete a photo from the library, click Photo Library in the Source pane, select the photo from the list, and then press the Delete key or choose Photos ➜ Move to Trash. (You must select a photo in the library, not one from an album, to use this command.)

Changing the slideshow settings

You can change the speed of the slideshow and other settings in the Slideshow window. Follow these steps:

1. **In Organize mode, select a photo album from the albums list.**

   To define slideshow settings, you have to use a photo album as the basis for your slideshow.

2. **Click the Slideshow icon in the tools pane (the second icon from the left).**

   The Slideshow window appears, as shown in Figure 15-4.

3. **Make as many changes to the options as you want.**

   You can set a transition style and direction for the slides, change the speed of the slideshow's photos, display your ratings with the photos, and change the music. The following list covers some of the major options for the Slideshow window:

   - **Transitions:** Use this option to choose a transition between slides. The Dissolve transition, a popular one, dissolves one slide into another. But the Cube and Mosaic Flip transitions are also cool. You can experiment with transitions and see a preview in the tiny window.

   - **Direction:** The Direction option specifies which direction the transition occurs from; for example, a

wipe generally moves the new slide into position while "wiping" the old slide out, from left to right. You can change the direction to right-to-left, top-to-bottom, and so on.

- **Speed:** The Speed slider specifies the speed of the transition relative to the overall speed of the slideshow.

- **Preview window:** As you choose a transition, the miniature preview uses slides from the selected album to show you how the transition will appear.

- **Play each slide for . . . seconds:** Your slideshows don't have to run endlessly, or show for only two seconds per slide. You can set the slideshow so the audience has a chance to listen to your excellent music as they look at each photo. In the Slideshow window, you can change the "Play each slide for . . . seconds" setting so that slides appear onscreen for the duration you want before fading. The up and down arrows allow you to adjust the duration in seconds of each transition, with a maximum of 30 seconds between photos. If you want more than 30 seconds between photos, you can type a number higher than 30, but not higher than 60 seconds. The number of seconds you choose applies to each slide in the slideshow; you can't set different timings for different slides (if you need that level of control, use iMovie, described later in this chapter). The number of seconds you choose for playing each slide also affects the transition time between slides: choosing a longer playing time produces longer transitions.

▼ **Tip**

The timing is saved with the photo album used for the slideshow. You can try different timings by setting up multiple photo albums and changing the settings for each one.

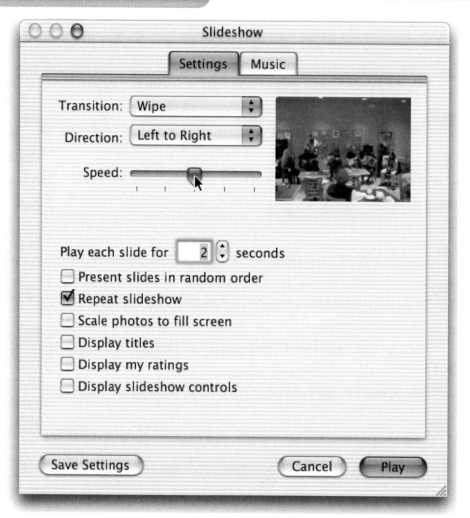

Figure 15-4
Changing slideshow settings in iPhoto

■ **Repeat slideshow:** When this option is turned off, iPhoto plays the slideshow and, at the end, returns to the viewer pane in Organize mode. This may be useful for previewing, but you may want your slideshows to repeat, especially if you are using a slideshow in an exhibit or on a demonstration table. Turn on this option to make the slideshow repeat over and over. The viewer can always end a slideshow by clicking the mouse or pressing the Esc key.

4. **Click Save Settings.**

The settings are saved with the photo album.

Adding music

Slides come alive with music. In fact, without music, slides are fairly dull. Apple thoughtfully provided very nice music to go along with your slideshows, but you can quickly change from that boring stuff to something else by clicking the Music tab of the Slideshow window.

The Source pop-up menu in the Music pane typically starts out with the Sample Music option, as shown in Figure 15-5; the songs available in this category (as of this writing) are Bach's "Jesu, Joy of Man's Desiring," performed by Leo Kottke (our favorite), and "Minuet in G," performed by Harvey Reid.

Apple only provides the samples as suggestions. You can select your own GarageBand songs, or even an entire playlist, from your iTunes library. Follow these steps:

1. **Open the Slideshow window by selecting a photo album in Organize mode and clicking the Slideshow icon in the tools pane.**

   The Slideshow window appears.

2. **Click the Music tab to open the Music pane.**

   The Music pane appears in the Slideshow window (refer to Figure 15-5).

3. **Click the Music pane Source pop-up menu to select an iTunes playlist, or select iTunes Library to see the entire music library.**

   Selecting a playlist is useful if you already defined a playlist in iTunes to use for slideshows (as described in Chapter 12), and you want to play the entire playlist with the slideshow. The songs stored in the playlist appear in the box below the Source menu, as shown in Figure 15-6.

   If you click the iTunes Library, you can sort the song list and select a particular song from the entire library.

However, if you choose an iTunes playlist, the *entire playlist* is assigned to the slideshow, unless you then click a particular song within that playlist.

4. **Click the triangular play button to hear your selection.**

 Tip

Clicking the Song column header sorts the list alphabetically by song title, and clicking the Time column header sorts the songs by duration (from shortest to longest). If you know the specific song you want to add to the slideshow, type the title in the Search box to narrow the choices.

You can choose one song or an entire playlist for a slideshow. iPhoto continues playing the song or playlist until either the song or the slideshow ends. If the slideshow repeats endlessly, the song (or entire playlist) also repeats. The slideshow and playlist play independently: the songs and the slides are not synchronized. If you want to synchronize sound with photos, use iMovie to create a video, described later in this chapter.

When you are satisfied with your slideshow settings, you can save them by clicking Save Settings in the Slideshow window. iPhoto saves the slideshow settings for the entire photo album. When you view your photo album, the slideshow information appears in the viewer pane underneath the Source list.

Playing a slideshow

Here's how to control your slideshow while you're reviewing it:

- **To play the slideshow:** Select a photo album and click the Play button underneath the Source list. The slideshow runs according to the settings you defined in the Slideshow window.

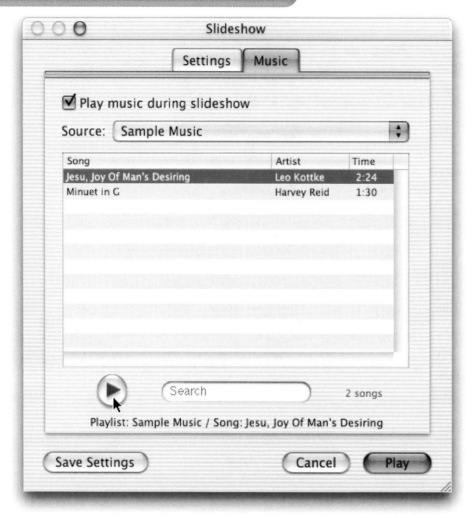

Figure 15-5
Checking out the sample music that comes with iPhoto

● **To pause a slideshow while playing:** Press the space-bar. A pause indicator appears briefly onscreen and then disappears, leaving the slideshow paused on the photo. When you pause a slideshow, the music keeps playing, which means you can't really synchronize photos to music (to create a slideshow synchronized to music, use iMovie).

● **To resume playing after pausing:** Press the spacebar again. When the slideshow resumes, a play indicator appears briefly and then disappears, and the slideshow continues.

Usually slideshows run in auto-play mode with the timing you set in the Slideshow window. However, you can override

Figure 15-6
Selecting a tune from your iTunes library for the slideshow's music

the settings by manually advancing or reversing the slides, and increasing or decreasing the speed of the slideshow:

- **To advance manually, slide-by-slide:** Press the Right Arrow key on your keyboard. The slideshow jumps to the next slide, and then pauses while the music continues to play.

- **To manually go backwards:** Press the Left Arrow key.

- **To speed up a slideshow:** Press the Up Arrow key. This decreases the time each slide is shown.

- **To slow down a slideshow:** Press the Down Arrow key. This increases the time each slide is shown.

- **To return to normal playback speed (after pressing an arrow key):** Press the spacebar to bring the slideshow out of pause mode.

▼ Note

When you manually speed up or slow down a slideshow, the slideshow continues at that speed until you change the speed again with the Up or Down arrow keys. However, this speed change is temporary: speeding up or slowing down the slideshow does not affect the slide playback timing you defined in the Slideshow window. When you rerun the slideshow after stopping it, iPhoto uses the saved settings for timing the presentation.

EVERY PICTURE TELLS A STORY — SO SHARE THEM

A slideshow on your computer is wonderful for those who can pull up a seat and watch. To reach a larger audience, or different audiences at different times, you have some options:

- **Share your slideshow online with the .Mac service.** You can make the entire slideshow available online for others to use as a screen effect (anyone using .Mac, that is). See the .Mac service (www.mac.com) for details.

- **Export your slideshow as a QuickTime movie.** You can post a QuickTime movie on a Web page and include it with other scenes in an iMovie presentation, as described in "Publishing Quick-Time on the Web" later in this chapter.

- **Create a DVD of the slideshow.** You can export the entire slideshow (including music) to iDVD, the DVD-authoring portion of iLife, which gives you tools to improve the slideshow and burn a DVD disc (see Chapter 16).

A PEEK AT IMOVIE

Yo, get out the makeup, leather jackets, whips, and chains — it's time to make your video debut for the talent shows. (Okay, hold the whips and chains). With iMovie, not only can you edit your video clips, you can improve them by adding transitions and special effects, matching the audio with the video or adding music, and creating a final movie with just the scenes you want. You can make all the changes you want to make in the digital format without the use of videotape and without any loss in quality. You can then copy the movie to your DV camcorder's tape cassette, watch the movie on TV, save the movie as a QuickTime file for use elsewhere, or use it with iDVD to burn a DVD disc that can play in any DVD player.

Here's a quick summary of how you would use iMovie with a DV camcorder to create digital movies:

- **Shoot video and transfer it to iMovie.** iMovie automatically separates the video scenes into clips you can organize any way you want.

- **Edit the video clips in a timeline viewer that uses a precise time code to synchronize sound to the video.**

- **Add scene transitions and visual effects like Lens Flare, Aged Film, Letterbox, and Electricity.** You can also use pan and zoom effects to give professional, documentary-style impact to images imported from iPhoto.

- **Edit the soundtrack with fade-ins and fade-outs, voice-overs, narration, sound effects, and music from your iTunes library.**

- **Add credits, titles, and even rolling commentary.** You can choose from several styles, fonts, and colors.

- **Copy your movie to digital videotape, use iDVD to burn your movie onto a DVD, or export your movie as a QuickTime file for publishing on the Web or for importing into a professional video application.**

A quick tour of the iMovie interface

You need plenty of display space to run iMovie, and your display must be capable of at least 1024 x 768 pixel resolution or higher. iMovie appears as in Figure 15-7, except that when you first launch it on your Mac, the iMovie monitor is black and your Clips pane is empty.

iMovie divides its window into three sections:

- **iMovie monitor:** Your video clip plays in the iMovie monitor, whether you select the clip in the Clips panes, timeline, or clips viewer.

- **Media panes including Clips pane:** iMovie stores incoming clips in the Clips pane. The Clips pane is one of the media panes; you switch media panes by clicking the media panes buttons. The media pane buttons give you access to media elements and effects by switching panes when you click them:

  - **Clips:** Switches to the Clips pane, which holds transferred video clips and imported movies.

  - **Photos:** Switches to the Photos pane, which provides access to your iPhoto library and the Ken Burns photo effects.

  - **Audio:** Switches to the Audio pane, which provides iMovie sound effects and access to your iTunes library.

  - **Titles:** Switches to the Titles pane, which offers a set of animation effects for creating frames with text, such as movie titles and credits.

  - **Trans:** Switches to the Trans pane, which offers a set of transitions to use between video clips.

  - **Effects:** Switches to the Effects pane, which offers a set of special effects for livening up video clips and images.

- **iDVD:** Switches to the iDVD pane, which enables you to define chapter markers for a movie and create an iDVD project (see iDVD in Chapter 16).

- **Timeline or clip viewer:** The timeline viewer displays the video clips over a period of time (refer to Figure 15-7). When you click the clip viewer mode button, the timeline viewer switches to the clip viewer, which shows individual clips in the sequence.

You can use the following tools to edit and play video clips and monitor hard drive space while editing:

- **Scrubber bar:** Drag the triangle along the scrubber bar to move through (or scrub through) a clip or sequence of clips frame by frame. Whatever the scrubber bar plays shows up in the iMovie monitor. You can scrub through either a single clip from the Clips pane, or a sequence you created in the timeline or clip viewer.

- **Camera/edit mode switch:** iMovie provides two modes of operation; you can switch from one mode to the other by clicking the camera/edit mode switch:

  - **Camera mode:** Click the switch on the camera side for camera mode. Use this mode only when you're connecting a camcorder and transferring video. You can control the camera with the playback controls.

  - **Edit mode:** Click the switch on the scissors side for edit mode. Use this mode when you're editing the movie. (Note: You can't edit your movie when in camera mode.) All Clip panes, editing tools, and views are available in edit mode.

- **Clip viewer/timeline viewer button:** The clip viewer/timeline viewer button on the far left switches the lower pane from clip viewer mode to timeline viewer mode and vice versa.

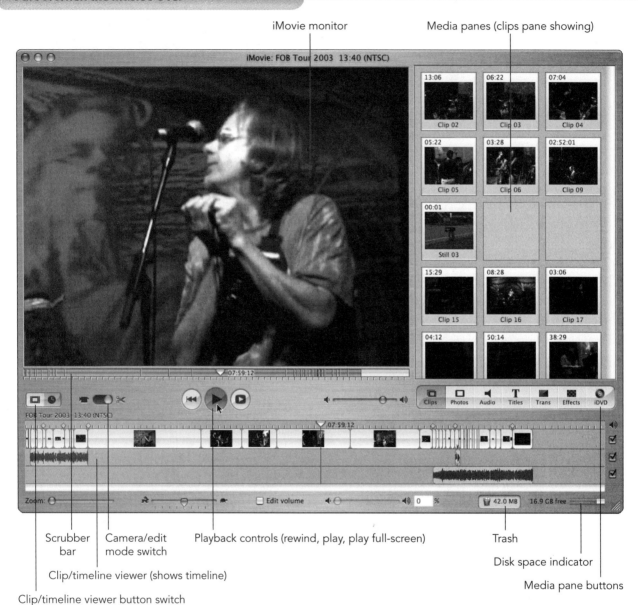

iMovie monitor

Media panes (clips pane showing)

Scrubber
bar

Camera/edit
mode switch

Playback controls (rewind, play, play full-screen)

Trash

Disk space indicator

Clip/timeline viewer (shows timeline)

Media pane buttons

Clip/timeline viewer button switch

Figure 15-7
iMovie offers the Clips pane for organizing video clips, and a viewer for arranging clips in a timeline

- **Playback controls:** Use the playback controls to skip to the beginning of a selected clip, play the clip in the iMovie monitor, or play the clip using the entire screen. The playback controls do the following:

    - **Play button:** Plays the movie in the iMovie monitor.

    - **Rewind button:** Moves back to the beginning of the movie.

    - **Play full-screen button:** Plays the movie using the entire Mac display. Click your mouse to stop full-screen playback and return to the iMovie window.

    - **Arrow keys on your keyboard:** Steps through the movie one frame at a time. The Right Arrow key moves forward and the Left Arrow moves backward. Hold down the Shift key while pressing the Right or Left Arrow key to play the movie faster (ten frames at a time).

- **Trash:** Drag unwanted video clips to the Trash to delete them and reclaim hard drive space. However, if you empty the Trash, you can no longer restore video clips to their original, unedited state. To empty the Trash, choose File ➜ Empty Trash.

- **Disk space indicator:** You can see how much hard drive space you use as you work. You need at least 2GB of free storage space at any time while using iMovie. The hard drive space indicator turns yellow when you start running out of memory. When it turns red, you must free up some space (usually by emptying the Trash) in order to continue working in iMovie.

Accessing your iTunes music library

With iLife, your music in iTunes is always, as Mick Jagger might say, just a click away. Click the Audio button, which is in the list of the media pane buttons. The Clips pane is replaced with the Audio pane, and your entire iTunes music library appears, ready for use in your movie (as shown in Figure 15-8).

The music in the library appears in a list in the same order as you sorted it in iTunes. You can click the Artist heading to sort the list alphabetically by artist, or click the Song heading to sort the list by song. You can also select a playlist from the pop-up menu to see only the songs in the playlist. You can also rc-sort the playlist by clicking the Song or Artist heading. Sorting in the iMovie Audio pane does not change your iTunes library.

With iMovie, you can make a video look as professional as a TV broadcast. Shooting techniques have not changed much with the advent of digital video; you just have more capability to experiment now, without wasting film or videotape. And you can take the results of your iMovie experiments directly to iDVD to burn a DVD disc, convert them to a QuickTime file for use on a Web site, or use them in a professional digital editing application or video studio.

Importing video clips

Bringing video into iMovie is simple; even Orson Welles could do it by himself. To start a new project, choose File ➜ New Project. To open an existing project, choose File ➜ Open Project.

 Tip

Deciding what hard drive you use to save the project folder is important. iMovie uses the project folder to store copious amounts of video data, which occupy about 3.6MB of storage space per second, and roughly 7GB for 30 minutes. If you have more than one hard drive, pick the fastest one; an internal hard drive is usually faster than an external FireWire hard drive, unless you are using high-performance external drives. Don't save your project file onto removable media, such as Zip or Jaz drives, which are not fast enough for digital video recording.

Figure 15-8
Opening your iTunes library in iMovie

To import video using iMovie with your camcorder, follow these steps:

1. **Locate the FireWire cable (your digital camcorder most likely came with one).**

   These cables are also available commercially. FireWire is also known as IEEE 1394 DV terminal or i.Link; the cable has a camcorder-style (very small) square connector on one end and a standard FireWire connector (also known as a six-pin connector) for the Mac on the other end.

2. **Use the FireWire cable to connect the camcorder to the Mac.**

   Locate the FireWire connection on the camcorder and plug the square connector into it. Find the FireWire port on your Mac (marked with the Y radiation symbol), and plug the larger six-pin connector into it.

3. **Turn your camcorder to camera mode or VTR/VCR mode.**

   If you are recording video directly to a hard drive, without using DV tape, choose camera mode. If you are importing prerecorded video from DV tape cassette, choose VTR/VCR mode.

4. **In iMovie, click the camera/edit mode switch on the camera side to switch to camera mode (if iMovie didn't automatically switch modes).**

   If iMovie already detects the camcorder, it may switch to camera mode automatically. The Import button appears under the monitor window when iMovie is in camera mode.

5. **If you are importing from DV cassette, press the Rewind button on the camcorder to rewind the camcorder's cassette to the beginning.**

6. **In iMovie, click Import.**

   And away it goes. iMovie controls the camcorder and copies the video directly to the hard drive, and a new clip appears in the Clips pane for each new scene, as shown in Figure 15-9.

7. **Click Import again, or press the spacebar to stop capturing video.**

   When the importing stops, iMovie automatically sets itself up like a faithful butler to store another clip in the Clips pane. You can repeatedly click Import to start and stop recording; each time you start over, you create a new clip. When iMovie reaches the end of the prerecorded video, it stops capturing to the hard drive; however, the camcorder may continue playing blank tape. Stop the camera by pushing its Stop button.

When you import video into iMovie from DV tape, each scene you record automatically separates into video clips in the Clips pane. iMovie does this magic by checking the date and time stamp that the DV camcorder puts into every frame of video on tape. When iMovie detects a break in time — which happens when you stop recording with the camcorder, even for a few seconds — the next piece of footage is imported as a new clip.

Arranging video in the timeline

You shot concert footage with D.A. Pennebaker, organized the video clips with Martin Scorsese, and selected the clips that don't show your nose in profile. You also trimmed the clips of any inappropriate backstage scenes and added some effects — for information on how to do these things, see *The iLife '04 Book* (Wiley) by Andy Ihnatko and yours truly. Now you're ready to edit the sequence of clips along with the music you created in GarageBand.

The timeline viewer gives you more control over the entire movie, enabling you to adjust the duration of any clip in the sequence and control audio tracks. To show the timeline viewer, click the clock icon in the clip viewer/timeline viewer button. The timeline viewer arranges the video clips along a timeline, with each clip clearly indicated by a thumbnail. Here are some fun things you can do in the timeline:

- Select any clip and play only that clip by clicking the Play button, or click the Rewind button and then the Play button to play the entire movie.

- Drag clips from the Clips pane to the timeline viewer and add them to the end of the sequence, or insert them between other clips.

- Move to any point in the movie by dragging the playback head in the scrubber bar, or by dragging the playback head in the timeline, which appears like a ruler above the clips in the timeline viewer.

Figure 15-9
Importing video clips from a digital camcorder into the Clips pane

The timeline viewer displays the sequence of clips horizontally. Drag the scroll slider along the bottom of the timeline viewer to scroll forward and backward though the entire sequence. If you want a closer view of the frames so that you can move to an exact position, zoom in or out of the timeline viewer by dragging the Zoom slider at the

bottom left of the iMovie window. Drag the slider to the right to zoom in and to the left to zoom out.

You can perform clip-editing operations, such as trimming and cropping, from the timeline viewer. As you perform such operations, the timeline viewer automatically adjusts to reflect the editing changes. To trim a video clip, follow these steps:

TIME IS ON YOUR SIDE

As a GarageBand user, the iMovie time measurements should not be too difficult to understand. iMovie displays the time code on the scrubber bar and in the timeline, and displays the total time for each clip in the Clips pane. The frame counter and other time measurements use *mm:ss:ff*, where *mm* is minutes, *ss* is seconds, and *ff* is number of frames. U.S. NTSC Video records at 30 frames per second, but this counting scheme starts at zero; the first second of video is from 00:00 to 00:29, and the next second is 01:00 to 01:29. If a clip is shorter than a minute, the minutes are left off.

1. Move your pointer to one end of the clip until the pointer turns into a double-arrow (as shown in Figure 15-10).

2. Drag toward the center to trim the clip with one move.

   The trimmed video is not deleted, just hidden; you can drag the end of the clip to adjust it without removing any video.

3. Choose File ➜ Empty Trash to remove the trimmed part permanently and reclaim hard drive space.

   The trimmed part of the clip is preserved until you empty the iMovie Trash.

▼ **Tip**

You can also overlap clips, trimming the clip underneath. Move your pointer near the center of the clip, hold down the Command key, and drag toward an adjacent clip. The clip you are dragging overlaps the adjacent clip, trimming the adjacent clip in one move. All subsequent clips adjust along with it, so that you don't leave a gap by accident.

Editing the sound in a clip

Editing the sound of a video is as important, if not more important, than editing the picture (especially for a music video). Viewers usually don't notice flaws in a moving picture compared to flaws in the sound, which linger in the mind until they become irritating.

You can do a number of editing tricks with the soundtrack of your video:

- **Lower the volume or remove the sound in the video clips.** If you are creating a music video, you probably don't want the sound that was recorded with the video clips, except in the case of interviews or scenes requiring the original sound. By far the most common editing technique for doing away with unwanted audio is to simply lower the volume of the video's sound track, which you can do on a clip-by-clip basis.

- **Add two more tracks of sound.** In addition to the sound in the video clips, you can add two more tracks of sound and control the volume of each track. The two lower tracks in the timeline viewer are reserved for sound and can't be used for anything else. Since you can overlay sounds in a single track, and iMovie automatically mixes all of the sound for playback, the possibilities are endless.

- **Fade the soundtrack in or out.** You can fade the sound in at the beginning, and fade it out at the end or when you don't want to hear it (such as when you would rather hear the video clip's sound).

- **Adjust the sound in the soundtrack or in video clips.** Weave the soundtrack in and out of sound from the video clips, or lower the sound in places where it is too loud. iMovie gives you ultimate control over every moment of sound.

Figure 15-10
Trimming video clips in the iMovie timeline viewer

To control the volume of the sound in a video clip, follow these steps:

1. **Click the video clip in the timeline viewer.**

2. **Click the Edit Volume checkbox at the bottom center of the timeline viewer.**

   The Edit Volume option should have a check mark next to it. A purple volume level bar appears across the middle of the clip, as shown in Figure 15-11.

3. **Drag the volume slider (located next to the Edit Volume option).**

   Drag the volume slider to the right for louder volume, to the left for lower volume, or all the way to the left to mute the volume. As you drag this slider, the purple volume level bar rises or falls to reflect the change.

Figure 15-11
Reducing the volume of the sound in the selected video clip

To fade the sound from full volume to mute at the beginning of a clip, follow these steps:

1. **Select the video clip in the timeline viewer.**

2. **Click the Edit Volume checkbox at the bottom center of the timeline viewer.**

3. **Click a point in the volume level bar in the clip, and drag the marker that appears (up for louder or down for softer).**

The purple volume level bar allows you to adjust the volume directly. If you want to gradually fade and then mute the volume, click the point where you want the volume to be muted, and then drag that point to the bottom of the track.

Tip

You can select multiple video clips and adjust the volume for all the clips at once. To adjust the volume in multiple clips, click the first clip in the timeline viewer, and then Shift+click the last clip. With the Edit Volume option selected, drag the volume slider (next to the Edit Volume option).

Adding a music soundtrack

To lay in music from your iTunes library (including any songs you exported from GarageBand), follow these steps:

1. **Click the clock icon to switch to the timeline viewer.**

2. **Click the Audio button.**

   The Audio pane displays a pop-up menu for selecting superbad iMovie sound effects, your rockin' iTunes library, or a playlist within your library (refer to Figure 15-8).

3. **Select a song.**

   Choose the iTunes library from the pop-up menu (if not already selected), and click a song (or scroll the song list if the song you want is not visible, then click the song). You can pick a playlist in your iTunes library from the pop-up menu and click a song in that playlist.

4. **Drag the song to the timeline viewer, as shown in Figure 15-12, or click the Place at Playhead button.**

   If you already moved the playback head to the exact spot where you want the music to begin, clicking the Place at Playhead button is the easiest way to create an audio clip in the audio track.

The timeline viewer's audio tracks work the same way as the video clip track; drag horizontally to adjust the position of a sound clip relative to the video clips.

Sound clips can display waveforms within them, so that you can see where the sound is loud or soft (or completely silent). To show waveforms within sound clips, choose iMovie ➔ Preferences and click the Show Audio Track Waveforms option. This is optional because the waveform display may slow down performance a bit.

 Tip

You can use a snap-to line to line up a sound clip with a video clip, using the waveform as a guide. As you scrub through the timeline or drag clips in the timeline while holding down the Shift key, a yellow snap-to line appears that acts like a magnet for lining up clips. The line appears just as you reach the end of a clip while scrubbing, to make lining up the next clip or aligning a sound clip to a video clip easier. A snap-to line also appears if you reach the playhead, a timeline bookmark, or three or more frames of silence in a sound clip — that is, if the Show Audio Track Waveforms option is selected.

You can adjust the volume of the audio track the same way as a video track. To change the volume of the entire audio track, follow these steps:

1. **Select the sound clip in the audio track of the timeline viewer.**

2. **Turn on the Edit Volume option by clicking to add a check to the checkbox.**

   A purple volume level bar appears across the middle of the audio track.

3. **Drag the volume slider next to the Edit Volume option.**

   Drag the volume slider to the right for louder volume, or to the left for lower volume. As you drag this slider, the purple volume level bar rises or falls to reflect the change.

Figure 15-12
Dragging a song to one of the timeline viewer's two audio tracks

You can directly manipulate the volume level bar in the sound clip to control the volume at different places in the sound clip, just like a GarageBand track volume curve. Follow these steps:

1. **Select the sound clip in the audio track of the timeline viewer.**

2. **Turn on the Edit Volume option by clicking to add a check to the checkbox.**

3. **In the clip, click a point in the volume level bar and drag the marker that appears (up for louder or down for softer).**

Sometimes splitting a sound clip into two clips is useful. For example, you may want to use part of a song at the beginning of a movie, and another part at the end.

To split a sound clip into two clips, follow these steps:

1. **Select the clip in the audio track of the timeline viewer.**

2. **Move the playback head to the place in the clip where you want the split.**

3. **Choose Edit ➜ Split Selected Audio Clip at Playhead.**

After splitting the sound clip, iMovie saves the second clip with the same name, but with "/1" appended to it. You can rename the clip if you want. You can also drag either sound clip somewhere else in the movie.

Synchronizing sound and video

As you trim and rearrange video clips to fit the music soundtrack, you should remember to play the entire movie from beginning to end to see how the video clips are synchronized with the music. Make sure that a particular part of a video clip plays exactly at a particular part of the soundtrack. In order to make sure this happens, you can lock the audio clip to that video clip.

Locking audio to video is especially useful if you've done a lot of editing of the video's sound, and you discover that you need to shorten or lengthen a video clip or add another clip. If you go ahead and edit the video clips without locking the audio, the audio clips will most likely be out of synchronization with the video. You would then have to drag all the clips back to their original positions for them to be synchronized. A tedious job — and you're likely to forget a clip or drag a clip too far.

To lock an audio clip to a video clip, move the playback head to where you want to lock the audio to the video, and choose Advanced ➜ Lock Audio Clip at Playhead. Yellow pushpins appear to indicate that the audio clip is locked to the video, as shown in Figure 5-13.

You can always unlock the audio clip by simply dragging it. But while the audio is locked to the video clip, if the video clip moves, the audio clip moves with it, so that they stay in sync. Nothing you do to other video clips — including inserting, deleting, cropping, trimming, or changing their speed — changes the synchronized audio and video.

Adding titles and credits

Even music videos start with some kind of title and credits, usually during the opening scene. iMovie gives you lots of choices for titles and credits, including the typical kind you see on MTV.

iMovie simplifies the making of titles and credits, which can appear superimposed over the video, or against a plain black background. iMovie creates a clip in the timeline viewer to represent the title or credits section.

To create a title or credits clip, follow these steps.

1. **In the timeline viewer, click the Titles button.**

   The Titles pane appears, providing a list of effects (from 3D Spin to Zoom), Speed and Pause controls, a Font pop-up menu and character size slider, and text fields for typing in text (as shown in Figure 15-14).

2. **Choose a title effect, such as Music Video, and type your text in the lower text field.**

   Some title effects are part of a set, such as Centered, which includes Centered Title and Centered Multiple. Click the triangle next to the set name to open a set of effects. The title effect you choose appears in the small preview window. Experiment with different effects before making your choice.

3. **Set the Speed and Pause settings.**

   The Speed slider allows you to set the speed of the title effect, which is the actual speed of the animation. The Pause slider (not available with the Music Video

Figure 15-13
Synchronizing the audio clip to the video clip

effect) allows you to set the pause time of the title effect, which is how long the title remains completely 100 percent visible and readable. The total duration of the title effect is the sum of these settings. iMovie conveniently adds these for you at the bottom of the small preview screen.

4. **Choose a font and size for the text.**

The Font pop-up menu allows you to select any font in your system; use the Size slider (to the right of the pop-up menu) to make the characters larger or smaller.

5. **Optional: Click the Color button (if you want a color other than black for the title text).**

The Color window appears; select a color from the color wheel, or try the other color models, such as the spectrum or the crayons (available as buttons at the top of the Color window).

Figure 15-14
Entering a title and using the Music Video title effect in iMovie

6. **Drag the title effect's name from the list to the timeline.**

   You may want to zoom into the timeline viewer to see the clips better, especially if you want to insert the title effect at the very beginning. The title appears in the timeline viewer as a clip.

   If you plan to create a DVD of your movie, you can create chapter markers in advance, so that viewers can jump directly to their favorite scenes. When you use the movie with iDVD, your chapter markers are automatically assigned to the DVD menu of scenes in the movie. Follow these steps for each chapter marker you want to add:

1. **Select a clip in the timeline viewer, and if necessary, move the playback head to the beginning of the clip.**

When you select a clip in the clip viewer and then switch to the timeline viewer, the playback head is already at the beginning of the clip you selected.

2. **Click the iDVD button.**

The iDVD pane opens, as shown in Figure 15-15.

3. **Click the Add Chapter button and type a chapter title.**

Type the chapter title next to the thumbnail that appears in the iDVD pane. The chapter markers appear in the timeline viewer as diamonds.

Figure 15-15
Adding chapter buttons in the iDVD pane

4. **Move the playback head to another position you want to mark as a chapter and repeat Step 3.**

   With the iDVD pane open, you can continue to move the playback head and add chapter markers.

After you create these chapter markers in iMovie, you can use them to jump around the movie and start playing from any chapter. To move the playhead to a marked chapter in a movie, click the chapter name in iMovie's iDVD pane.

With the post-production finishing touches complete, you are ready to export your movie as a QuickTime file, or transfer the movie to iDVD for burning onto DVD, which is described in Chapter 16.

EXPORTING QUICKTIME

You can play your slideshow or music video in iMovie, but you need to export the file to another format so that other people can view it. QuickTime is a digital video file format that offers many choices for quality, compression, picture size, and playback format. QuickTime provides the key to Internet distribution, and increases your audience to millions of potential viewers.

Exporting slideshows with music

QuickTime is like a container for multimedia built into every Mac (and available to any PC user intelligent enough to know what's best). When you create a QuickTime movie file, even those dudes with Dells and geeks with Gateways can play it. You can send it out on a CD or DVD, or you can publish a QuickTime file on a Web site for anyone to play.

To put your slideshow into a QuickTime file, follow these steps:

1. **In Organize mode, select an album from the Source pane, or individual photos used in a slideshow.**

2. **Choose File ➜ Export.**

   The Export Photos window appears, with tabs for different types of export functions, as shown in Figure 15-16.

   ▫ **File Export:** Export versions of your photos using file formats such as JPG (for JPEG, the standard image format for Web pages) and TIFF (the standard format for desktop publishing software).

   ▫ **Web Page:** Export photos or an entire album to a Web page.

   ▫ **QuickTime:** Export photos or an album set up as a slideshow to the QuickTime format.

3. **Click the QuickTime tab.**

   The QuickTime pane appears.

4. **Change the movie options however you want.**

   You can change the following settings in the Quick-Time pane of the Export Photos window:

   ▫ **Width and Height:** In the QuickTime pane's Images section, specify the pixel resolution of your movie. You may want to use the suggested resolution settings of 640 x 480 pixels.

   ▫ **Display Image for... seconds:** Type a number in this option box to control the amount of time each photo takes to show. This setting overrides the settings for the slideshow defined in the Slideshow

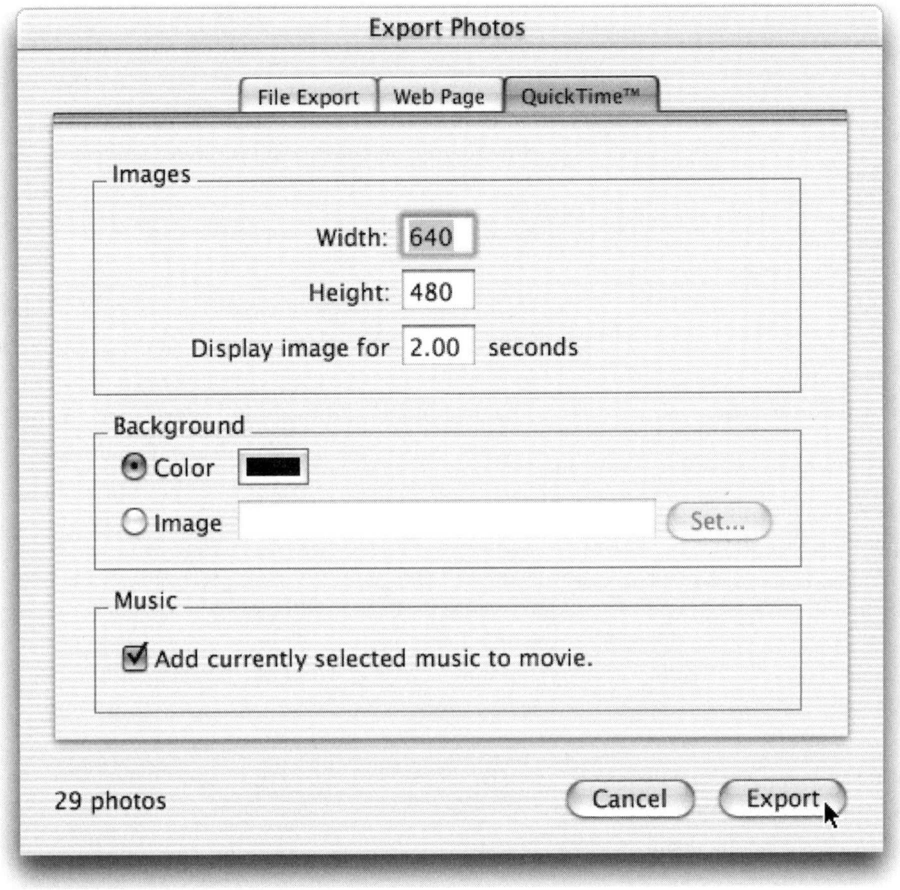

Export Photos

File Export | Web Page | QuickTime™

Images

Width: 640

Height: 480

Display image for 2.00 seconds

Background

● Color ▮

○ Image [   ] Set...

Music

☑ Add currently selected music to movie.

29 photos   Cancel   Export

Figure 15-16
Exporting a slideshow as a QuickTime movie from iPhoto

window. You can select the exact number of seconds the image displays, down to hundredths of a second. In fact, you can make a QuickTime movie that displays images so fast it can pass for a light show at a rock concert. The maximum amount of time is 60 seconds.

- **Background color:** To add a background color, click the Color option in the Background section of the QuickTime pane and then click the color

preview box. The Colors window appears with multiple ways to select a color. To set a color, drag the color you chose in the Colors window to the preview box in the QuickTime pane.

- **Background image:** An alternative to a background color is a background image, preferably one that doesn't clash with the photos themselves (unless you are trying for that effect). To set an image as the background, click the Image button in the Background section of the QuickTime pane, and then click the Set button to select an image from your hard drive.

- ▪ **Music:** The "Add currently selected music to movie" option turns on the music you defined in the Slideshow window.

5. **Click Export to create the QuickTime movie.**

   The Save As dialog box opens.

6. **Type a name for the QuickTime movie, choose where to save it on your hard drive, and then click Save.**

To view the finished movie, open the movie file using QuickTime Player or any other application that plays QuickTime movies. Your slideshow looks like a professional presentation, and now you can share it with the world.

Exporting videos

iMovie offers multiple ways of sharing a QuickTime movie on the Internet. Using the built-in settings, you can export movies and send them out via email or by publishing them on the Web. You can export QuickTime movies that you have streamed from Web sites; streaming movies start playing immediately after you click on them, and keep playing while the rest of the movie continues to download from the Internet. You can export QuickTime movies for CD-ROM playback, and as digital video files at the highest possible quality for professional use. iMovie even lets you export movies to your DV camcorder, or to iDVD, or to QuickTime with custom settings for professional editing.

Choose File ➜ Share, and iMovie displays the share dialog box, as shown in Figure 15-17. Click the buttons at the top of the dialog box to see the sharing panes, each of which offers different export settings:

- ○ **Email:** Exports to a small QuickTime file (160 x 120 pixels) at 10 frames per second. The pop-up menu enables you to choose what email program to use to send the movie. The Email pane has settings shrinking the movie down using video and audio compression — reducing the picture size as well as compressing the audio — to create a QuickTime movie file small enough to attach to an email message.

- ○ **HomePage:** Exports to a small QuickTime file (160 x 120 pixels) at 10 frames per second in the streaming format. The sound is compressed by resampling at a rate of 22.05 kHz (16-bit sample size), which is good but not the best quality. With this option, iMovie launches your browser and automatically publishes the movie on the Web using the .Mac service.

- ○ **Videocamera:** Export to your DV camcorder's digital videocassette to archive the edited movie or to use it with other projects. Both audio and video export at absolute high quality with no degradation or compression.

- ○ **iDVD:** Export the movie to iDVD to create a DVD that plays with any DVD player.

- ○ **QuickTime:** QuickTime files play on almost any computer (and certainly any Mac).

- ○ **Bluetooth:** You can use Bluetooth wireless technology to transfer movies to other computers, mobile phones, or personal digital assistants (if the devices can play movies).

After choosing the export options, click Share to export the movie.

It's nice to have choices — you can export a tiny video small enough to send to others or publish on a Web page, or you can export the full-size monster in formats the professionals understand and use. iMovie is built on

Figure 15-17
Exporting a movie from iMovie

QuickTime technology, and can make available all of the QuickTime export options for compressing and encoding the movie in different formats, so that your music video can be as full-sized as the pros.

QuickTime is used extensively in the digital video production world for creating high-quality video production, making DVDs, and producing movies for the Web. Those who know a lot about QuickTime can tweak the movie

files to gain performance advantages, adjust settings for the highest possible quality, or make tradeoffs in performance or quality.

To get access to the wizardly QuickTime features for exporting, click the QuickTime button. The Compress Movie For pop-up menu, as shown in Figure 15-18, lets you choose a built-in compression format. Your choices are the following:

- **Email:** Your movie is compressed to 10 frames per second, with a picture size of 160 x 120 pixels, and mono (rather than stereo) sound.

- **Web:** The standard Web setting creates a QuickTime movie that has, at 240 x 180 pixels, a slightly larger picture than the e-mail setting for QuickTime, but the larger size is much more viewable. Files are still

quite large — our 6-minute movie came out to 32.3MB — and Web users must download the entire movie before starting to play it.

- **Web Streaming:** Streaming video does not download to your computer: it starts playing as soon as the user clicks the Play button, no matter how long the video is. The video streams into the computer from the

Figure 15-18
Exporting from iMovie using QuickTime options

Internet in short bursts (called buffering), which are enough to start the movie playing while the computer receives more streaming data. The streaming format is the most useful QuickTime format for large-scale movies because it provides instant gratification for the viewer. However, it requires the use of the QuickTime Streaming Server, which is available from Apple; otherwise, the Web Streaming setting is the same as the Web setting, except that the file size is slightly larger because of the additional *hint track* for controlling streaming. The hint track maps key frames in the video to time signatures so that you can navigate to any part of a streaming movie and wait only for buffering to occur before seeing that part.

- ⊙ **CD-ROM:** Your movie is compressed to 15 frames per second, with a picture size of 320 x 240 pixels, and full-quality stereo sound — suitable for playback from CD-ROM.

- ⊙ **Full-Quality DV:** Your movie copies to a disk file in digital video format with full-quality picture and sound, suitable for professional video editing programs and video services. The QuickTime file takes up a lot of hard drive space in this format because no compression is involved. To give you an idea of how large the file can get, we saved a movie that is 6:11 (6 minutes and 11 seconds), with a file size of 1.24GB.

- ⊙ **Expert Settings:** This option provides several windows of options for specifying picture size, frame rate, compression methods, and various custom settings for streaming and other features. In short, it gives you access to the entire menu of QuickTime settings.

To gain access to the full range of QuickTime settings, choose Expert Settings in the Compress Movie For pop-up menu, and then click the Share button. The Save

Exported File As dialog box appears, as shown in Figure 15-19, with an Options button and two pop-up menus: Export and Use.

The Export pop-up menu (refer to Figure 15-19) offers a wide variety of QuickTime export formats. Each format offers its own dialog box — which you access by clicking the Options button — providing options specific to that type of file. The Use pop-up menu, shown in Figure 15-20, provides convenient settings that help you fine-tune QuickTime movies for the Web. The pop-up menu also offers the Default Settings choice that resets all your custom settings back to their defaults.

Publishing QuickTime on the Web

So you want to be a rock and roll star? It used to be that all you needed was an electric guitar and a tight pair of jeans (according to Roger McGuinn of the Byrds). Over the last two decades, that guitar and those jeans were the highlights of the music video that appeared briefly on MTV. Now you can "publish" the videos on the Web for everyone to watch anytime they want (short videos, about one or two songs' length, are best).

The .Mac service provides an easy way to create and publish a Web page from iMovie. With HomePage on the .Mac service, viewers can download your movie from your home page.

Publishing your movie with the HomePage feature of .Mac is a snap; you don't need a separate publishing or FTP application. iMovie exports the movie file when you click the Share button in the HomePage pane, and the .Mac HomePage service does the rest for you. Follow these steps:

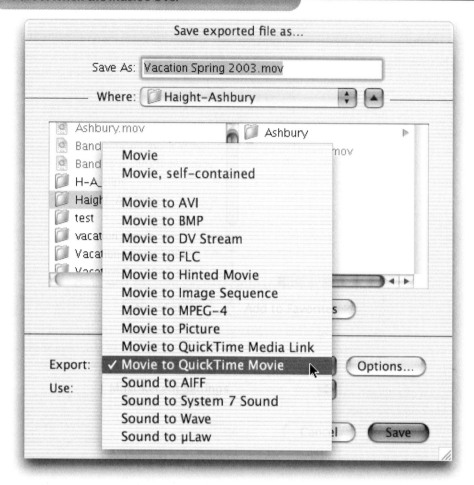

Save exported file as...

Save As: Vacation Spring 2003.mov

Where: Haight–Ashbury

Ashbury.mov
Band
Band
H-A
Haigh
test
vacat
Vacat

Ashbury

Movie
Movie, self-contained

Movie to AVI
Movie to BMP
Movie to DV Stream
Movie to FLC
Movie to Hinted Movie
Movie to Image Sequence
Movie to MPEG-4
Movie to Picture
Movie to QuickTime Media Link
✓ Movie to QuickTime Movie
Sound to AIFF
Sound to System 7 Sound
Sound to Wave
Sound to μLaw

Export:
Use:

Options...

Save

Figure 15-19
Picking a QuickTime export format after choosing Expert Settings

1. **Choose File → Share and click the HomePage button.**

2. **Type a name for your movie (or use the name conveniently provided).**

   The HomePage pane, as shown in Figure 15-21, lets you type a name for your movie.

3. **Check your iDisk space, and buy more space if you need it.**

   In the HomePage pane (refer to Figure 15-21), the message describes how the movie is compressed, and offers an estimate of the resulting file size (which depends on the size of your movie). Make sure you have enough disk space in iDisk. You can click the Buy More Space button to purchase more.

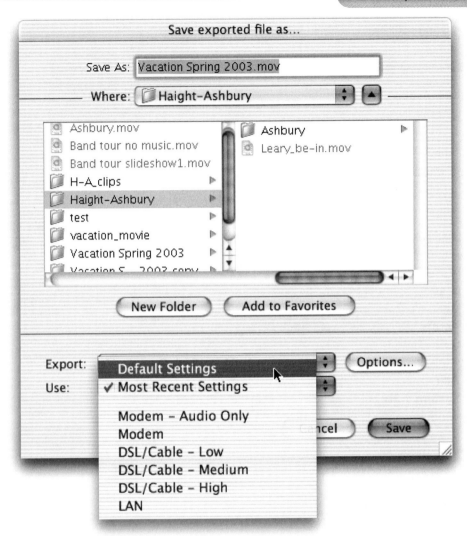

Figure 15-20
Fine-tuning a QuickTime movie for the Web

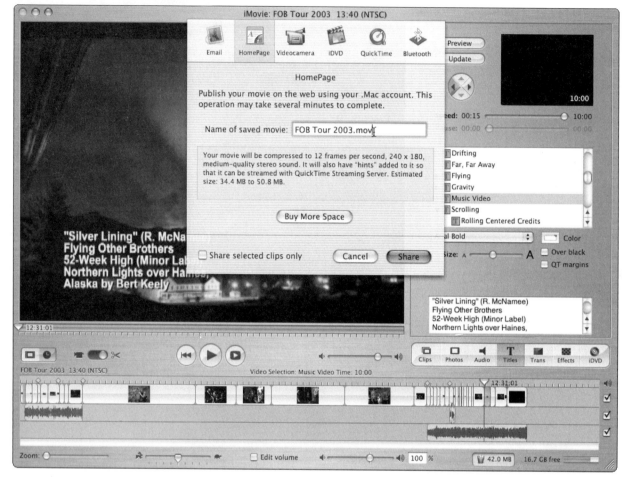

Figure 15-21
Exporting from iMovie using the HomePage feature of the .Mac service

4. **Click Share.**

   iMovie automatically compresses your movie into the proper QuickTime format and transfers it to your iDisk. After this is finished, iMovie automatically launches your browser and connects you to the .Mac log-in page.

5. **Type your .Mac ID and password, and then click Enter.**

   The HomePage service page opens in your browser with your movie shown in a small QuickTime player, ready for previewing, as shown in Figure 15-22.

PUBLISHING IS NOT BROADCASTING

Broadcasting is MTV or any type of video broadcast network — for that, you need to export your video using a QuickTime format a broadcaster accepts (see "Exporting videos" in the previous section), or export it to your camcorder's DV cassette. *Web broadcasting* is something else: videos are published on the Web using a streaming format — frames of video appear without having to wait for the entire movie to download. You can use the streaming format to blast your video out like a television show to anyone foolish enough to click on the link. The streaming format requires the QuickTime Streaming Server, available from Apple, and some expertise in setting up Web servers.

As of this writing, the .Mac HomePage feature does not yet offer streaming video. However, the movie files you upload to your HomePage are exported with a hint track to take advantage of a streaming server, for when the .Mac HomePage service eventually provides one (if ever). Streaming video works best when the viewer has a high-bandwidth connection.

To publish a QuickTime movie on the Web, you can use the HomePage feature of the .Mac service, or export your movie from iMovie to the Site folder on your hard drive, where you can make the movie available directly to people on your network, or use Web publishing software (such as Macromedia Dreamweaver MX) to create a Web page for the movie and upload both the page and the movie to the Web. You can also create your own Web page and use an FTP (file transfer protocol) application (or FTP function built into the publishing application) to transfer the movie file and Web page to your Web site. For more information, we recommend *Web Design For Dummies* by Lisa Lopuck (Wiley).

6. Click the play button to preview your movie.

The play button turns into a pause button; click it to pause the movie, and click it again to resume playing.

7. Click Themes and select from the available thumbnails.

The thumbnail images in the lower part of the page (refer to Figure 15-22) represent iMovie themes. (Make sure the iMovie theme type is selected on the lower-left side of the page; if another type is selected, click iMovie in the list of theme types.) Click a thumbnail to select a theme. Your custom page opens with your movie embedded in the page (as shown in Figure 15-23, which uses the Projector theme). The movie starts playing almost immediately, and you can use the player controls under the picture to control playback. Three buttons appear in the upper-right corner of the HomePage window: Themes, to switch to other themes; Edit, to edit titles on the page; and Publish, to publish the page.

8. Click Edit to edit the titles on the page.

When you click Edit, the page changes to an editable version. Click inside the title section of the page and type your own title for the movie; then click inside the description section and write a few descriptive lines of text. You can also click the Choose button in the layout to choose a different QuickTime movie.

9. Click Publish to publish your Web page containing the movie.

After clicking Publish, your page is on the Web. The HomePage service displays a message with a link to the page. Click the link to see the page.

Figure 15-22

Using the HomePage feature of the .Mac service to publish a QuickTime movie

10. Announce your page to others.

You can announce your page to others by sending an iCard from the .Mac service, which includes a link to your movie page. Click the right-arrow button to send an iCard.

Your movie is now up on the Web, viewable by anyone, anywhere, anytime. All users need to do is find the movie on your Web site and click it, and you're in business.

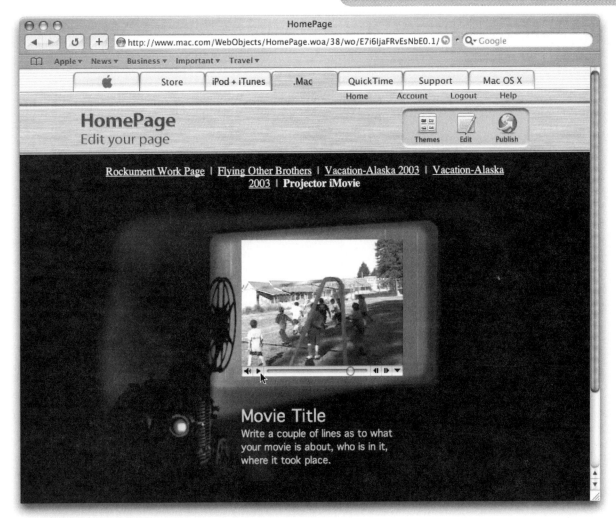

Figure 15-23
A custom movie page with a HomePage theme (Projector) for playing the QuickTime video

16

Putting Music Videos on DVD

In This Chapter

Importing movies from iMovie and slideshows and photos from iPhoto • Creating buttons
and menus with your original music • Including your song projects in the DVD
burn operation • Burning DVDs with movies, slideshows, and song projects

Now that you've created a music video and slideshow to support your new album of GarageBand songs, what's the best way to distribute the video and slideshow?

DVD is taking off as the medium of choice for movies. The cost of DVD players has come down to under $250, and the older VHS-based VCRs are disappearing from the electronics stores. The simple reason is that DVD is so much better: unlike VHS tapes, DVDs don't break so easily or wear down after a few plays.

DVD stands for Digital Versatile Disc (not digital videodisc, an older medium that has joined Betamax and 8-track cartridges in my dusty closet). DVDs can hold anything from video to music to photos. DVD is the first consumer medium that lets you interact with the content by using menus to navigate the disc's movies, excerpts, photos, and multiple soundtracks.

CHECKING OUT IDVD

iDVD lets you create DVDs with menus and buttons to navigate the contents of the disc. Besides offering professionally designed menu themes with spectacular special effects, iDVD allows you to grab your photos from iPhoto, import your QuickTime movies from iMovie, and use your music from iTunes. iDVD requires a Mac with a factory-installed Apple SuperDrive, which is a DVD-R (recordable DVD) burner.

With iDVD, you can put movies on DVD, and you can also add several features to the DVD (besides just a menu with a button to play a movie):

- Mark sections of a movie you create with iMovie as chapters, so that viewers can jump to specific sections. The chapter titles you use can be automatically turned into a scene menu to access the specific sections of the movie. See Chapter 15 to find out how to add chapter titles with iMovie.

- Create nifty menus animated with scenes from the movie, adding your original GarageBand music or other music from your iTunes library. You can define up to 30 menus in one iDVD project, and you can define up to six buttons in a menu that link to sub-menus, slideshows, or movies.

- You can create a slideshow of your photographs that is accompanied by music or narration (or both). Each slideshow can contain up to 99 images, and a DVD can contain up to 99 slideshows or movies in any combination.

iDVD fits well with the iLife suite. When you export a movie from iMovie to iDVD, iMovie automatically launches iDVD with the movie ready to be placed in a menu. iPhoto also has an iDVD button to launch iDVD with a ready-made slideshow, as shown in Chapter 15.

When you launch iDVD, its main window appears as shown in Figure 16-1, with the menu for just the DVD you intend to make. iDVD's inauspicious start may be confusing at first: what you see is what someone viewing the DVD might see, only in a small window.

To see what iDVD can do, click Customize. A Customize drawer slides out to the left of the main window, displaying the Themes pane (the default) with buttons for the Settings, Media, and Status panes (as shown in Figure 16-2).

I GOT YOUR MTV RIGHT HERE, ON DISC

Don't think for a moment that a DVD-R disc you create with iDVD is not as professional as a DVD you can buy in stores. To create a commercial DVD, you still have to burn a DVD-R of some kind with the content. Somewhere there is a high-quality "authoring" DVD-R that serves as a "master" for each DVD in the store. With iDVD, software from Roxio (www.roxio.com) called Toast, and the right type of DVD-R burner (such as the under $5,000 Pioneer DVR-S201 DVD Recordable Drive a.k.a. "DVD Writer"), you can burn a high-quality "authoring" DVD-R that can be used as a master for a commercial DVD.

The iDVD window consists of the following elements:

- **Main window:** iDVD shows the DVD project in the main window and allows you to arrange buttons and edit slideshows. This window changes to a preview window when you click Preview.

- **Customize:** The Customize drawer (refer to Figure 16-2) offers the following:

  - **Themes:** Browse and select themes.

  - **Settings:** Customize the buttons, titles, and backgrounds of a theme.

  - **Media:** Browse your iMovie projects and Quick-Time movies you want to use in your iDVD project; browse your iTunes library to add music to slideshows or menu elements to enhance a theme; or browse your iPhoto library to create slideshows with your photos.

  - **Status:** Check the status of the imported movie's encoding process (iDVD encodes digital video for the DVD format).

Figure 16-1
Starting iDVD and displaying a DVD's opening menu

- **Folder:** Click Folder to create a submenu for your DVD project.

- **Slideshow:** Click Slideshow to create a slideshow using photos from iPhoto.

- **Motion:** Click Motion to turn off the motion in menus and buttons; click it again to turn motion back on. Motion slows down the performance of iDVD, and you may want to turn it off until you are ready to preview and burn your DVD project.

- **Map:** Open a map view of your iDVD project to navigate more easily through menus and submenus.

- **Preview:** Click Preview to preview the DVD project in the main window.

- **Burn:** Click Burn to burn a DVD-R.

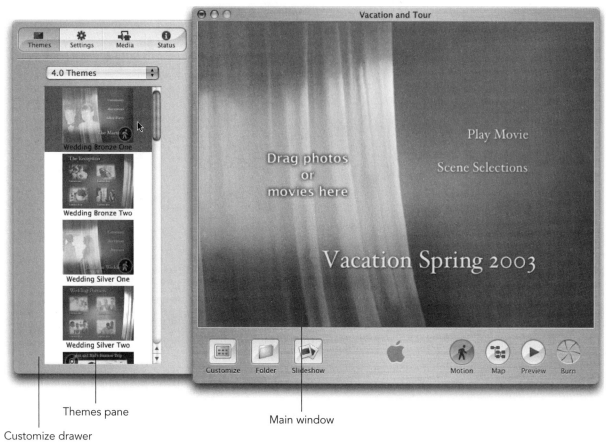

Customize drawer

Themes pane

Main window

Figure 16-2
Click Customize to see the Customize drawer

Importing movies and slideshows

Before burning your movie to a DVD, you have to import the video into iDVD. When you import digital video, iDVD automatically prepares the video to be burned to a DVD by encoding and compressing it.

Your first step is not with iDVD at all: use iMovie to export your finished movie, or use iPhoto to export your finished slideshow, and iDVD automatically compresses the file and makes it available in your iDVD project. Using iMovie to export your movie greatly reduces the possibility of error in making high-quality DVDs, and using iPhoto to export your slideshow is simply more convenient than bringing the photos into iDVD one by one (although iDVD has slideshow-making tools as well).

To export your movie to iDVD from iMovie, follow these steps:

1. **Open iMovie and export your movie.**

   See Chapter 15 if you're not sure how to export.

   iMovie automatically transfers your movie to iDVD, where a project with a link to the movie is created.

   If you use slow motion, reverse clips, or other special effects, you may get a message reminding you to render them before exporting your movie. Click Render and Proceed to export a high-quality movie to iDVD; otherwise, the movie may not be as good as expected. The rendering process may take some time, depending on your processor speed, the amount of RAM installed in your system, and the speed of your hard drive. For example, a dual-processor Power Mac G5 will easily outperform an eMac G4.

2. **Optional: In iDVD, click Motion to turn off animation and sound temporarily.**

   Turning off motion and sound improves the iDVD performance during the authoring phase. You can enable motion before previewing and burning the disc.

3. **Click Customize.**

   The Customize drawer slides out to the left of the main window.

4. **Click Status to see the status of the imported movie's encoding process.**

   iDVD takes time — a *lot* of time — to compress and encode your movie — a 60-minute movie might take three hours or more. The Status pane shows a progress bar, which is nice if you also enjoy watching grass grow. You can continue working in iDVD, doing other things while the encoding process continues. (Maybe eat lunch — I've been known to take very long lunches.) When the status shows Done, the movie is ready.

5. **Click Media and choose Movies from the pop-up menu to see the icon for the movie.**

   The Media pane shows icons for the movie files in your Movies folder, as shown in Figure 16-3. Not all of them are encoded yet: only the movies you assign to buttons in iDVD are actually encoded for DVD.

To import a QuickTime movie into iDVD, simply drag it from the Finder to the background of an iDVD menu, or to the iDVD Media pane (refer to Figure 16-3). Click Media at the top of the Customize drawer to open the Media pane, and then choose Movies from the pop-up menu. Or, if you prefer, choose File ➔ Import ➔ Video.

To import a slideshow from iPhoto into iDVD and automatically create a new iDVD project with the slideshow, follow these steps:

1. **With iPhoto open, click the Organize mode button and select a photo album prepared as a slideshow.**

   See Chapter 15 to find out how to create a slideshow in iPhoto.

2. **Click the iDVD icon in the iPhoto tools pane.**

   iDVD opens a new iDVD project with a link to the slideshow in iPhoto. The title is the name of the slideshow photo album in your iPhoto library.

3. **Click Preview to see the slideshow.**

   The slideshow plays as it would from a DVD. The DVD remote control appears for selecting menu items and advancing through the slideshow manually.

   To stop the preview, click Preview again.

Figure 16-3
Using iDVD to browse movies in your Movies folder

If you don't have slideshows ready to go in your iPhoto library, you can use iDVD to create a slideshow with images in iPhoto. You can also rearrange and adjust a slideshow imported from iPhoto. Follow these steps to access your photos in the iPhoto library:

1. **In iDVD, click Customize, or choose Project →**
   Show Customize Panel.

   The Customize drawer slides out, providing access to the Media pane.

2. **Click Media in the Customize drawer, and choose**
   Photos from the pop-up menu.

   The Media pane displays your entire iPhoto library, including albums and slideshows.

3. **Click Slideshow in the iDVD window.**

   iDVD creates a link to the slideshow, as shown in Figure 16-4. The text button is named My Slideshow until you rename it (as I did, to Band Tour slideshow).

4. Double-click the slideshow link.

The slideshow editing window appears, as shown in Figure 16-5.

5. Drag photos directly from the Media pane into the slideshow editing window, using the order you want for your slideshow.

Each photo appears in a list of thumbnails, numbered consecutively to represent the slideshow order, and you can then drag the thumbnail images into any order you want.

One of the most important decisions that you must make about your slideshow is how you want it to play: either manually, so that the viewer has to click the Next button to move to the next slide, or automatically, so that the slideshow advances according to a specified slide duration. You set the duration with the Slide Duration pop-up menu in the slideshow editing window. The slideshow is set by default to the Manual setting, unless you add sound — in which case it is automatically set to the Fit to Audio setting.

Figure 16-4
Using iDVD to create a slideshow with iPhoto images

Figure 16-5
Dragging photos to the iDVD slideshow window

The Fit to Audio setting in the Slide Duration menu matches the duration to the length of the audio clip. You can also select the Loop Slideshow option so that the slideshow repeats, and choose a transition to use between slides from the Transition pop-up menu. The transitions are the same as the ones available for iPhoto slideshows.

▼ Cross-Reference
See Chapter 15 for more information about setting slide transitions.

You can use any song or playlist in your iTunes library as part of your DVD. You can even set an entire playlist for the background of a menu to play songs in a sequence while displaying the menu — an excellent way to present your music collection on DVD.

If you don't already have music associated with the slideshow — if you imported the slideshow from iPhoto, for example — you can add music from your iTunes library to a slideshow by following these steps:

1. **Click the link for your slideshow to open the slideshow editing window.**

2. **Click Media in the Customize drawer, and then choose Audio from the pop-up menu.**

   The iTunes library opens in the Media pane, as shown in Figure 16-6.

3. **Drag a song (or an entire iTunes playlist) from the iTunes library to the Audio icon in the slideshow editing window.**

   The Audio icon in the slideshow editing window changes to reflect the type of sound file you're dragging — an MP3 icon for an MP3 file, for example, or an AIFF icon for an AIFF sound file. You can also drag an entire iTunes playlist to the Audio icon to play multiple songs.

   You can also import a sound file by dragging it directly over the Audio icon from the Finder. iDVD imports the sound file and changes the icon to reflect the type of sound file.

4. **In the slideshow editing window, select a duration setting from the Slide Duration pop-up menu.**

   The Fit to Audio setting in the Slide Duration pop-up menu matches the duration of the slideshow to the length of the song or playlist. You can use a timed duration for each slide by choosing a duration from the Slide Duration pop-up menu. The sound loops back and plays again if you have more slides to show than music to play.

5. **Click Preview to preview your slideshow.**

   To stop the preview, click Preview again.

Figure 16-6
Dragging a song from the iTunes library to add music to the slideshow

Creating menus and buttons

With iDVD, you can create menus and backgrounds for your DVD project that are similar to the ones you see in commercial DVDs. iDVD provides plenty of ready-made themes to use, but also gives you a great deal of control over menus, buttons, and backgrounds, enabling you to customize these elements for a unique presentation that can include your original GarageBand music.

The themes in iDVD supply motion buttons and backgrounds, and iDVD allows you to customize these themes into unique menus for your DVDs. In iDVD, a *theme* consists of a professionally designed combination of background elements, music clips, and menu button styles. Typically, the menu is designed with typefaces and images to match the theme, and the text selections are set to readable font sizes and placed in areas on the page that attract attention.

Start with a theme and then customize it; you can change the music for musical themes, change the background picture and text, change the buttons, and add your own movies and slideshows to areas in the background or to buttons. You can then save your customized theme and burn it to a DVD.

To see the themes, click Customize. A drawer slides out to the left of the main window. If the Themes pane is not already open, click the Themes button to open it. The Themes pane offers a pop-up menu to select sets of themes. Thumbnails of the themes appear in the pane as a list that you can scroll through. Thumbnails that show a silhouette of a walking man in the lower-right corner offer motion.

To select a theme, click its thumbnail. The theme replaces whatever theme was displayed before in the main window, as shown in Figure 16-7. Click Motion to view the motion for themes that display the walking man silhouette.

What's cool is that if you already created some buttons for a menu, the new theme has the same buttons. It's as if the themes were intelligent — they know where buttons should be, what size they should be, and what font to use for the button's text.

Themes come in several types, including

- **Picture-only:** These themes offer a background style with a static image you can change. Examples include Your Photo Here, Brushed Metal One, and Parchment.

- **Picture with audio:** These themes offer a picture-only style and image, accompanied by music or sound, all of which you can change. One example is Claim Check. You can customize most themes to include your own music.

- **Motion:** These themes offer short repeating video clips in the background (with or without audio). Motion themes sport a silhouette of a running man within a circle. Examples include Global, Sky, and Baby Blue.

- **Drop zone:** These themes reserve sections of the main background called *drop zones* for running movies and slideshows. Drop zones are not links to movies: they show only part of the movie in your menu. Examples include Postcard, Projector, and Theater. You know a theme is a drop zone when you see a section of the background that says "Drag photos or movies here." Drop zone themes are designed so that movies or slideshows play within frames.

You can change the background of any theme. Some themes, such as the Your Photo Here theme, are designed specifically for you to add your own photo as a background. Others, such as the Global theme, are designed to play a movie in the background (but you can replace this movie with your own).

Figure 16-7
After selecting the Projector theme, the DVD menu changes automatically

To replace the background of a theme with either a photo from your iPhoto library or a movie from iMovie, follow these steps:

1. **Select the theme.**

   If you don't already have the Themes pane open, click Customize to open the Customize drawer, and then click Themes.

   iDVD changes the menu in the main window to reflect the new theme.

2. **Click Media to open the Media pane, and then choose either Photos or Movies from the pop-up menu.**

   The Photos option in the Media pane provides access to your iPhoto library, and the Movies option provides access to any movies exported from iMovie.

3. **Select a photo or movie and drag it over the Settings button until the Settings pane appears, and then drop your photo or movie into the Background well.**

   The Background well fills with the photo or movie you selected, as shown in Figure 16-8. The image now appears as the background of your menu, as shown in Figure 16-9.

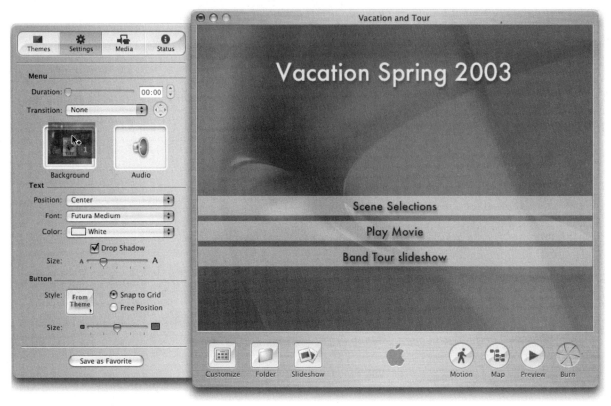

Figure 16-8
Dragging a photo from the iPhoto library to a theme's background

The Settings pane provides options for the background, including pop-up menus that control the position, font, size, and color of the text.

For movies used in the background, you can control the duration of the movie's loop with the Duration slider. This sets how long the movie plays before repeating in a loop. A movie in a background can play up to 30 seconds before looping.

Menus offer buttons that you click to play movies and slideshows and to access submenus. When you export a movie from iMovie or a slideshow from iPhoto, iDVD

automatically creates a button for your menu in whatever theme you used the last time you used iDVD. If you open iDVD for the first time, the theme is usually the Theater theme.

To create a button, you can do any of the following:

- **Button for a movie:** Drag a movie from the Movies pane in the Customize drawer — or drag a QuickTime file from the Finder — to any area of the background that is not a drop zone. When the menu appears on the DVD (and also when you use Preview to preview the DVD), clicking the button plays the movie.

Button for a slideshow: Drag an existing slideshow from the iPhoto browser in the Customize drawer to any area of the background that is not a drop zone. If you don't have a slideshow already prepared, click the Slideshow button to create the button, and then double-click the button to open the slideshow editing window.

Some themes provide text buttons, which are useful if the sections of your movie have long chapter titles, because you can fit more text in the label of the button. You can change the label of the text button by clicking the label to select it and typing a new name.

Using music in menus

All of the themes allow you to add your music to your menu background (or replace the sound already there). To add a song or playlist from your iTunes library, follow these steps:

1. **Select the theme.**

   If you don't already have the Themes pane open, click Customize to open the Customize drawer, and then click Themes. iDVD changes the menu in the main window to reflect the new theme.

Figure 16-9
The custom background photo is now set for the theme

2. **Click Media and choose Audio from the pop-up menu to open the Audio pane.**

   The Audio pane opens with your iTunes library and playlists.

3. **Select a song or playlist and drag it over the Settings button until the Settings pane appears, and then drop it into the Audio well.**

   The song or playlist appears in the Audio well. The music plays in the background and repeats in a loop until the user clicks a button in the menu.

PUTTING SONG PROJECTS ON DVD

Besides using iDVD to create movies, you can also use it to back up your GarageBand song projects, as well as photo and image archives, or to put just about any digital file on the DVD-ROM portion of the DVD-R (the part not accessible with a commercial DVD player).

You can check the available disc space in the Status pane. Open the Status pane by clicking Status in the Customize drawer. You can check the DVD capacity and the amount of space taken up by motion menus, tracks, and other menus.

 Tip

You may not want the recipients of your DVD-R (or the DVD created from it, if you plan on making multiple copies) to be able to access these files — which they can do, if they use the disc with a Macintosh. But if you want to archive your song projects, and possibly other files associated with a DVD-R project, you can add them to the disc.

To include song project files and other data files on the same disc, follow these steps:

1. **Choose Advanced → Edit DVD-ROM Contents.**

2. **Click New Folder to create a new folder.**

   You can add as many folders as you like and type a new name for each folder, as shown in Figure 16-10.

3. **Drag files or folders to the new folder in the DVD-ROM Contents window.**

   Dragging the files does not actually copy them, but establishes links to them so that when the DVD-R is burned, the files are copied. After you burn the disc, these files appear in the DVD-ROM portion of the disc.

BURNING DVDS

The discs you can create with the Apple SuperDrive are called DVD-R because they are a recordable format. DVD-Rs should play in all new DVD players purchased since 2003. Some older players and some inexpensive models can't play DVD-R media, or play them only marginally well, with picture defects and sound or navigation problems. The Apple SuperDrive burns standard 4.7GB 2.0 General DVD-Rs.

You can technically fit up to 90 minutes of video on a DVD-R, including still images, backgrounds, music, and movies. However, if you put more than 60 minutes of video on a DVD-R, the picture quality may suffer because iDVD uses stronger compression with a slower bit rate. Limiting the video you burn to each DVD-R to a total duration of 60 minutes or less is the best approach.

Figure 16-10
Creating folders for song projects to be included on the DVD-R as data files

▼ Tip

Before you start burning a disc, close all other projects you may have open. Burning a DVD takes a lot of processing power, and may also tie up your computer for a while. Let the computer do its disc-burning thing with the SuperDrive unimpeded by any other tasks.

Here's a checklist of things to do before burning your DVD-R:

- Add song project files to the DVD-ROM portion of the disc.

- Make sure the Motion button is active.

  While you may prefer to work without the menus and buttons moving because they slow down iDVD's performance, menus and buttons must be in motion if you want them to remain in motion on the DVD-R.

- Change the name of the DVD (optional) by choosing Project → Project Info and typing a new name in the Project Info window.

  By default, iDVD uses the name of your iDVD project as the name for the DVD.

Follow these steps to burn your DVD:

1. **Click Burn once.**

   The Burn button starts pulsating, its icon replaced with the symbol for radioactivity (Apple at least has a sense of humor), as shown in Figure 16-11. This is your fail-safe point. Should you proceed? Why not? As Dr. Hunter S. Thompson might have said at some point, *Mac ipsa loquitor*. Live as dangerously as you please. You can afford to botch a DVD-R that probably cost only about $1.

2. **Click Burn a second time to start the burn process.**

   When prompted, insert a blank DVD-R. (Make sure that the label side is up.) iDVD then burns the new DVD-R, rendering and encoding the menu and movie files if necessary. You may want to take a break now; the progress bar tells you the number of minutes the burning process will take.

   At the end of the process, iDVD spits out your newly burned DVD-R and displays a message asking if you want to burn another one just like it.

3. **Click OK to burn another identical disc; otherwise, click Cancel.**

Figure 16-11
The DVD-R burn process renders, encodes, and burns the DVD-R

Tip

Although you may be tempted to fire off a dozen more copies of a DVD-R for your friends, I recommend testing the disc first *before* you make any duplicates. You can always open iDVD and burn more copies later.

The best way to test your newly burned DVD-R is to pop it right back into your SuperDrive or similar DVD drive on your Mac. It should play just like any commercial DVD.

The DVD Player application, supplied with every Mac that has a DVD drive, provides a simulated remote control for controlling playback. DVD Player also has the ability to play the DVD in a half-screen, normal-size, or maximum-size window (depending on your display) by choosing options from the Video menu. You can resize the viewer to take over the entire screen by choosing Window → Viewer, or press Command+0 (zero) to toggle between full-screen and the viewer window. You can control the sound volume by dragging the slider in the remote control.

You can also double-click the disc's icon in the Finder to see the contents of the DVD-ROM portion of the DVD-R — if you included your GarageBand project files, for example. You can then copy the folders and files to your hard drive using the Finder and edit your GarageBand project.

After you test the DVD-R on a Mac, test the DVD-R with a commercial DVD player. If it works on the Mac but not on the commercial player, there may be a compatibility problem with the commercial player and DVD-Rs.

WHAT IF THE DVD-R DOESN'T WORK?

The problem just might be a bum disc — it happens. However, try it with another DVD player first, or with a computer that supports DVD. Some older DVD players may not be able to read DVD-R. DVD-R discs use a dark dye layer to absorb the high-powered laser in DVD burners that creates the tiny pits or holes for encoding video and music. This dye layer causes problems for some inexpensive and older DVD players that can play commercial discs. Those silver and gold DVDs you can buy in stores for movies and games are actually made from aluminum coatings over a clear layer that has been mechanically pressed with pits or holes to encode the information that lasers in the DVD players decode into music and video signals. DVD Video discs don't require the light sensitive dye layer used in DVD-R discs for burning, so they appear clear on the bottom, or nearly so. Most of today's DVD players — over 97 percent — can play both.

After burning your music video, musical slideshow, and GarageBand project files onto a DVD-R, burn just the music video and slideshow onto another DVD-R — you can use a DVD replicating service to make multiple copies from *that* one (the disc without the project files) for your audience. iDVD is now an important part of your GarageBand repertoire and your iLife.

Tips and Resources

In This Chapter

Performance tips for getting the most out of GarageBand • Finding information and support
for GarageBand and iLife • Joining GarageBand communities and uploading songs
• Finding musical instruments, MIDI gear, and music communities

This chapter is about getting by with a little help from your friends. Whether you're fixing a hole or just getting better all the time, any day in your iLife may require the tips and techniques gleaned from the sources listed here. I show you how to improve the performance of GarageBand (or at least keep it from giving up in exasperation when you add too many tracks). I also provide a compendium of Web sites and resources to look for further advice — including sites that specialize in particular instruments and equipment.

PERFORMANCE TIPS

GarageBand eats just about all your memory and quite a lot of disk space for breakfast and is still hungry at lunch. Other than purchasing a faster Mac, you really have only one way to wring the best possible performance from GarageBand: make more memory available. Having more than 256 MB RAM improves the performance of not only GarageBand but everything else. In GarageBand, more memory lets you increase the maximum number of instrument tracks you can have in your songs.

You can change the maximum number of Real Instrument and Software Instrument tracks in GarageBand by choosing GarageBand ➜ Preferences; in the Preferences window that appears, click Advanced, as shown in Figure 17-1. In the Advanced pane, choose the number of Real Instrument tracks (8, 16, 32, 64, or 255) from the Maximum Number of Real Instrument Tracks pop-up menu, or the number of Software Instrument tracks (8, 16, 32, 64) from the Maximum Number of Software Instrument Tracks pop-up menu. But don't set these numbers higher than your computer can support, as Apple says performance will be affected (and I don't mean *your* performance). I recommend that you set them to Automatic so that GarageBand figures out what's best for your system, and if performance suffers, try the lowest setting of 8 and work your way up.

▼ Tip

You should refrain from opening other applications or even having them open in the background when using GarageBand. If you use a virus protection program, check for viruses, then disconnect from the Internet if you want to feel safe, and turn off the antivirus program.

You may be cruising right along with your song and then abruptly see the message "System Overload," "Disk is too slow," or even the helpful "The hard disk is not fast enough to deliver all audio data in time. Try muting some tracks." Here are some tips for getting around this problem:

- **Try muting some tracks, like the Mac said.** Only problem is, you lose the music in those tracks. If this solves the problem, you can mix down the tracks that are muted, and then add them back as one mixdown track, as described in Chapter 11.

- **Optimize the performance of GarageBand and your MIDI keyboard by choosing GarageBand → Preferences and clicking the Audio/MIDI tab.** In the "Optimize for" section of the Audio/MIDI pane, click the Maximum number of simultaneous tracks

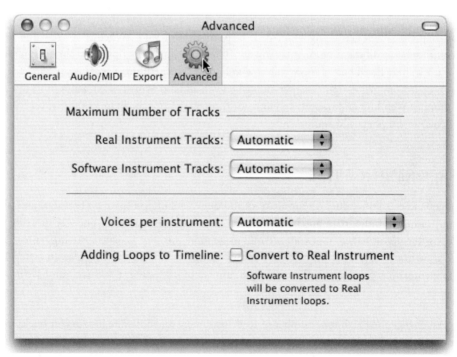

Figure 17-1
Changing advanced settings to improve performance

option. (In version 1.0 of GarageBand, click the Better performance option.)

○ **You can use fewer tracks and fewer voices per type of instrument to reduce GarageBand's overhead.** Choose GarageBand ➜ Preferences and click Advanced in the Preferences window. Choose lower settings for the Real Instrument Tracks, Software Instrument Tracks, and Voices per instrument pop-up menus.

○ **Reduce the pixel resolution of your display to 1024 x 768 pixels, and your colors to less than millions.** This action improves the performance of displaying changes, which may help a bit. Choose System Preferences from the Apple menu, click Displays, and select a resolution from the Resolutions list. Then choose Thousands from the Colors pop-up menu, as shown

in Figure 17-2. Your display changes immediately. Choose System Preferences ➜ Quit System Preferences (or Command+Q) to leave System Preferences.

○ **Turn off unused effects.** Many Real Instrument types (including No Effects) have effects that are turned on but not used: their sliders are set to create no change in the sound. For example, the Echo effect may be turned on, but its slider is set to zero. Open the Track Info window for that track (double-click the track's header, or select the track and choose Track ➜ Show Track Info), and turn off any effects you don't need. You can also turn off the Echo and Reverb effects in the Master track, as described in Chapter 10. Even if you want to use certain effects, you can turn them off temporarily, and then turn them back on when you create the final mix, as described in Chapter 11.

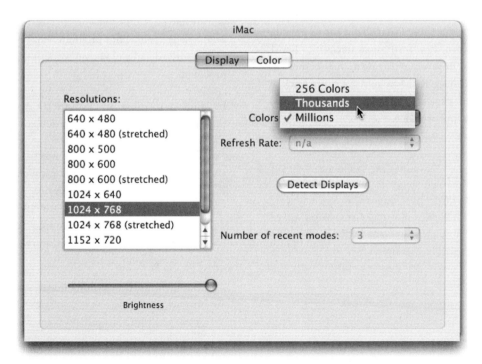

Figure 17-2
Changing display settings to improve performance

● **Delete the silent parts of Real Instrument tracks.** If you have multiple Real Instrument tracks with your recorded performances, chances are you have silent sections within those tracks taking up space and processing time. While you can record directly into a track at precisely the right point in the timeline, you may have recorded some tracks by performing and then remaining silent while GarageBand recorded the silence in those tracks for the entire song. If so, you can delete the silent portions without affecting the rest of the track. To delete a silent section of a region, first split the region into several regions (one of which has just the silent section) as described in Chapter 3, and then delete the silent region. You can also delete sections of silent audio in the Track Editor, as described in Chapter 9.

● **Store the song project on a faster hard drive, such as a FireWire drive, or your Mac's built-in drive (if you are using an external drive).** A faster data transfer rate can help because GarageBand has to periodically load parts of Real Instrument tracks into RAM from the hard drive while playing a song, as there typically is not enough RAM to hold the entire track. A faster hard drive speeds up this transfer to RAM and helps increase performance.

▼ **Tip**

If you turned on FileVault in the Security pane of System Preferences, it may slow down the process of retrieving files from your home folder. You may want to turn FileVault off, or save your GarageBand songs in a folder outside of your home folder. To turn off FileVault, choose System Preferences from the Apple menu, and click the Security icon. Click the Turn Off FileVault button.

GARAGEBAND AND ILIFE INFORMATION

The Apple Web site provides a wealth of information on the various iLife applications, including GarageBand, and on the current Mac OS and the iPod. You can go to the individual product pages (`www.apple.com/ilife/productname` — replace *productname* with GarageBand, iTunes, iPhoto, iMovie, iDVD, or iPod, as the case may be). These product pages are actually mini-Web sites on their own, with links to pages that show off the technology in QuickTime tutorials and demos, and offer free downloads for extras and add-ons. You can go to the Apple Feedback pages and report bugs or tell what you like and don't like about a particular program.

Search the extensive Knowledge Base (`http://kbase.info.apple.com/index.jsp`) to satisfy your curiosity or to find answers to questions about issues that frustrate you — like bugs. The Knowledge Base articles frequently acknowledge anomalous program behavior and, more importantly, detail any known workarounds for the problem.

In addition, there are pages within the Apple Web site I find useful (though the URLs are subject to change):

● **GarageBand Support** (`www.apple.com/support/garageband/`). I have found excellent information here, including compatible devices, tutorials on using features, and tips for getting around performance problems. You can search the Knowledge Base articles from this page, and download software upgrades and the GarageBand Jam Pack.

● **GarageBand Discussions** (`http://discussions.info.apple.com/webx/garageband/`). You can find messages from GarageBand users everywhere, discussing features or solving problems.

- **GarageBand Hot Tips** (www.apple.com/ilife/ garageband/hottips/). Everything from browsing loops to recording guitars to changing the number of Software Instruments you can play at once.

- **Apple Store** (http://store.apple.com/). Buy the accessories you need, such as a Monster Cable adapter, audio interface, or MIDI keyboard.

Other sites useful for iLife users include:

- **Apple iLife: The Digital Hub** (www.apple.com/ ilife/). You can find all the information you need about the iLife suite of software for creating digital music, photography, movies, and DVDs.

- **Apple .Mac Service** (www.mac.com/). Sign on to the .Mac service for automatic iDisk backup, Web pages for hosting slideshows and videos, and the ability to share files, photos, and calendars over the Internet.

- **Apple Downloads** (www.info.apple.com/support/ downloads.html). You can find the latest versions of software upgrade packages and other free software from Apple on this page.

- **iPodHacks** (www.ipodhacks.com). Visit iPodHacks for comprehensive iPod information, tips and tricks, and a lively user forum.

- **iPoding** (www.ipoding.com). iPoding is an excellent source of information about iPod accessories and third-party products (including software downloads), and includes an iPod Products Guide that lists major iPod-related third-party products.

- **iPod Lounge** (www.ipodlounge.com). This site is an excellent source of information about iPod third-party products, downloads, hacks, and tips.

GARAGEBAND COMMUNITIES

Independent sites have sprung up to provide information and host songs created in GarageBand. Want to be an Internet pop star? You can literally post your creations and then see if your songs climb the charts; the sites that allow submissions have contests and measure how many times the songs are played by visitors.

- **The Garage Door** (www.thegaragedoor.com/ index.html). This site offers tips and tricks and a newsletter emailed every three months (containing extra tips and an in-depth look at some important aspects of digital audio and home recording).

- **iCompositions** (www.icompositions.com/). This site hosts GarageBand music submitted by members who join the community, as well as discussion groups about GarageBand. The site offers 150MB of free upload space for every member as well as access to forums. Over 2,371 compositions have been uploaded from 3,012 artists as of this writing.

- **Mac Idol** (www.macidol.com/tips.php). The Mac Idol site hosts a Mac music community with a GarageBand page that offers news, discussions, and tips.

- **MacJams** (www.macjams.com/). The MacJams music community site ("We Be Jammin'") offers a forum on GarageBand, tips, music resources, and a buyer's guide, and it also lets you submit your songs. It lists mystery picks — GarageBand creations submitted by visitors — and contest winners. I found a great tutorial on using Native Instrument instruments and loops.

- **MacMusic.org** (http://macmusic.org/). One of the largest Mac music community sites, MacMusic.org is a noncommercial, nonprofit site that hosts reviews, links, and resources supplied by members. Services for members include news, articles, classifieds, forums, downloads, links, and mailing lists.

DOWNLOADABLE LOOPS AND EFFECTS

This is almost scary: the Internet is loaded to the gills with loops and effects. It's MIDI soup out there. There are lots of great sounds, sound effects, and instrument plug-ins in the Audio Unit (AU) format (see Chapter 10 for AU information).

- **Bitshift Audio** (www.bitshiftaudio.com/). Bitshift Audio's beat programmer, Art Gillespie (also known as bitshift), is so excited about GarageBand and the new Apple Loops file format that he put together a collection of free electro/breakbeat drum and synth loops from his forthcoming Apple Loops CD *bitshift's bangin' beats* for everyone to download for free. Bitshift also publishes iDrum, which turns your Mac into a drum machine; iDrum runs as both a stand-alone native OS X application, and as a plug-in for GarageBand, Soundtrack, and Logic applications.

- **Directions in Music** (www.directionsinmusic. com/news.html). This site offers free drum and percussion loops played by Michael Blair (Lou Reed, Tom Waits, Elvis Costello, Ryan Adams, and so on) and recorded, mixed, and produced by Chris Bell.

- **Drums on Demand** (www.drumsondemand.com/). A commercial site offering a collection of nearly 900 live, acoustic drum loops in the Apple format, organized into 41 easy-to-use Song Sets — all designed to help you quickly put together a drum track that sounds like you hired a pro session drummer in a high-end studio.

- **House of Samples free samples page** (www.mtlc. net/freesamples/freesamples.php). Stop by and download a new sample every day; you won't find these sounds anywhere else. The free samples are provided by Northeastern University's Music Technology Program in cooperation with House of Samples.

- **MIDISite** (www.midisite.co.uk/). Now with over 800,000 free indexed MIDI files, all you need to do is type in the name of the song or artist you are looking for and click MIDI Search. The MIDI search engine gives you a list of MIDI music pages that contain free MIDI files.

- **Native Instruments** (www.native-instruments. com/). You can add professional-quality software synthesizers and instrument generators to your Garage-Band palette. See Chapter 10 for information on how to install them.

- **Pro Loops** (www.proloops.com/). Pro Loops offers over 10,800 professional loops and samples (hundreds of them for free), free updates for active members, and an online store.

- **Sample Arena** (www.samplearena.com/download. htm). Loads of free royalty-free samples are available on this site.

- **Samples4.com** (www.samples4.com/catalog/). This site has an extensive catalog of commercial samples for GarageBand.

- **Sound-Effects Library** (www.sound-effects-library.com/free/mp3.html). This site is one of the world's largest libraries of sound effects, music samples, and music tracks.

RESOURCES FOR MUSICIANS

- **Drum!** (www.drummagazine.com/). News, product reviews, forums, and commentary for drummers.

- **Garageband.com** (www.garageband.com/). The site that licensed its name to Apple charts emerging music and offers a range of free and paid services to musicians, such as gig promotion and advice from industry experts. At the core of these services is its unique review process: hundreds of thousands of listeners test and critique new songs. Sir George Martin, producer of The Beatles, is the chairman of the www.garageband.com advisory board.

- **Guitarists.net** (www.guitarists.net/). This site hosts a community of guitar players of all ages, styles, and abilities, all exchanging their ideas, tips, and experiences. You can take part in a guitar-related discussion, take guitar lessons, discover new tunings, and research equipment.

- **HarmonicaLinks** (www.harmonicalinks.com/). Links galore for harmonica fans and players.

- **Harmony Central** (www.harmony-central.com/). One of the most popular Internet resources for musicians, Harmony Central offers valuable information, from news and product reviews to classified ads, discussion forums, and chat rooms. It also provides access to OLGA (On-Line Guitar Archive) with its extensive database of lyrics and guitar tablature (sheet music that shows a six-line staff graphically representing the guitar fingerboard).

- **MIDI.com** (www.midi.com/). This site provides access to the huge MIDI community, and offers extensive information about the MIDI standard and MIDI equipment.

- **Modern Drummer** (www.moderndrummer.com/). The online version of the newsstand magazine provides news, reviews, feature articles on drummers, and drumming techniques.

- **Musician's Friend** (www.musiciansfriend.com/). This site may well be the largest online music gear shop in the world (as they claim). Currently, Musician's Friend offers over 36,000 products in its mail-order catalogs and on its Web site, including guitars, basses, keyboards, percussion, and amps, as well as recording, mixing, lighting, and DJ gear. Hundreds of new products are added monthly. Musician's Friend is affiliated with the Guitar Center stores, where you might find good deals on instruments and equipment.

- **MusicianResources.org** (www.musicianresources.org/). This site provides a comprehensive directory of Web sites dedicated to musical instruments.

- **PianoMix** (www.pianomix.com/). PianoMix is a creative community of pianists, keyboard players, teachers, artists, and wannabes. Go there to exchange ideas, get to know fellow musicians, browse piano and keyboard resources, get inspired, or simply hang out.

- **Sonic State** (www.sonicstate.com/). Sonic State is a group of sites catering to electronic musicians. Founded in 1995, Sonic State is now firmly established as one of the top ten destinations for musicians online. It includes the Synth Site, a resource for information on synthesizers, featuring an exhaustive database of 900 models; The Gas Station, an electronic musicians knowledgebase; The Directory, a comprehensive database of musicians, studios, stores, and related products and services; and assorted classified ads for electronic equipment.

- **TAXI** (www.taxi.com/). Want a record deal? Want your song to be featured in a movie? TAXI is an independent A&R company helping unsigned bands, artists, and songwriters get record deals, publishing deals, and placement in films and TV shows.

18

Twenty GarageBand Questions from Aunt Estelle

My Aunt Estelle, bless her, spent 30 years as part of Staxx Records' legendary stable of session musicians collectively known as the "Fabulous Nineteen." We're all really proud of her; Estelle's smoking tremolo-punched lead guitar riffs, all performed on her trademark 1959 Les Paul Goldtop Custom, can be heard on over 50 Top Ten records. Eddie Van Halen needn't bother turning away from the audience during his guitar solos because there ain't any noise he can coax from a Stratocaster that Estelle didn't crank out back during the Johnson administration, while perched atop a Marshall in front of 90,000 mud-caked hippies. She also makes a peach cobbler that'll knock you flat on your duff.

Every book in this series has a collection of questions from Estelle. The questions are the sort of basic but befuddling kind that friends, relatives, and friends of relatives will ask you once word starts to spread that you know a little something about hardware and software. With the other subjects in this series — learning the Mac OS, figuring out how to work a digital camera and import photos, making playable DVDs with iMovie and iDVD — Estelle was pretty much out of her element, but where GarageBand is concerned the lady has all the madd skilz anyone could ever want, and only needs to figure out how to work the app.

I'm taking time out to mention this because she promised to teach me how to play the rhythm line on "All Along The Watchtower" (which she recorded in 1970, called into the studio to sweeten Bob Dylan's live performance for his 1971 *Greatest Hits* album). I'm hoping to win big at this year's Technology Pundit and Industry Commentator Talent Show, so I'm well motivated to keep the old dear happy. Here are the most common GarageBand questions that turn up in my Inbox:

How do I export the performances I created in GarageBand so I can use them with other MIDI apps, or other studio hardware?

You, um... well, you can't. GarageBand can only export into audio files. They're very *nice* audio files, but you can't turn a brilliant keyboard performance into a MIDI file, for example. GarageBand is just an iApp: it wasn't designed to be an all-in-one digital recording studio. It's the app you use at your beach house to create a demo of the song you want to record "for real" when you get to the studio.

That said, exporting your GarageBand MIDI performances is such an obvious feature that I'd be shocked if Apple didn't provide professional musicians and Amateurs With Ambition with some sort of a solution in the near future, be it an extra-cost utility or an expanded, stand-alone version. (Two-Car GarageBand?)

For now — and only if you imagine that you're about to capture lightning in a bottle — you may want to use your keyboard's built-in sequencing features, or plug another box into your MIDI stream, so that essentially you're making two separate recordings as you go.

Can I at least import a MIDI file?

Come on. Why would you want to import a MIDI file? Oh. Yes, I suppose it *would* be handy to download the score from *The Mikado* and work on your own arrangements and vocals. Okay, yes, yes, yes, you work with other people in your band and they don't all use Macs and swapping MIDI files would be the best way to collaborate on a piece. And... well, at this stage, I concede the point and admit that importing MIDI would be a good thing.

GarageBand doesn't support MIDI import, but if you visit `http://homepage.mac.com/beryrinaldo/`, you can download a third-party utility called Dent du MIDI which will take a standard MIDI file and convert it into a GarageBand track, retaining nearly all of the track's original properties.

GarageBand keeps stopping in the middle of a recording, telling me it can't continue.

Yeah, it probably also dissed your Macintosh, didn't it? Throwing out an error alert claiming that there aren't enough system resources available? If it could have thrown in a couple of "Your mama is so fat..." jokes, it would have.

GarageBand is a very resource-intensive app, particularly when you're working with Real Instruments (recorded sound, as opposed to MIDI data). Your Mac has to do a boatload of signal processing to make your $69 Sears guitar sound like Joe Satriani's $23,000 combination of custom axe and perfectly matched amp, and it can only keep up the pace if you have a meaty CPU and a ton of RAM. GarageBand gives you a hint that things are starting to get overheated: the playhead changes color from white to orange to red as the app puts more and more stress on your Mac's resources.

If you skimped on memory when you bought your Mac, now's the time to upgrade. Whether you're using Garage-Band or not, you should cram as much RAM into your computer as you can. Memory is cheap, and the performance difference between a Mac with the most RAM possible and one with just the stock 256MB is like the difference between the 1967 Mets and every lineup since.

If you're using a G3 Mac, it's time to buy a new machine. If you're using a G4 Mac with one processor, it's time to see if you can use GarageBand as an excuse to get your boss or spouse or both to buy you a G5. And if you're using a PowerBook, go to Energy Saver in System Preferences (you'll find it under the Options tab) and make sure the Processor performance pop-up menu is set to Highest.

At any rate, you'll have the best results by restarting your Mac and then running GarageBand as the only app.

The other possibility is that GarageBand is trying to tell you "*ENOUGH* with 'Louie, Louie' already, for God's sake!!!" And it has a point. Everybody knows that the only reason why the song enjoys any popularity at all is because it only has three chords. This song is in no way a pit stop on any musician's path to glory.

I'm trying to record a Real Instrument, but I can't get any sound.

Assuming that you really *are* recording a Real Instrument — if you've selected a Software Instrument track, GarageBand ignores the microphone — the instrument you've plugged into your Mac's sound-in port probably needs a preamp. As it is, the signal is too weak for the Mac to pick up. Use Griffin Technology's iMic (a $40 USB sound interface that sports its own preamp circuit) and all shall be golden.

Nope, that wasn't it.

Ah. Okay. You probably have the wrong sound source selected. Go to System Preferences, select Sound, and then click the Input tab. You'll see a list of all the different places your Mac can record sound from, including its built-in microphone if it has one. If you have an iMic, for instance, you'll see "iMic audio system" in the list. Click it and close System Preferences. Return to GarageBand, open Preferences, and click Audio/MIDI. If the input device isn't already selected in the Audio Input pop-up menu, select it and you should be good to go.

Still nothin'.

Have you adjusted the input volume levels correctly? You can adjust the inputs in two different places, and many users forget to check the slider for the master input level in System Preferences. If that's been sloughed down to the left, adjust it back upward. The Preference panel gives you a live level meter so you can determine (a) that the hardware is working and (b) what the approximate level is.

Nope.

Okay, we've exhausted all of the simple and logical solutions, which means we fall back on what you nearly always do when your Mac is doing something you don't approve of: quit GarageBand and launch it again. If that doesn't work, try restarting your Mac. Possibly something has clobbered the piece of system software that controls sound input, and we're trying to make the OS restart that bit of code from scratch.

If there's still no joy, then clearly God is telling you that your parents were right: you'll never make a living as the trombone player in a Duran Duran tribute band, and it's time to go back to technical college. As omens go, it isn't exactly a burning bush, but all that matters is that you'll finally have that welding and carpentry proficiency certificate in your back pocket and be well on your way to owning a much better class of used car.

I've changed the tempo of the song, and now a lot of my tracks are out of sync with each other.

That's because some of your tracks are loops, some are Virtual Instruments, and some are Real Instruments. Your Mac records the first two kinds of tracks as streams of note, velocity, and tempo data, and GarageBand can transmogrify those until a Schubert string quartet sounds like speed metal. An audio recording is what it is, and that's all it is. GarageBand can't keep an audio recording aligned with the rest of the tracks when you change their speed, so you're sort of stuck.

The only solution is preparation: if you know you're recording a mixture of Real and Virtual Instrument tracks, record all of the Virtual Instrument tracks first and monkey with the tempo until you've finally decided whether "Crowbar Massage" is going to be a sweet ballad or a spasmodic sprint to the bridge. Then and only then should you record your Real Instrument tracks.

I'm using GarageBand to convert some of my LPs to digital, but the sound is all muted and junky.

Assuming you have all of your sound inputs set up correctly, it's probably because you tried to plug the turntable straight into your Mac's sound-in jack. The reason why home stereos have a special jack for record players is because the tone is entirely different, and requires its own kind of processing by the preamp. Drag your home stereo over next to your Mac (or vice versa) and use the amp's outputs instead of the turntable's.

If I've created a song using GarageBand's built-in loops, can I publish and sell it?

Sure. All of the loops that come with GarageBand are royalty-free, so you're good to slap them onto a commercial CD, upload the loops to your Web site where anybody can download them, or use your latest opus as the soundtrack to a movie or a presentation. Just make absolutely sure you haven't incorporated loops you've downloaded or purchased from other sources: many of those loops are free only for noncommercial use. Even the ones that are *free*

can be problematic. Once Miramax buys your independent film for a low six figures, simply *claiming* that you have the right to use those loops is not enough. You need proof, and maybe by then you'll have forgotten where you downloaded the loops from. So definitely tread cautiously.

I'm trying to line up a clip precisely, but dragging it around with the mouse I'm always just a little bit early or late. Can't I just tell GarageBand that this clip should come in at one minute, thirty-four point seven seconds?

Nope. The only real way to solve this problem is to turn off Snap To Grid so that GarageBand isn't making any assumptions about lining up the clip straight on the beat, and then use the Zoom tool to view the timeline at its highest magnification. This is another one of those things that defines the difference between a music app that retails for $200 and one that's part of a $50 suite of lifestyle apps.

When are you going to learn a *proper* instrument?

With all due respect, Auntie, the ukulele *is* a proper instrument. Long before the first commercial electric guitar hit the marketplace, ukuleles were the rage of the Jazz Age, you know.

Can I create my own loops?

Yes and no. GarageBand doesn't have this feature, but if you go to Apple's developer site (`http://developer.apple.com/sdk/`), you'll find a kit named AppleLoops SDK. It contains a tool for building loops that are compatible with both GarageBand and Soundtrack.

There are a bunch of third-party utilities for making loops, but I don't think any of them are necessarily easier to use than AppleLoops SDK (says the guy who isn't a professional musician), and you can't beat Apple's price (free).

Is there a way I can turn off my Mac's fan so everything's nice and quiet when I record Real Instrument tracks?

Man alive, if there were, you'd have a fantabulously simple way to turn your $2,000 Mac into a $20 smoke machine; the fan is the bane of audio recording with a Mac. There are three common workarounds:

Try rotating your microphone 90 degrees. Many mics are highly directional, and hopefully with a little trial and error you can find its "cone of silence." If that doesn't work, buy a longer patch cable and put some distance between yourself and the Mac: five feet ought to do it. If you want to get super fancy, buy yourself a wireless (Bluetooth or RF) mouse so you can start and stop the recording without putting so much wear and tear on your Reeboks.

If neither of these ideas works — which is likely, if you're recording longhair acoustic guitar junk, for example — you need to break out the heavy weapons. Some folks actually spend $20 or $30 building a soundproof (well, soundproof*ish*) enclosure for their Macs. Take a few sheets of lightweight foamcore, upholster it with eggshell foam (which you can find at any packing store), and you've made a nice portable shroud of silence to surround your Mac.

Two very serious warnings accompany this tip, though: First, don't make the enclosure so small that absolutely no air flows around and through your Mac. (Remember, the cooling fan is all that stands between a happy healthy Mac and the reason why you're on your way to your closest

Apple store with the machine in the backseat, rehearsing your innocent "I don't know, it just stopped working all of a sudden" speech with increasing desperation.) Second, packing foam is highly flammable, and you sure don't want to keep it stacked up in your office.

Recording with a quiet Mac, such as an iMac or a PowerBook, is the only foolproof way to eliminate noise from the fan. Better yet, shut down your Mac, or head off someplace quiet and record your Real Instrument tracks onto tape instead of onto the hard drive. If you have a camcorder, you already have a very high-quality audio recording deck (just plug the mic right into the camera's input jack). Later, plug the camera into your Mac as an audio device and press Play.

When I say that I'm a closet musician, I mean it literally. The only times I've ever recorded anything good were when I just walked into a closet with my ukulele and a MiniDisc recorder and shut the door behind me.

Hey, it says here that GarageBand has more than a thousand built-in loops. But I've never seen more than a handful, and some don't do anything when I click 'em!

That's because you're a skinflint who settled for a 17-inch display instead of popping for the 40,960-x-30,720-pixel wall-sized screen, designed to be big enough to display 1,000 buttons at once (plus the Dock). The chapter on loops explains how to adjust the viewer to access the entire collection of loops.

As for buttons that don't do anything: again, this is GarageBand looking out for number one (which is you, apparently). The app automatically disables any loops that are in the wrong key or tempo to work effectively with the current project.

Wow! Using these loops, I can create music that sounds exactly like Philip Glass!

Not quite. Your music is just as dry, just as emotionless, and just as tedious and endless, but it doesn't have the added *oomph* that comes when the listener is thinking, "Cripes! I paid *40 bucks plus parking* to come hear this?" It just goes to show you that there's always that line between the true professional and a mere enthusiastic amateur.

You're not embarrassed to be seen playing an instrument that looks like it plays "Pop Goes The Weasel" when you turn a little crank on the side of it? I have an old Flying V I can loan you, you know.

Honest, I like my ukulele. It's small enough to travel with, it's self-contained, it's easy to pick up and strum when I'm sitting behind my computer searching for Le Mot Juste. I appreciate where you're coming from, having received a Grammy nomination for your work on The Doors's third album, but I'm going to stick with what I have.

I'm all finished recording and mixing, but now that I've exported the song to iTunes it sounds... unprofessional. Or something.

My first tendency is to refer you back to an earlier question in which I broke the tough but crucial news that three chords and the bass line to "Smoke On The Water" do not a guitar hero make. Some people pick up an instrument as the first step to creating masterful works that throw a spotlight on the human condition and in time cause us all to coalesce into a tighter, friendlier society. For other people, it's the last step in deciding that perhaps you were meant to promote music and not play it. Chin up; it only stings until you see what an Exploiter Of Creative Visionary pays. You never read about a record industry executive suing a musician for unpaid royalties, do you?

This is, of course, a question with far too many variables to answer directly. But when people try to articulate it, I ask them to show me their GarageBand file. I nod as they continue to explain, but all the while I'm selecting the Master Track and pulling up the Track Info dialog box. I open Details, click Compressor, and move the slider all the way to its maximum setting. By the time they pause to take another breath, I've pressed Play and suddenly their song sounds right.

The Compressor is sort of a magic wand of music production: it boosts the soft bits to make them clearer, and dampens the loud bits slightly so they don't get out of control. This does indeed have an immediate and positive impact on your song, but it also makes your project sound like it's been "produced." Nearly all studio recordings are run through a compressor and the process imparts a certain flavor that people recognize, even if they can't specifically identify it.

At any rate, changing the Compressor's setting requires no work on your part, so it's always worth a whirl.

How do I lock a track so that my collaborator (or even I myself!) can't ruin it by continuing to change things around?

You can't lock a track per se. The only practical way to prevent further editing is to export the track as an AIFF file and then re-import it. Instead of dealing with 18 perfectly recorded, tweaked, and mixed Real and Software instruments (each of which is attempting to seduce you...*adjuu-uust meeee...re-recooooorrrrd meeee...*) and being constantly confronted with all that screen clutter, you now have one schmooshed-together Real Instrument track containing everything recorded so far. Now you only have to focus on adding the tambourine and the handclaps and then huzzah: your all-skiffle version of The Who's "Tommy" is ready to ship.

Two words, Andy: "Tiny Tim."

A Flying V, you say? Do you tune it G-C-E-A, like a concert-scale uke? I mean, I won't have to learn all those chords over again, will I?

Index